Pocke BUSINESS SPANISH DICTIONARY

second edition

English-Spanish/Spanish-English
Inglés-Español/Español-Inglés

General Editor
PH Collin

Spanish Editor
Lourdes Melcion

A & C Black

Originally published by Peter Collin Publishing

Second edition published 2003
First edition published 1995

A&C Black Publishers Ltd
38 Soho Square
London WID 3HB

British Library Cataloguing in Publications Data

A Catalogue record for this book is
available from the British Library

ISBN 0 7136 7734 1

Text computer typeset by A&C Black

Preface

This pocket dictionary is designed for any business person, business student or traveller who needs to deal with the language of business. It contains over 5,000 essential business terms in Spanish and English with clear and accurate translations.

Abbreviations

adj	adjective
adv	adverb
f	feminine
fpl	feminine plural
m	masculine
mf	masculine or feminine
mpl	masculine plural
n	noun
v	verb

Prefacio

Este diccionario tiene como objetivo facilitar la comunicación a toda persona que se relacione o viaje por asuntos de negocios. Contiene más de 5.000 términos básicos de negocios con sus correspondientes traducciones.

Abreviaturas

adj	adjetivo
adv	adverbio
f	femenino
fpl	femenino plural
m	masculino
mf	masculino o femenino
mpl	masculino plural
n	nombre
v	verbo

Contents

Índice

English-Spanish
Inglés-Español

Aa

A1 de primera clase
abandon abandonar
o renunciar a
abandon an action
desistir de una
acción
abatement
disminución (f)
abroad (en el)
extranjero (m)
absence ausencia (f)
absent ausente
absolute monopoly
monopolio
(m) absoluto
abundance
abundancia (f)
**accelerated depre-
ciation** amorti-
zación (f) acelerada
accept (v) aceptar
accept a bill
aceptar una letra
**accept delivery of a
shipment** aceptar
la entrega de
mercancías

**accept liability for
something** aceptar
la responsabilidad
de algo
acceptable
aceptable o
admisible
acceptance
aceptación (f)
**acceptance of an
offer** aceptación
(f) de una oferta
**acceptance sam-
pling** muestreo
(m) de aceptación
access (n) acceso (m)
accessible accesible
**accommodation
address** dirección
(f) postal
**accommodation
bill** pagaré (m) o
efecto (m) de favor
according to según
account cuenta
account executive
ejecutivo (m) de
cuentas
account for
justificar o
responder de

account in credit
cuenta (f) con saldo
positivo *o* cuenta
acreed *or* a
account on stop
cuenta (f) bloqueada
account: on
account a cuenta
accountant
contable (mf)
accounting
contabilidad (f)
accounts depart-
ment departamento
(m) de contabilidad
accounts payable
cuentas (fpl) a
pagar *o* por pagar
accounts receivable
cuentas (fpl)
a cobrar *o* por cobrar
accrual
acumulación (f)
accrual of interest
acumulación (f)
de interés
accrue acumularse
o devengar
accrued interest
interés (m)
acumulado

accumulate acumu-
lar *o* acumularse
accurate exacto,
-ta *o* correcto, -ta
accusation (n)
acusación (f)
accuse (v) acusar
acknowledge
receipt of a letter
acusar recibo de una
carta
acknowledgement
acuse (m) de recibo
acquire adquirir
acquisition
adquisición (f)
across-the-board
general
act (v) actuar
act (v) [do some-
thing] tomar medidas
act of God fuerza
(f) mayor
acting interino, -na
o en funciones
acting manager
director (m) en
funciones
action acción (f)
action [lawsuit]
acción (f) legal

action for damages
demanda (f) por
daños y perjuicios
active (adj) activo, -va
activity (n)
actividad (f)
actual real *o*
efectivo, -va
actuals cifras (fpl)
reales
actuarial tables
tablas (fpl) actuari-
ales *o* tablas de
mortalidad
actuary actuario, -ria
ad valorem ad
valorem
ad valorem tax
impuesto (m) ad
valorem
add añadir
add on 10% for
service añadir el
10% por el servicio
add up a column of
figures sumar una
columna de cifras
addition suma (f) *o*
adición (f)
additional adicional
o suplementario, -ria

additional charges
cargos (mpl)
adicionales
additional premium
sobreprima (f)
address (n) direc-
ción (f) *o* señas (fpl)
address (v) dirigir
address a letter *or* a
parcel poner las
señas *o* la dirección
address label eti-
queta (f) (de señas)
address list lista
(f) de direcciones
addressee
destinatario, -ria
adequate
adecuado, -da
adjourn aplazar *o*
diferir
adjourn a meeting
aplazar una reunión
adjudicate in a
dispute arbitrar un
litigio
adjudication
adjudicación (f)
adjudication
tribunal tribunal
(m) de justicia

adjudicator árbitro (mf) o juez (mf)

adjust ajustar o reajustar

adjustment ajuste (m) o reajuste (m)

administration administración (f)

administrative administrativo, -va

administrative body or authority órgano (m) administrativo

administrative expenses gastos (mpl) adminis-trativos

admission entrada (f) o ingreso (m)

admission charge precio (m) de entrada

admit admitir

advance (n) [loan] anticipo (m)

advance (n) [progress] avance (m)

advance (v) [lend] anticipar

advance (v) [progress] avanzar

advanced (adj) anticipado, -a o adelantado, -a

advance booking reserva (f) anticipada

advance on account anticipo (m) a cuenta

advance payment pago (m) anticipado

advertise anunciar o publicar

advertise a new product anunciar un nuevo producto

advertise a vacancy anunciar una vacante

advertisement anuncio (m)

advertiser anunciante (mf)

advertising publicidad (f)

advertising agency agencia (f) de publicidad

advertising budget presupuesto (m) de publicidad

advertising campaign campaña (f) publicitaria

advertising manager jefe (m) de publicidad

advertising rates tarifas (fpl) publicitarias

advertising space espacio (m) publicitario

advice note nota (f) de aviso

advise [suggest] aconsejar

advise [tell what happened] informar

advise against desaconsejar o disuadir

adviser *or* **advisor** asesor, -ra o consejero, -ra

affidavit acta (f) notarial

affiliated afiliado, -da o filial

affiliation (n) afiliación (f)

affirmative afirmativo, -va

afford permitirse un gasto o tener tiempo

after-sales service servicio (m) posventa o de postventa

after-tax profit beneficios (mpl) netos de impuestos

agency agencia (f)

agenda orden (m) del día

agent [in an agency] agente (mf)

agent [representative] representante (mf)

AGM (= annual general meeting) junta general anual

agree [accept] aceptar

agree [approve] acordar

agree [be same as] corresponder o coincidir

agree to do something aceptar hacer algo

agree with [be same as] corresponder *o* coincidir con

agree with [of same opinion] estar de acuerdo

agreed acordado, -da *o* convenido, -da

agreed price precio (m) acordado *o* precio convenido

agreement convenio (m) *o* acuerdo (m) *o* contrato (m) *o* pacto (m)

agricultural agrícola *o* agropecuario, -ria *o* agrario, -ria

aim (n) objetivo (m) *o* propósito (m)

aim (v) proponerse *o* aspirar a

air aire (m)

air freight flete (m) aéreo *o* carga (f) aérea

air freight charges *or* rates tarifas de carga aérea

air letter aerograma (m)

air terminal terminal (f) de aeropuerto

airfreight (v) enviar por carga aérea

airline línea (f) aérea

airmail (n) correo (m) aéreo

airmail (v) enviar por correo aéreo

airmail sticker etiqueta (f) de correo aéreo

airport aeropuerto (m)

airport bus autobús (m) del aeropuerto

airport tax tasas (fpl) de aeropuerto

airport terminal terminal (f) del aeropuerto

airtight packaging embalaje (m) hermético

all expenses paid todos los gastos pagados

all-in todo incluido
all-in price precio (m) todo incluido
all-risks policy póliza (f) a todo riesgo
allocate asignar
allocation of funds provisión (f) de fondos
allow permitir
allow [accept] aceptar
allow [give] conceder o dar
allow for dejar un margen o tener en cuenta
allow 10% for carriage dejar un margen del 10% para el porte
allowance for depreciation cuota (f) de depreciación
alphabetical order orden (m) alfabético
alter modificar
alteration modificación (f)

alternative (adj) alternativo, -va
alternative (n) alternativa (f)
amend enmendar
amendment enmienda (f)
American (adj) americano, -na o estadounidense
American (n) americano, -na o estadounidense (mf)
amortization amortización (f)
amortize amortizar
amount [of money] importe (m) o cantidad (f)
amount owing importe (m) debido
amount paid importe (m) pagado
amount to ascender a
analyse or analyze analizar
analyse the market potential analizar las posibilidades del mercado

analysis análisis (m)
annexe anexo (m)
announce anunciar
o comunicar
announcement
anuncio (m) o
declaración (f)
annual anual
annual accounts
cuentas (fpl)
anuales
**annual general
meeting (AGM)**
junta general anual
annual report
informe (m) anual
annually
anualmente
answer (n)
contestación
(f) o respuesta (f)
answer (v) contes-
tar o responder
answer a letter
contestar una carta
**answer the tele-
phone** contestar el
teléfono
answering machine
contestador (m)
automático

answering service
servicio (m) de
contestación
antedate antedatar
anticipate anticipar
o prever
apartment
apartamento (m)
apologize discul-
parse o presentar
excusas o pedir
perdón
apology disculpa
(f) o excusa (f)
**appeal (n) [against
a decision]**
apelación (f)
**appeal (n) [attrac-
tion]** atractivo (m)
o interés (m)
**appeal (v) [against
a decision]** apelar
**appeal to (v)
[attract]** atraer o
interesar
appear parecer
appendix
apéndice (m)
applicant for a job
candidato, -ta a un
puesto de trabajo

application
aplicación (f)
application [request]
solicitud (f)
application [for a job] solicitud (f) de trabajo
application form impreso (m) o formulario (m) de solicitud
apply (v) aplicar
apply for [ask for] solicitar
apply for a job solicitar un trabajo
apply in writing solicitar por escrito
apply to [affect] referirse a
appoint nombrar
appointment [job] empleo (m)
appointment [meeting] cita (f) o compromiso (m)
appointment [to a job] nombramiento (m)
appointments book agenda (f)

appointments vacant ofertas (fpl) de trabajo
appreciate [how good something is] apreciar o valorar
appreciate [increase in value] subir (en valor)
appreciation [how good something is] apreciación (f) o aprecio (m) o valoración (f)
appreciation [in value] aumento (m) o subida (f)
apprentice aprendiz, -za
appropriate (adj) apropriado, -da
appropriate (v) [funds] asignar o consignar
approval aprobación (f)
approval: on approval a prueba

approve the terms of a contract aprobar los términos de un contrato
approximate aproximado, -da
approximately aproximadamente
arbitrate arbitrar
arbitrate in a dispute arbitrar un litigio *o* en una disputa
arbitration arbitraje (m)
arbitration board *or* **arbitration tribunal** comisión (f) *o* tribunal (m) de arbitraje
arbitrator árbitro (mf)
area área (f)
area [of town] distrito (m) *o* zona (f)
area [region] región (f) *o* zona (f)
area [subject] campo (m)
area code código (m) postal *o* territorial

area manager director, -ra regional
argument discusión (f) *o* argumento (m)
arrange [meeting] organizar
arrange [set out] ordenar *o* disponer *o* acomodar
arrangement acuerdo (m) *o* acomodo (m) *o* arreglo (m)
arrangement [system] plan (m)
arrears atrasos (mpl)
arrival llegada (f)
arrivals llegadas (fpl)
arrive llegar
article artículo (m)
article [clause] cláusula (f)
articles of association estatutos (mpl) *o* escritura (f) de constitución
articulated lorry *or* **articulated vehicle** camión (m) con remolque

as per advice
según nota de
expedición
as per invoice
según factura
as per sample
según muestra
**asap (= as soon as
possible)** lo antes
posible
ask [inquire]
preguntar
ask [request] pedir
ask for solicitar *o*
pedir
ask for a refund
exigir el reembolso
**ask for further
details *or* particu-
lars** pedir más
detalles
assembly asamblea
(f) *o* reunión (f)
**assembly
[putting together]**
montaje (m)
assembly line
cadena (f) de
montaje
assess valorar *o*
evaluar

assess damages
fijar los daños
assessment
valoración (f)
**assessment of
damages** valoración
(f) de daños
asset activo (m)
asset value valor
(m) de activo
**assets and liabili-
ties** activo (m) y
pasivo (m)
assign asignar
**assign a right to
someone** adjudicar
un derecho a alguien
assignee
cesionario, -ria
assignment
asignación (f)
assignment [work]
tarea (f)
assignor
cedente (mf)
assist asistir *o*
ayudar
assistance asisten-
cia (f) *o* ayuda (f)
assistant ayudante
(mf) *o* auxiliar (mf)

assistant manager
subdirector, -ra
**assisted: computer-
assisted** asistido
por ordenador
associate (adj)
asociado, -da *o*
afiliado, -da
associate (n)
socio, -cia
associate company
compañía (f) afiliada
association
asociación (f)
assurance seguro
(m) (de vida)
assurance company
compañía (f) de
seguros
assurance policy
póliza (f) de seguros
**assure someone's
life** asegurar la
vida de alguien
attach adjuntar *o*
sujetar
attachment (n)
[email] adjunto (m)
attack atacar
attend [meeting]
asistir

attended asistido, -da
attend to ocuparse de
attention atención (f)
attorney apoder-
ado, -da *o* procu-
rador, -ra
attract atraer
attraction atrac-
tivo (m)
attractive salary
salario (m)
interesante
auction (n)
subasta (f)
auction (v) subastar
auction rooms sala
(f) de subastas
audit (n) auditoría
(f) *o* intervención
(f) *o* revisión (f) de
cuentas
audit (v) auditar *o*
intervenir
audit the accounts
revisar las cuentas
auditing auditoría (f)
auditor auditor, -ra
o censor, -ra *o*
interventor, -ra
authenticate aut-
entificar *o* legalizar

authority
autoridad (f)
authorization
autorización (f)
authorize autorizar
authorize payment
autorizar el pago
authorized
autorizado, -da
availability
disponibilidad (f)
available dis-
ponible o asequible
available capital
capital (m)
disponible
average (adj)
medio, -dia o
mediano, -na
average (n)
promedio (m)
**average (n) [insur-
ance]** avería (f)
average (v) calcu-
lar el promedio
average price pre-
cio (m) medio o
precio corriente
avoid evitar
await instructions
esperar instrucciones

award (n) premio (m)
award (v) conceder
o adjudicar o otorgar
**award a contract
to someone** adju-
dicar un contrato a
alguien

Bb

back (n) dorso (m)
o reverso (m)
back orders
pedidos (mpl)
pendientes
back payment pago
(m) atrasado
back tax impuesto
(m) atrasado
back up (v) respal-
dar o apoyar
**back up (v) [com-
puter file]** archivar
o guardar
backdate antedatar
backer garante (m)

backhander soborno (m)

backing respaldo (m) *o* apoyo (m) financiero

backlog acumulación (f) de trabajo atrasado

backup (adj) [computer] de reserva

backup copy copia (f) de reserva *o* de seguridad

backwardation margen (m) de cobertura

bad buy mala compra (f)

bad debt deuda (f) morosa *o* incobrable

bag saco (m) *o* bolsa (f)

bail someone out obtener la libertad de alguien bajo fianza

balance (n) equilibrio (m)

balance (n) [accounts] balance (m) *o* saldo (m)

balance (v) equilibrar

balance (v) [accounts] cuadrar *o* saldar

balance brought down *or* brought forward saldo (m)

balance carried down *or* carrried forward saldo (m) a cuenta nueva

balance due to us saldo (m) a (nuestro) favor

balance of payments balanza (f) de pagos

balance of trade balanza (f) comercial

balance sheet balance (m) general *o* de situación

ban (n) prohibición (f)

ban (v) prohibir

bank (n) banco (m)

bank (v) ingresar *o* depositar

bank account cuenta (f) bancaria

bank balance
estado (m) de
cuenta
bank base rate tipo
(m) base de interés
bancario
bank bill (GB) letra
(f) bancaria *o* giro
(m) bancario
bank bill (US)
billete (m) de banco
bank book libreta
(f) de ahorros
bank borrowings
préstamos (mpl)
bancarios
bank charges gas-
tos (mpl) bancarios
bank credit crédito
(m) bancario
bank deposits
depósitos (mpl)
bancarios
bank draft giro (m)
bancario
bank holiday fiesta
(f) oficial
bank loan prés-
tamo (m) bancario
bank manager
director, -ra de banco

bank mandate
orden (f) de pago
bank statement
extracto (m) de
cuentas
bank transfer
transferencia (f)
bancaria
bankable paper
efecto (m) negociable
banker banquero, -ra
banker's draft giro
(m) bancario
banker's order
orden (f) de domi-
ciliación (bancaria)
banking banca (f)
banking hours
horario (m) bancario
banknote billete
(m) (de banco)
bankrupt (adj) en
bancarrota *o* en
quiebra *o* insolvente
bankrupt (n)
quebrado (m)
bankrupt (v)
arruinar
bankruptcy quiebra
(f) *o* insolvencia (f)
o bancarrota (f)

bar chart gráfico (m) de barras
bar code código (m) de barras
bargain (n) [cheaper than usual] ganga (f)
bargain (n) [deal] trato (m) o negocio (m)
bargain (n) [Stock Exchange] venta (f) en la bolsa
bargain (v) negociar o regatear
bargain offer oferta (f) de ocasión
bargain price precio (m) de ocasión o precio irrisorio
bargaining negociación (f)
bargaining position postura (f) negociadora
bargaining power poder (m) de negociación
barrier barrera (f)
barter (n) trueque (m)

barter (v) trocar
bartering trueque (m) o cambio (m) en especie
base (n) base (f)
base (v) basar
base (v) [in a place] radicar o establecer
base year año (m) base
basic (adj) básico, -ca
basic (adj) [most important] fundamental
basic discount descuento (m) básico
basic tax impuesto (m) básico
basis base (f)
batch (n) [of orders] serie (f) o remesa (f) o partida (f)
batch (n) [of products] lote (m)
batch (v) agrupar
batch number número (m) de lote
batch processing procesamiento (m) por lotes

bear (n) [Stock Exchange] bajista (mf)

bear (v) [carry] llevar

bear (v) [interest] devengar *o* rendir

bear (v) [pay for] pagar (costes)

bear market mercado (m) bajista

bearer portador, -ra

bearer bond título (m) al portador

begin empezar *o* comenzar

beginning comienzo (m)

behalf: on behalf of en nombre de

belong to pertenecer

below abajo

benchmark punto (m) de referencia

beneficiary beneficiario, -ria

benefit (n) beneficio (m) *o* subsidio (m)

benefit from (v) beneficiarse de

berth (n) amarradero (m)

berth (v) atracar

best (adj) lo mejor

best (n) (el, la) mejor

best-selling car coche en gran demanda

bid (n) oferta (f)

bid (n) [at an auction] oferta (f) *o* puja (f)

bidder postor (m) *o* licitador (m)

bidding ofertas (fpl) *o* subasta (f) *o* licitación (f)

big (adj) grande

bilateral (adj) bilateral

bill (n) (US) billete (m)

bill (n) [draft] letra (f)

bill (n) [in a restaurant] cuenta (f)

bill (n) [in Parliament] proyecto (m) de ley

bill (n) [invoice] factura (f)

bill (v) facturar

bill of exchange letra (f) de cambio

bill of lading conocimiento (m) de embarque

bill of sale contrato (m) de venta

billing facturación (f)

billion mil millones (mpl)

bills for collection letras (fpl) por cobrar

bills payable letras (fpl) a pagar

bills receivable letras (fpl) a cobrar

binding obligatorio, -ria o vinculante

black economy economía (f) sumergida

black list (n) lista (f) negra

black market mercado (m) negro

blacklist (v) poner en la lista negra

blame (n) culpa (f)

blame (v) culpar o echar la culpa

blank (adj) en blanco

blank (n) blanco (m) o espacio (m) en blanco

blank cheque cheque (m) en blanco

blister pack embalaje (m) de plástico tipo burbuja

block (n) [building] manzana (f)

block (n) [of shares] paquete (m)

block (v) bloquear

block booking reserva (f) en bloque

blocked currency moneda (f) bloqueada

blue chip acción (f) de primera categoría

blue-chip investments inversiones (fpl) en valores seguros

board (n) [group of people] consejo (m) (de administración)

board (v) abordar o embarcarse

board meeting reunión (f) del consejo de administración

board of directors junta (f) directiva

board: on board a bordo

boarding card *or* **boarding pass** tarjeta (f) de embarque

boardroom sala (f) de juntas

bona fide de buena fe

bond (n) bono (m) o título (m)

bonded warehouse depósito (m) aduanero

bonus prima (f) o bonificación (f)

bonus issue emisión (f) gratuita

book (n) libro (m)

book (v) reservar

book sales ventas (fpl) registradas

book value valor (m) contable

booking reserva (f)

booking clerk taquillero, -ra

booking office taquilla (f) o despacho (m) de billetes

bookkeeper contable (mf)

bookkeeping contabilidad (f)

boom (n) auge (m) o 'boom' (m)

boom (v) prosperar o aumentar

boom industry industria (f) próspera o en pleno auge

booming próspero, -ra o floreciente

boost (n) estímulo (m) o impulso (m)

boost (v) estimular o impulsar

border frontera (f)

borrow pedir o tomar prestado

borrower prestatario, -ria

borrowing
préstamo (m)
borrowing power
capacidad (f) de
endeudamiento
boss (informal)
jefe, -fa *o* amo (m)
bottleneck atasco
(m) *o* embotel-
lamiento (m)
bottom fondo (m)
bottom line saldo
(m) final *o* total
bought ledger libro
(m) mayor de compras
bought ledger clerk
encargado (m) del
libro de compras
bounce [cheque]
devolver por falta de
fondos
box number número
de apartado de
correos
boxed set juego
completo en caja
de presentación
boycott (n)
boicot (m)
boycott (v)
boicotear

bracket (n) [tax]
categoría (f) *o*
clase (f)
bracket together
agrupar
brake (n) freno (m)
branch (n) sucursal
(f) *o* rama (f)
branch manager
director (m) de
sucursal
branch office
sucursal (f)
brand marca (f)
brand image ima-
gen (f) de marca
brand loyalty fidel-
idad (f) a la marca
brand name marca
(f) *o* nombre (m)
comercial
brand new comple-
tamente nuevo, -va
breach of contract
violación (f) de
contrato
breach of warranty
violación (f) de
garantía
break (n)
des-canso (m)

break (v) [con-tract] infringir o incumplir

break an agree-ment romper un acuerdo

break down (v) [itemize] desglosar o detallar

break down (v) [machine] estropearse o averiarse

break down (v) [talks] romperse

break even (v) cubrir gastos

break off negotia-tions romper las negociaciones

break the law infringir la ley

breakages roturas (fpl) o desperfectos (mpl)

breakdown (n) [items] desglose (m)

breakdown (n) [machine] avería (f)

breakdown (n) [talks] ruptura (f) o interrupción (f)

breakeven point punto (m) muerto

bribe (n) soborno (m)

bribe (v) sobornar

brief (v) informar o dar instrucciones

briefcase cartera (f) o maletín (m)

bring traer

bring a civil action constituirse parte civil

bring in producir

bring out lanzar al mercado

British británico, -ca o inglés, -esa

brochure folleto (m) publicitario

broke (informal) sin dinero o arruinado, -da

broker agente (mf) o intermediario, -ria

brokerage or **bro-ker's commission** corretaje (m) o comisión (f)

brown paper papel (m) de estraza

bubble pack embalaje (m) de plástico tipo burbuja

budget (n) presupuesto (m)

budget (n) [government] presupuesto (m) del Estado

budget (v) presupuestar

budget account [in bank] cuenta (f) presupuestaria

budgetary presupuestario, -ria

budgetary control control (m) presupuestario

budgetary policy política (f) presupuestaria

budgeting preparación (f) de presupuestos

build construir

building society sociedad (f) hipotecaria o de crédito hipotecario

built-in incorporado, -da

bulk volumen (m)

bulk buying compra (f) a granel

bulk shipments envíos (mpl) a granel

bulky voluminoso, -sa

bull [Stock Exchange] alcista (mf)

bull market mercado (m) alcista

bulletin boletín (m)

bullion oro (m) o plata (f) en lingotes

bureau de change agencia (f) de cambio

bureaucracy burocracia (f)

bus autobús (m)

business negocios (mpl)

business [company] empresa (f) o negocio (m)

business [discussion] asunto (m)

business address dirección (f) comercial

business call visita (f) de negocios

business card
tarjeta (f)
business centre
centro (m) comercial
business class
clase (f) preferente
(en aviones)
business equipment
equipos (mpl) de
oficina
business hours
horas (fpl) de oficina
business letter
carta (f) comercial
business lunch
almuerzo (m) de
negocios
business premises
local (m) comercial
business school
escuela (f)
empresarial
business strategy
estrategia (f)
comercial
business transac-
tion transacción
(f) o trámite (m)
business trip
viaje (m) de
negocios

business: on busi-
ness por asuntos
de negocios
businessman
hombre (m) de
negocios
businesswoman
mujer (f) de
negocios
busy ocupado, -da
buy (v) comprar o
adquirir
buy back volver a
comprar o rescatar
buy for cash
comprar en efectivo
o al contado
buy forward
comprar a futuros
buyer [for a store]
encargado, -da de
compras
buyer [person]
comprador, -ra
buyer's market
mercado (m) de
compradores
buying compra (f)
buying department
departamento (m)
de compras

by-product subpro-ducto (m) *o* pro-ducto (m) derivado

Cc

cable address dirección (f) telegráfica
calculate calcular
calculation cálculo (m)
calculator calcu-ladora (f)
calendar month mes (m) civil
calendar year año (m) civil
call (n) [for money] demanda (f) de pago
call (n) [phone] llamada (f)
call (n) [Stock Exchange] demanda (f) *o* petición (f) de pago (de acciones)

call (n) [visit] visita (f)
call (v) [meeting] convocar (una reunión)
call (v) [phone] llamar (por telé-fono)
call off a deal suspender *o* anular un acuerdo
call on (visit] visitar
call rate frecuencia (f) de visitas de un representante
callable bond obligación (f) redimible
campaign campaña (f)
cancel cancelar *o* suspender *o* anular
cancel a cheque anular un cheque
cancel a contract rescindir *o* anular un contrato
cancellation cancelación (f) *o* anulación (f)

cancellation clause
cláusula (f) de
rescisión
**cancellation [of an
appointment]** can-
celación (f) de una cita
cancelled
cancelado, -da
candidate
candidato, -ta o
aspirante (mf)
canvass solicitar
votos
canvasser persona
(f) que busca clientes
o solicita votos
canvassing
búsqueda (f) de
clientes o solicitación
(f) de votos
**canvassing tech-
niques** técnicas
(fpl) de sondeo
capable capaz o
competente
capable of capaz de
capacity capacidad (f)
capacity [ability]
aptitud (f)
capacity [output]
rendimiento (m)

capacity utilization
empleo (m) de la
capacidad
capital capital (m)
capital [heritage]
patrimonio (m)
capital account
cuenta (f) de capital
capital assets bie-
nes (mpl) de capital
capital equipment
bienes (mpl) de
equipo
capital expenditure
gastos (mpl) de
capital
capital gains
plusvalía (f)
**capital gains
tax** impuesto (m)
sobre las plusvalías
capital goods
bienes (mpl) de
capital
capital loss pérdi-
das (fpl) de capital
o minusvalías (fpl)
**capital-intensive
industry** industria
con alto coeficiente
de capital

capitalist (n)
capitalista (mf)
capitalization
capitalización (f)
**capitalization of
reserves** capital-
ización (f) de las
reservas
capitalize capitalizar
capitalize on
aprovechar
captive market
mercado (m) cautivo
capture acaparar
carbon copy copia
(f) carbón
carbon paper papel
(m) carbón
carbonless sin
papel carbón
**card [business
card]** tarjeta (f)
card [material]
cartulina (f)
card [membership]
carnet (m)
card [postcard]
postal (f) o tarjeta
(f) postal
card index (n)
fichero (m)

card-index (v)
pasar información a
un fichero
card-index file
fichero (m) de
tarjetas
card-indexing paso
(m) de información
a un fichero
cardboard
cartón (m)
cardboard box caja
(f) de cartón
card phone telé-
fono (m) de tarjeta
care of (c/o) para
entregar a
cargo carga (f)
cargo ship barco
(m) de carga
carnet [document]
carnet (m)
carriage porte (m)
o transporte (m)
carriage forward
porte (m) debido
carriage free
franco de porte
carriage paid porte
(m) pagado o franco
a domicilio

carrier empresa (f) de transportes o transportista (mf)

carrier [vehicle] vehículo (m) de transporte

carry llevar o transportar

carry [a motion] aprobar

carry [have in stock] tener en existencia

carry [yield] producir

carry forward pasar a cuenta nueva

carry on a business llevar un negocio

carry out [fulfil] cumplir

carry over a balance pasar a cuenta nueva

cartel cartel (m)

carton cartón (m)

carton [box] caja (f) de cartón

case (n) [box] caja (f)

case (n) [suitcase] maleta (f)

case (v) [put in boxes] poner en una caja o embalar

cash (adv) en efectivo o al contado

cash (n) [money] dinero (m) efectivo

cash a cheque cobrar un cheque

cash account cuenta (f) de caja

cash advance anticipo (m) de caja a cuenta

cash and carry autoservicio (m) mayorista

cash balance saldo (m) de caja

cash book libro (m) de caja

cash card tarjeta (f) de cajero automático o tarjeta de dinero

cash deal transacción (f) en efectivo

cash deposit imposición (f) en efectivo

cash desk caja (f)
cash discount descuento (m) por pago al contado
cash dispenser cajero (m) automático
cash float fondo (m) de caja
cash flow flujo (m) de caja o 'cash flow' (m)
cash flow statement estado (m) de flujo de caja
cash in hand efectivo (m) en caja
cash offer oferta (f) en metálico
cash on delivery (c.o.d.) cobro (m) a la entrega o contra reembolso
cash payment pago (m) en efectivo
cash price precio (m) al contado
cash purchase compra (f) al contado
cash register caja (f) registradora
cash reserves reservas (fpl) de caja
cash sale venta (f) al contado
cash terms pago (m) al contado
cash transaction operación (f) al contado
cash voucher vale (m) de caja
cashable cobrable
cashier cajero, -ra
cashier's check (US) cheque (m) de administración
casting vote voto (m) de calidad
casual work trabajo (m) eventual
casual worker trabajador, -ra eventual o temporero, -ra
catalogue catálogo (m)
catalogue price precio (m) de catálogo
category categoría (f)

cater for abastecer
caveat emptor
por cuenta y riesgo
del comprador
ceiling techo (m) o
límite (m)
ceiling price precio
(m) tope o precio
máximo autorizado
cellular telephone
teléfono (m) celular
o móvil
central central
central bank banco
(m) central
central purchasing
centralización (f) de
las compras
centralization
centralización (f)
centralize centralizar
centre centro (m)
CEO (= chief execu-
tive officer) jefe
(m) ejecutivo o
director (m) general
certificate
certificado (m)
certificate of
approval certificado
(m) de aprobación

certificate of
deposit certificado
(m) de depósito
certificate of guar-
antee certificado
(m) de garantía
certificate of origin
certificado (m) de
origen
certificate of regis-
tration certificado
(m) de registro
certificated
titulado, -da o
diplomado, -da
certificated bank-
rupt quebrado (m)
rehabilitado
certified account-
ant censor jurado
de cuentas
certified cheque
cheque (m)
conformado
certified copy
compulsa (f) o copia
(f) auténtica o
certificada
certify certificar
cession cesión (f)
chain cadena (f)

chain store tienda (f) de una cadena *o* sucursal (f)

chairman presidente, -ta

chairman and managing director presidente y director gerente

Chamber of Commerce Cámara (f) de Comercio

change (n) cambio (m)

change (n) [cash] dinero (m) suelto *o* moneda (f) suelta

change (n) [in a shop] vuelta (f)

change (v) cambiar

change hands cambiar de dueño

change machine máquina (f) de cambio

channel (n) canal (m)

channel (v) dirigir *o* encauzar

channels of distribution canales (mpl) de distribución

charge (n) coste (m) *o* precio (m) *o* cargo (m)

charge (n) [in court] acusación (f) *o* cargo (m)

charge (n) [on account] débito (m)

charge (v) cargar

charge (v) [in court] acusar

charge (v) [price] cobrar

charge a purchase cargar una compra en cuenta

charge account cuenta (f) abierta *o* cuenta de crédito

charge card tarjeta (f) de crédito

chargeable (to) a cargo de

charges forward gastos (mpl) a cobrar a la entrega

chart (n) gráfico (m), gráfica (f)

charter (n) flete (m) *o* alquiler (m)

charter (v) fletar *o* alquilar
charter an aircraft fletar un avión
charter flight vuelo (m) chárter
charter plane avión (m) chárter
charterer fletador, -ra
chase perseguir
chase [an order] apremiar
cheap barato, -ta
cheap labour mano de obra barata
cheap money dinero (m) *o* crédito (m) barato
cheap rate tarifa (f) reducida
check (n) [examination] control (m) *o* comprobación (f)
check (n) [stop] freno (m)
check (v) [examine] comprobar *o* cotejar
check (v) [stop] parar *o* contener

check in [at airport] facturar el equipaje
check in [at hotel] registrarse
check-in (counter) [at airport] mostrador (m) de facturación
check-in time horario (m) de presentación en el aeropuerto
check out [of hotel] pagar la cuenta y marcharse
checkout [in supermarket] caja (f)
check sample muestra (f) de inspección
cheque cheque (m)
cheque (guarantee) card tarjeta (f) de crédito
cheque account cuenta (f) corriente
cheque book talonario (m) de cheques

cheque number
número (m) de
cheque
cheque stub matriz
(f) de un talonario
cheque to bearer
cheque (m) al
portador
chief (adj)
principal *o* jefe
chief clerk jefe (m)
de oficina
chief executive
jefe (m) ejecutivo
choice (adj)
escogido, -da *o*
selecto, -ta
**choice (n) [choos-
ing]** elección (f)
o selección (f)
**choice (n) [items
to choose from]**
surtido (m)
**choice (n) [thing cho-
sen]** preferencia (f)
choose elegir
Christmas bonus
paga (f) extraordi-
naria de Navidad
chronic crónico, -ca
o endémico, -ca

chronological order
orden (m) cronológico
**c.i.f. (= cost, insur-
ance and freight)**
cif (coste, seguro y
flete)
**circular (n) *or* circu-
lar letter** circular (f)
**circular letter of
credit** carta (f) de
crédito general
circulation
circulación (f) *o*
difusión (f)
**circulation [news-
paper]** tirada (f)
city centre centro
(m) de la ciudad
civil law derecho
(m) civil
civil servant
funcionario, -ria
claim (n)
reclamación (f) *o*
demanda (f) *o*
reivindicación (f)
claim (v) exigir *o*
reclamar *o*
reivindicar
claim (v) [suggest]
alegar *o* pretender

claimant
demandante (mf)
claims department
departamento (m)
de reclamaciones
claims manager
director, -ra de
reclamaciones
clarify (v) aclarar
o clarificar
class (n) clase (f)
o categoría (f)
classification
clasificación (f)
classified ads or
advertisements
anuncios (mpl) por
palabras
classified directory
directorio (m)
comercial
classify clasificar
clause cláusula (f)
clawback
devolución (f) (de
impuestos)
clear (adj) claro, -ra
clear (v) aclarar o
clarificar
clear (v) [stock]
liquidar existencias

clear a cheque
tramitar el pago de
un cheque
clear a debt
liquidar una deuda
clear profit
ganancia (f) neta
**clearance certifi-
cate** certificado
(m) de aduana
**clearance of a
cheque** tramitación
(f) del pago de un
cheque
clearing [paying]
liquidación (f) o
pago (m) de una
deuda
clearing bank
banco (m) comercial
clerical de oficina
clerical error error
(m) de copia o error
de oficina
clerical staff per-
sonal (m) de oficina
clerical work tra-
bajo (m) de oficina
clerk oficinista
(mf) o empleado,
-da de oficina

client cliente (mf)
clientele clientela (f)
climb subir o
aumentar
clinch cerrar un trato
clipping service
servicio (m) de
recortes de prensa
close (n) [end]
cierre (m)
close (v) [after
work] cerrar
close a bank
account cerrar una
cuenta bancaria
close a meeting
clausurar o levantar
una sesión
close an account
cerrar una cuenta
close down cerrar
close to cercano,
-na o próximo, -ma
closed cerrado, -da
closed circuit TV
circuito cerrado
closed market mer-
cado (m) cerrado
closing (adj) final
o al cierre
closing (n) cierre (m)

closing balance
saldo (m) final
closing bid oferta
(f) final
closing date fecha
(f) tope o fecha límite
closing price precio
(m) al cierre
closing stock exis-
tencias (fpl) finales
closing time hora
(f) de cierre
closing-down sale
liquidación (f)
total por cierre
closure clausura (f)
o cierre (m)
c/o (= care of)
para entregar a
co-creditor
coacreedor, -ra
co-director
co-director, -ra
co-insurance
coaseguro (m)
co-operate
cooperar
co-operation
cooperación (f)
co-operative (adj)
cooperativo, -va

co-operative (n)
cooperativa (f)
co-opt someone
nombrar por
coopción
co-owner
copropietario, -ria
co-ownership
copropiedad (f)
COD *or* c.o.d.
**(= cash on deliv-
ery)** cobro a la
entrega *o* contra
reembolso
code código (m)
code of practice
normas (fpl) de
conducta
coding codificación (f)
coin moneda (f)
cold call visita (f)
comercial sin cita
previa
cold start empezar
un negocio a cero
cold storage
almacenaje (m)
frigorífico
cold store almacén
(m) frigorífico
collaborate colaborar

collaboration
colaboración (f)
collapse (n)
hundimiento (m) *o*
derrumbamiento (m)
collapse (v)
hundirse *o*
derrumbarse
collateral (adj)
colateral
collateral (n)
garantía (f)
collect (v) [fetch]
recoger
collect (v) [money]
cobrar
collect a debt
cobrar una deuda
collect call (US)
llamada (f) a cobro
revertido
collection
recogida (f)
**collection [of
money]** cobro (m)
collection charges
or **collection rates**
cobro (m) por
recogida
collective
colectivo, -va

collective owner-ship propiedad (f) colectiva

collective wage agreement convenio (m) salarial colectivo

collector cobrador, -ra o recaudador, -ra

commerce comercio (m)

commercial (adj) comercial

commercial (n) [TV] emisión (f) publicitaria o anuncio (m)

commercial attaché agregado, -da comercial

commercial college escuela (f) superior de comercio

commercial course curso (m) comercial

commercial directory guía (f) comercial

commercial district distrito (m) comercial

commercial failure quiebra (f) comercial

commercial law derecho (m) mercantil

commercial traveller representante (mf)

commercial under-taking empresa (f) comercial

commercialization comercialización (f)

commercialize comercializar

commission [com-mittee] comisión (f) o comité (m)

commission [money] comisión (f)

commission agent comisionista (mf)

commission rep representante (mf) a comisión

commit [crime] cometer

commit funds to a project asignar fondos a un proyecto

commitments
compromisos (mpl)
commodity
mercancía (f)
commodity
exchange lonja (f)
o bolsa (f) de
contratación o de
comercio
commodity futures
materias primas
cotizadas en el mer-
cado de futuros
commodity market
lonja (f) o bolsa (f)
de contratación
common [frequent]
corriente o
frecuente
common [to more
than one] común o
público, -ca
common carrier
empresa (f) de
transporte público
Common Market
Mercado Común
Europeo
common ownership
propiedad (f)
colectiva

common pricing
fijación (f) colectiva
de precios
communicate
comunicar o
comunicarse
communication
comunicación (f)
communication
[message]
comunicado (m)
communications
comunicaciones (fpl)
community
comunidad (f)
commute [exchange]
conmutar
commute [travel]
viajar diariamente al
trabajo
commuter viajero
diario o viajera
diaria
companies' register
registro (m) de
compañías
company compañía
(f) o sociedad (f)
company director
director, -ra de una
empresa

company law ley (f) de sociedades anómimas
company secretary secretario, -ria de una empresa
comparability posibilidad (f) de comparación
comparable comparable
compare comparar o cotejar
compare with comparar con
comparison comparación (f)
compensate compensar o indemnizar o resarcir
compensation compensación (f)
compensation for damage indemnización (f) por daños y perjuicios
compete (with) competir (con)
competent competente

competing (adj) competitivo, -va
competing firms empresas (fpl) rivales
competing products productos (mpl) en competencia
competition competencia (f)
competitive competitivo, -va
competitive price precio (m) competitivo
competitive pricing fijación (f) de precios competitivos
competitive products productos (mpl) competitivos
competitively priced con precio competitivo
competitiveness competitividad (f)
competitor competidor, -ra
complain (about) quejarse
complaint queja (f)

**complaints depart-
ment** oficina (f) de
reclamaciones
complementary
complementario, -ria
complete (adj)
completo, -ta
complete (v)
completar o acabar
completion
finalización (f)
completion date
fecha (f) de
cumplimiento
**completion of a
contract** firma (f)
de un contrato
compliance
conformidad (f) o
acuerdo (m)
complimentary de
favor
**complimentary
ticket** entrada (f)
de favor
compliments slip
saluda (m) o
tarjeta (f) de
saludo
comply with
obedecer

**composition [with
creditors]** aco-
modamiento (m)
compound interest
interés (m) compuesto
comprehensive com-
pleto, -ta o global
**comprehensive
insurance** seguro
(m) a todo riesgo
compromise (n)
compromiso (m) o
acuerdo (m)
compromise (v)
transigir
compulsory
obligatorio, -ria
**compulsory liqui-
dation** liquidación
(f) forzosa
**compulsory pur-
chase** expropiación
(f) forzosa
computer
ordenador (m)
computer bureau
oficina (f) de
informática
**computer depart-
ment** departamento
(m) de informática

computer error
error (m) de
ordenador
computer file
archivo (m) *o*
fichero (m)
computer language
lenguaje (m)
informático *o* de
ordenador
computer listing
listado (m) de
ordenador
computer printer
impresora (f)
computer printout
copia (f) impresa
(de ordenador)
computer program
programa (m) de
ordenador
**computer program-
mer** programador,
-ra de ordenadores
**computer program-
ming** programación
(f) de
ordenador
computer services
servicios (mpl) de
informática

computer system
sistema (m)
informático
computer terminal
terminal (m) de
ordenador
computer time
tiempo (m)
invertido por el
ordenador
computer-readable
legible por
ordenador
**computer-readable
codes** códigos (mpl)
legibles por
ordenador
computerize
informatizar
computerized
informatizado, -da *o*
informático, -ca
**concealment of
assets** encubrim-
iento (m) de activos
**concern (n) [busi-
ness]** negocio (m)
o empresa (f)
concern (n) [worry]
preocupación (f) *o*
inquietud (f)

concern (v) [deal with] concernir
concession [reduction] desgravación (f)
concession [right] concesión (f) o agencia (f) exclusiva
concessionaire concesionario, -ria
conciliation conciliación (f)
conclude [agreement] concluir
conclusion conclusión (f)
condition condición (f)
condition: on condition that a condición de que
conditional condicional
conditions of employment condiciones (fpl) de empleo
conditions of sale condiciones (fpl) de venta
conduct negotiations llevar negociaciones

conference [large] congreso (m)
conference [small] asamblea (f) o conferencia (f)
conference phone teléfono (m) de conferencias
conference room sala (f) de conferencias
confess confesar
confidence confianza (f)
confidential confidencial
confidential report informe (m) confidencial
confidentiality confidencialidad (f)
confirm confirmar
confirm a booking confirmar una reserva
confirm someone in a job confirmar a alguien en su puesto de trabajo
confirmation confirmación (f)

conflict of interest conflicto (m) de intereses
conglomerate conglomerado (m)
congress congreso (m)
connect conectar *o* relacionar
connecting flight vuelo (m) de correspondencia
connection vínculo (m) *o* relación (f) *o* enchufe (m)
consider considerar
consign consignar
consignee consignatario, -ria
consignment [sending] consignación (f) *o* envío (m) *o* expedición (f)
consignment [things sent] envío (m) *o* remesa (f)
consignment note nota (f) de expedición *o* nota de envío

consignor remitente (mf) *o* consignador, -ra
consist of constar de
consolidate consolidar
consolidate [shipments] agrupar
consolidated consolidado, -da
consolidated shipment envío (m) agrupado de mercancías
consolidation agrupación (f)
consortium consorcio (m)
constant constante *o* invariable *o* continuo, -nua
consult consultar
consultancy asesoría (f)
consultancy firm asesoría (f) *o* consultoría (f)
consultant asesor, -ra *o* consejero, -ra
consulting engineer técnico (m) asesor *o* técnica (f) asesora

consumables
bienes (mpl) de
consumo
consumer
consumidor, -ra
consumer credit
crédito (m) al
consumidor
consumer durables
bienes (mpl) de
consumo duraderos
consumer goods
bienes (mpl) de
consumo
consumer panel
equipo (m) de
consumidores
**consumer price
index** índice (m)
de precios al
consumo (IPC)
**consumer protec-
tion** protección (f)
al consumidor
consumer research
investigación (f)
sobre el consumo
consumer spending
gastos (mpl) del
consumidor o de
consumo

consumption
consumo (m)
contact (n)
contacto (m)
**contact: useful
contact**
enchufe (m)
contact (v)
contactar
contain contener
container [box, tin]
recipiente (m) o
envase (m)
**container [for ship-
ping]** contenedor (m)
container port
puerto (m) de
contenedores
container ship
buque (m) de
contenedores o por-
tacontenedores
container terminal
terminal (f) de
contenedores
containerization
contenerización (f)
**containerization
[shipping]**
transporte (m) en
contenedores

containerize poner en contenedores
containerize [ship in containers] transportar en contenedores
content significado (m)
contents contenido (m)
contested takeover oferta (f) de adquisición disputada o rebatida
contingency eventualidad (f) o contingencia (f)
contingency fund fondo (m) para imprevistos
contingency plan plan (m) de emergencia
continual continuo, -nua
continually continuamente
continuation continuación (f)
continue continuar o proseguir

continuous continuo, -nua
continuous feed alimentación (f) continua
continuous stationery papel (m) continuo
contra account cuenta (f) compensada
contra an entry anotar una contrapartida o un contraasiento
contra entry contrapartida (f) o contraasiento (m)
contract (n) contrato (m)
contract (v) contratar
contract law derecho (m) de contratos o de obligaciones
contract note contrato (m) de Bolsa
contract of employment contrato (m) de empleo

contract work trabajo (m) a contrata
contracting party parte (f) contratante
contractor contratista (mf)
contractual contractual
contractual liability responsabilidad (f) contractual
contractually según o por contrato
contrary contrario, -ria
contrast (n) contraste (m)
contribute contribuir o cotizar
contribution contribución (f) o colaboración (f)
contribution of capital contribución (f) de capital
contributor contribuyente (mf)
control (n) [check] control (m)

control (n) [power] control (m) o mando (m)
control (v) controlar
control a business controlar o dirigir un negocio
control key tecla (f) de control
control systems sistemas (mpl) de control
controlled economy economía (f) dirigida
controller [who checks] inspector, -ra
controller (US) contable (mf) jefe
controlling (adj) dominante
convene convocar
convenient cómodo, -da o conveniente
conversion conversión (f)
conversion of funds apropiación (f) indebida de fondos

conversion price *or* **conversion rate** precio (m) de conversión *o* tasa (f) de conversión

convert convertir

convertibility convertibilidad (f)

convertible currency moneda (f) convertible

convertible loan stock valores (mpl) convertibles en acciones

conveyance transmisión (f) del título de propiedad

conveyancer notario, -ria especialista en escrituras de trapaso

conveyancing transmisión (f) de títulos de propiedad

cooling off period (after purchase) periodo (m) de reflexión

cooperative society sociedad (f) cooperativa

copartner socio, -cia

copartnership coparticipación (f)

cope arreglárselas *o* hacer frente (a)

copier fotocopiadora (f)

copy (n) copia (f)

copy (n) [book, newspaper] ejemplar (m) *o* número (m)

copy (v) copiar

copying machine multicopista (f)

corner (n) [inside angle] rincón (m)

corner (n) [outside angle] esquina (f)

corner (n) [monopoly] monopolio

corner shop tienda (f) de barrio *o* de la esquina

corner the market acaparar el mercado

corporate image imagen (f) pública de una empresa

corporate name razón (f) social

corporate plan
plan (m) de trabajo
de una empresa
corporate planning
planificación (f)
empresarial
corporate profits
beneficios (mpl)
de la empresa
corporation
corporación (f) o
sociedad (f)
mercantil
corporation tax
impuesto (m) de
sociedades
correct (adj)
correcto, -ta
correct (v) corregir
o rectificar
correction
corrección (f) o
rectificación (f)
**correspond with
someone** escribir
a alguien
**correspond with
something**
corresponder a algo
correspondence
correspondencia (f)

correspondent
[journalist] corre-
sponsal (mf)
correspondent
[who writes let-
ters] correspondi-
ente (mf)
cost (n) costo (m)
o coste (m)
cost (v) costar o
valer
cost accountant
contable (mf) de
costes
cost accounting
contabilidad (f) de
costes
cost analysis análi-
sis (m) de costes
cost centre centro
(m) de costes
cost factor factor
(m) del coste
cost of living coste
(m) de vida
cost of sales coste
(m) de ventas
cost plus costo (m)
más honorarios o
porcentaje (m) de
comisión

cost price precio (m) de coste

cost, insurance and freight (c.i.f.) coste, seguro y flete o cif

cost-benefit analysis análisis (m) coste-beneficio

cost-cutting reducción (f) de costes

cost-effective rentable

cost-effectiveness rentabilidad (f)

cost-of-living allowance subsidio (m) de carestía de vida

cost-of-living bonus plus (m) de carestía de vida

cost-of-living increase aumento (m) de sueldo por coste de vida

cost-of-living index índice (m) del coste de vida

cost-push inflation inflación (f) de costes

costing cálculo (m) de costos

costly costoso, -sa

costs costas (fpl)

counsel abogado, -da

count (v) [add] contar o calcular

counter mostrador (m) o ventanilla (f)

counter staff personal (m) de atención al público

counter-claim (n) reconvención (f)

counter-claim (v) presentar una reconvención

counter-offer *or* **counterbid (n)** contraoferta (f)

counterfeit (adj) falso, -sa o falsificado, -da

counterfeit (v) falsificar dinero

counterfoil matriz (f) (de un talonario)

countermand revocar

countersign refrendar

country país (m)
country [not town] campo (m)
country of origin país (m) de origen
coupon cupón (m)
coupon ad cupón (m) de anuncio
courier [guide] guía (mf) de turismo
courier [messenger] mensajero, -ra
court tribunal (m) o juzgado (m)
court case proceso (m) o causa (f) o juicio (m)
covenant (n) pacto (m) o convenio (m)
covenant (v) pactar
cover (n) cubierta (f) o funda (f)
cover (n) [insurance] cobertura (f)
cover (v) cubrir
cover a risk cubrir un riesgo
cover charge [restaurant] (precio del) cubierto (m)

cover costs cubrir gastos
cover note póliza (f) provisional o nota (f) de cobertura
covering letter carta (f) adjunta o explicatoria
covering note carta (f) adjunta o explicatoria
crane grúa (f)
crash (n) [accident] choque (m) o colisión (f)
crash (n) [financial] 'crack' (m)
crash (v) chocar
crash (v) [fail] quebrar
crate (n) cajón (m)
crate (v) embalar
credit (n) crédito (m)
credit (v) abonar o acreditar
credit account cuenta (f) de crédito
credit agency agencia (f) de informes comerciales

credit balance haber (m) o saldo (m) acreedor o a favor

credit bank banco (m) de crédito

credit card tarjeta (f) de crédito

credit card sale venta (f) con tarjeta de crédito

credit ceiling techo (m) crediticio

credit column columna (f) del haber

credit control control (m) de crédito

credit entry abono (m)

credit facilities facilidades (fpl) de crédito

credit freeze congelación (f) de créditos

credit limit límite (m) de crédito

credit note nota (f) de abono o nota (f) de crédito

credit policy política (f) crediticia

credit rating clasificación (f) crediticia

credit side haber (m)

credit-worthy solvente

credit: on credit a crédito

creditor acreedor, -ra

cross a cheque cruzar un cheque

cross off or **cross out** tachar

cross rate tipo (m) de cambio cruzado

crossed cheque cheque (m) cruzado

crowd multitud (f)

cubic cúbico, -ca

cubic measure medida (f) de volumen o de capacidad

cum coupon con cupón de interés

cum dividend con dividendo

cumulative acumulativo, -va

cumulative interest
interés (m)
acumulativo
**cumulative prefer-
ence share** acción
(f) preferente
acumulativa
currency moneda (f)
**currency conver-
sion** conversión (f)
de divisas
currency note
billete (m) de banco
currency reserves
reservas (fpl) de
divisas
current actual *o*
corriente
current account
cuenta (f)
corriente
current assets
activo (m) circulante
**current cost
accounting**
contabilidad (f) de
costes actuales
current liabilities
pasivo (m) circu-
lante *o* obligaciones
(fpl) a corto plazo

current price pre-
cio (m) actual
**current rate of
exchange** tipo (m)
de cambio actual
current yield
rendimiento (m)
corriente
**curriculum vitae
(CV)** curriculum
(vitae) (m)
curve curva (f)
custom clientela (f)
custom-built *or* **custom-made** hecho a
medida *o* a la orden
customer cliente
(mf)
customer appeal
atractivo (m) para
los clientes
customer loyalty
fidelidad (f) a un
establecimiento
**customer satisfac-
tion** satisfacción
(f) del cliente
**customer service
department** depar-
tamento (m) de
atención al cliente

customs aduana (f)
Customs and Excise
Aduanas y Arbitrios
customs barriers
barreras (fpl)
arancelarias
customs broker
agente (mf) de
aduanas
customs clearance
despacho (m) adu-
anero o de aduanas
**customs declara-
tion** declaración
(f) de aduana
**customs declara-
tion form** impreso
(m) de declaración
de aduana
customs duty dere-
cho (m) de aduana
**customs entry
point** puesto (m)
aduanero
**customs examina-
tion** inspección
(f) aduanera
**customs
formalities**
formalidades (fpl)
aduaneras

customs officer
or **customs official**
aduanero, -ra o fun-
cionario, -ria de
aduanas
customs receipt
recibo (m) de
aduana
customs seal
precinto (m) de
aduana
customs tariff
arancel (m)
aduanero
customs union
unión (f) aduanera
cut (n) recorte (m)
o rebaja (f)
cut (v) recortar
**cut down on expen-
ses** reducir gastos
cut price (n) precio
(m) reducido
cut-price (adj) a
precio reducido
cut-price goods
mercancías (fpl) a
precio reducido
cut-price petrol
gasolina a precio
reducido

cut-price store
tienda (f) de rebajas
cut-throat competi-
tion competencia
(f) encarnizada
CV (= curriculum
vitae) curriculum
(vitae) (m) **cycle**
ciclo (m)
cyclical cíclico, -a
cyclical factors
factores (mpl)
cíclicos

Dd

daily diario, -ria
daisy-wheel printer
impresora (f) de
rueda de margarita
damage (n) daño (m)
damage (v) dañar
damage survey
inspección (f) de
daños

damage to property
daños (mpl)
materiales
damaged
dañado, -da o
tarado, -da o
deteriorado, -da
damages daños
(mpl) y perjuicios
data datos (mpl)
data processing
elaboración (f) o
proceso (m) de
datos
data retrieval
recuperación (f) de
datos
database base (f)
de datos
date (n) fecha (f)
date (v) fechar
date of receipt
fecha (f) de
recepción
date stamp
fechador (m)
dated [with date]
con fecha de
dated [old]
anticuado, -da
day día (m)

day [working day]
jornada (f)
day shift turno (m)
de día
day-to-day
cotidiano, -na o
diario, -ria
dead (adj) [person]
muerto, -ta o
fallecido, -da
dead account
cuenta inactiva
dead loss siniestro
(m) o pérdida (f)
total
deadline fecha (f)
tope o plazo (m)
límite (m)
deadlock (n) punto
(m) muerto
deadlock (v) estar
en punto muerto
deadweight peso
(m) muerto
deadweight cargo
carga (f) por peso
muerto
**deadweight ton-
nage** toneladas
(fpl) de peso
muerto

deal (n) transac-
ción (f) o negocio
(m) o trato (m)
deal in (v)
comerciar (en) o
negociar (en)
deal with an order
servir un pedido
deal with someone
tratar o comerciar
con alguien
dealer comerciante
(mf) o tratante (mf)
**dealing [Stock
Exchange]** opera-
ciones (fpl) en bolsa
dear caro, -ra
debate debate (m)
o discusión (f)
debenture bono
(m) o pagaré (m) de
interés fijo
debenture holder
obligacionista (mf)
debit (n) débito
(m) o debe (m)
debit an account
adeudar o cargar en
cuenta
debit balance saldo
(m) deudor

debit column
columna (f) del debe
debit entry asiento
(m) de débito o
adeudo
debit note nota (f)
de adeudo
debits and credits
debe y haber
debt deuda (f)
debt collection
cobro (m) de
morosos
**debt collection
agency** agencia
(f) de cobro de
morosos
debt collector
cobrador (m) de
morosos
debtor deudor, -ra
o prestatario, -ria
debtor side debe (m)
debts due deudas
(fpl) a pagar
decentralization
descentralización (f)
decentralize
descentralizar
decide decidir o
optar

**decide on a course
of action** optar por
una línea de conducta
deciding
decisivo, -va
deciding factor
factor decisivo
decimal (n)
decimal (m)
decimal point
punto (m) decimal
decision decisión (f)
decision maker
persona (f) que
toma las
decisiones
decision making
toma (f) de deci-
siones
**decision-making
body** órgano (m)
decisorio
**decision-making
processes**
procesos (mpl)
decisorios
deck cubierta (f)
deck cargo carga
(f) en cubierta
declaration
declaración (f)

declaration of bankruptcy declaración (f) de quiebra

declaration of income declaración (f) de renta

declare declarar *o* confesar

declare goods to customs declarar mercancías en la aduana

declare someone bankrupt declarar a alguien en quiebra

declared declarado, -da

declared value valor (m) declarado

decline (n) baja (f) *o* descenso (m)

decline (v) [fall] disminuir

decontrol liberalizar *o* suprimir controles

decrease (n) descenso (m) *o* reducción (f) *o* disminución (f)

decrease (v) disminuir *o* reducir

decrease in price bajada (f) de precio

decrease in value disminución (f) de valor

decreasing (adj) decreciente

deduct deducir *o* descontar

deductible deducible

deduction deducción (f)

deed título (m) *o* escritura (f)

deed of assignment escritura (f) de cesión

deed of covenant escritura (f) de convenio

deed of partnership escritura (f) de sociedad

deed of transfer escritura (f) de transferencia

default (n) incumplimiento (m)

default (v) incumplir
**default on pay-
ments** incumplir
los pagos
defaulter
deudor, -ra
defect defecto (m)
o tara (f)
defective [faulty]
defectuoso, -sa
**defective [not
valid]** defec-
tivo, -va
defence defensa
(f) o protección (f)
defence counsel
abogado (m)
defensor
defend defender o
proteger
defend a lawsuit
defenderse en juicio
defendant deman-
dado, -da o acusado,
-da o parte
demandada
defer aplazar o diferir
defer payment
diferir el pago
deferment
aplazamiento (m)

**deferment of pay-
ment** aplazamiento
(m) de pago
deferred
diferido, -da o
aplazado, -da
deferred creditor
acreedor (m)
diferido
deferred payment
pago (m) aplazado
deficit déficit (m)
deficit financing
financiación (f)
del déficit pre-
supuestario
deflation
deflación (f)
deflationary
deflacionista
defray [costs]
pagar o sufragar
**defray someone's
expenses** costear
los gastos de
alguien
del credere prima
(f) al comisionista
del credere agent
agente (mf) del
credere

delay (n) demora (f) o retraso (m)
delay (v) demorar o retrasar
delegate (n) delegado, -da
delegate (v) delegar
delegation delegación (f)
delete suprimir
deliver entregar o repartir
delivered price precio (m) de entrega
delivery entrega (f) o reparto (m)
delivery date fecha (f) de entrega
delivery note albarán (m)
delivery of goods reparto (m) de mercancías
delivery order orden (f) de expedición
delivery time plazo (m) de entrega

delivery van furgoneta (f) de reparto
deliveryman recadero (m)
demand (n) demanda (f)
demand (n) [for payment] reclamación (f) o requerimiento (m) de pago
demand (v) exigir o reclamar
demand deposit depósito (m) a la vista
demonstrate demostrar o mostrar (el funcionamiento de algo)
demonstration demostración (f) o prueba (f)
demonstration model modelo (m) de prueba
demonstrator exhibidor, -ra
demurrage gastos (mpl) de demora

department departamento (m) o sección (f)

department [in government] Departamento (m) de Estado o ministerio (m)

department [in shop] sección (de tienda)

department store grandes almacenes (mpl)

departmental departamental

departmental manager jefe, -fa de departamento o de sección

departure [going away] salida (f)

departure [new venture] novedad (f)

departure lounge sala (f) de embarque

departures salidas (fpl)

depend on depender de

depending on según

deposit (n) [in bank] depósito (m) o ingreso (m) o imposición (f)

deposit (n) [paid in advance] depósito o señal (f) o entrada (f)

deposit (v) depositar o ingresar

deposit account cuenta (f) de depósito o cuenta a plazo

deposit slip recibo (m) (de depósito)

depositor depositante (mf) o impositor, -ra

depository [place] almacén (m)

depot almacén (m) central o centro (m) de transporte

depreciate [amortize] amortizar o depreciar

depreciate [lose value] depreciarse o perder valor

depreciation [amortizing] amortización (f) o depreciación (f)

depreciation [loss of value] depreciación (f) o pérdida (f) de valor

depreciation rate coeficiente (m) o tasa (f) de amortización

depression depresión (f) o crisis (f) económica

dept (= department) dpto. (= departamento)

deputize for someone sustituir a alguien

deputy delegado, -da o adjunto, -ta o suplente (mf)

deputy manager subdirector, -ra o director, -ra adjunto, -ta

deputy managing director director, -ra general adjunto, -ta

deregulation liberalización (f) o desregulación (f)

describe describir o exponer

description descripción (f)

design (n) diseño (m)

design (v) diseñar o proyectar

design department departamento (m) de diseño

desk escritorio (m) o mesa (f) de despacho

desk diary agenda (f) de mesa (de despacho)

desk-top publishing (DTP) autoedición (f) o publicación (f) asistida por ordenador

despatch (= dispatch) destination destino (m)

detail (n) detalle (m)

detail (v) detallar

detailed detallado, -da

detailed account
cuenta (f) *o* factura
(f) detallada
determine determinar
Deutschmark
marco (m) alemán
devaluation
devaluación (f) *o*
desvalorización (f)
devalue devaluar *o*
desvalorizar
develop [build]
construir
develop [plan]
desarrollar
developing country
país (m) en vías de
desarrollo
development
desarrollo (m)
device aparato (m)
o dispositivo (m) *o*
estratagema (f)
diagram diagrama (m)
dial (v) marcar
dial a number
marcar un número
dial direct marcar
directamente
dialling acto (m)
de marcar

dialling code
prefijo (m)
dialling tone señal
(f) de línea
diary agenda (f)
dictate dictar
dictating machine
dictáfono (m)
dictation dictado (m)
differ diferir *o* ser
distinto
difference
diferencia (f)
differences in price
diferencias (fpl) de
precio
different distinto,
-ta *o* diferente
differential (adj)
diferencial
differential tariffs
tarifas (fpl)
diferenciadas
difficult difícil
difficulty
dificultad (f)
digit dígito (m)
dilution of equity
dilución (f) del capital
dimensions
dimensiones (fpl)

direct (adj)
directo, -ta
direct (adv)
directamente
direct (v) dirigir
direct cost coste (m)
directo
direct debit domi-
ciliación (f) bancaria
direct mail venta (f)
por correo
direct mailing
envío (m) de publi-
cidad por correo
direct selling venta
(f) directa
direct tax impuesto
(m) directo
direct taxation
imposición (f)
directa
**direct-mail adver-
tising** publicidad (f)
por correo
direction dirección (f)
directions for use
instrucciones (fpl) o
modo de empleo
directive directriz
(f) o directiva (f)
o instrucción (f)

director director,
-ra o consejero, -ra
directory
directorio (m)
disagreement
desacuerdo (m)
disburse
desembolsar
disbursement
desembolso (m)
**discharge (n) [of
debt]** pago (m) o
descargo (m)
**discharge (v)
[employee]**
despedir
discharge a debt
pagar una deuda
disclaimer
renuncia (f) o
abandono (m) de
responsabilidad
disclose revelar o
divulgar
**disclose a piece of
information**
revelar una
información
disclosure
divulgación (f) o
revelación (f)

**disclosure of confi-
dential information**
revelación (f) de
información
confidencial
discontinue sus-
pender o interrumpir
discount (n) des-
cuento (m) o rebaja (f)
discount (v)
descontar
**discount house
[bank]** banco (m)
de descuento
**discount house
[shop]** tienda (f)
de rebajas
discount price
precio (m) de
descuento
discount rate tipo
(m) o tasa (f) de
descuento
discount store
tienda (f) de rebajas
discountable
descontable
**discounted cash flow
(DCF)** cash flow
actualizado o flujo de
caja descontado

discounter banco
(m) de descuento
discredit (v)
desacreditar
discrepancy dis-
crepancia (f) o
diferencia (f)
discuss discutir
discussion discusión
(f) o debate (m)
dishonour
deshonorar
dishonour a bill
devolver una letra
disk disco (m)
disk drive
disquetera (f)
diskette disquete
(m) o diskette
**dismiss an
employee** despedir
a un empleado
dismissal despido (m)
**dispatch (n) [goods
sent]** envío (m)
**dispatch (n) [send-
ing]** despacho (m)
o envío (m)
dispatch (v) enviar
o consignar o
despachar o expedir

dispatch depart-ment oficina (f) de expedición

dispatch note nota (f) de expedición *o* de envío

display (n) exposición (f) *o* exhibición (f)

display (v) exhibir *o* exponer

display case vitrina (f)

display material material (m) de exposición

display pack embalaje (m) de exposición

display stand ordisplay unit estantería (f) *o* vitrina (f) de exposición

disposable desechable *o* de usar y tirar

disposal venta (f)

dispose of excess stock deshacerse de *o* vender las exis-tencias sobrantes

dissolve disolver

dissolve a partner-ship disolver una sociedad

distress merchan-dise efectos (mpl) embargados (vendidos a bajo precio)

distress sale venta forzosa *o* remate (m)

distributable profit beneficios (mpl) distribuibles

distribute dis-tribuir *o* repartir

distribution dis-tribución (f) *o* reparto (m)

distribution chan-nels canales (mpl) de distribución

distribution costs costes (mpl) de distribución

distribution man-ager jefe, -fa de distribución

distribution net-work red (f) de distribución

distributor
distribuidor, -ra
distributorship
distribución (f)
exclusiva
district distrito (m)
diversification
diversificación (f)
diversify
diversificar
dividend
dividendo (m)
dividend cover
cobertura (f) del
dividendo
dividend warrant
cheque (f) en pago
de dividendos
dividend yield
rentabilidad (f) del
dividendo
**division [part of
a company]**
sección (f) o
departamento (m)
**division [part of a
group]** división (f)
o sucursal (f)
do hacer
do business with
comerciar con

dock (n) muelle
(m) o dique (m)
**dock (v) [remove
money]** deducir o
descontar del sueldo
dock (v) [ship]
entrar en dársena o
atracar
docket lista (f) del
contenido de un
paquete
doctor's certificate
parte (m) de baja
document
documento (m)
documentary
documental
**documentary
evidence**
pruebas (fpl)
documentales
**documentary
proof** prueba (f)
documentada
documentation
documentación (f)
documents
documentos (mpl)
dollar dólar (m)
dollar area zona (f)
del dólar

dollar balance
reserva (f) en
dólares
dollar crisis crisis
(f) del dólar
domestic interior *o*
nacional
domestic market
mercado (m) inte-
rior *o* nacional
**domestic produc-
tion** producción (f)
interior *o* nacional
domestic sales
ventas (fpl)
nacionales
domestic trade
comercio (m)
interior
domicile
domicilio (m)
door puerta (f)
door-to-door de
puerta en puerta *o* a
domicilio
**door-to-door
salesman** vende-
dor, -ra a domicilio
**door-to-door
selling** venta (f) a
domicilio

dossier
expediente (m)
dot-matrix printer
impresora (f)
matricial
double (adj) doble
double (v) duplicar
o duplicarse
double taxation
doble imposición (f)
**double taxation
agreement** acuerdo
(m) de doble
imposición
double-book
reservar la misma
plaza a dos personas
double-booking
doble reserva (f)
down abajo
down payment
entrada (f) *o* depósito
(m) *o* pago (m) inicial
down time tiempo
(m) muerto
down-market
dirigido, -da a un
mercado popular
downside factor
factor (m) de riesgo
(en una inversión)

downtown (adv)
en el centro de la
ciudad *o* hacia el
centro
downtown (n) cen-
tro (m) de la ciudad
downturn
descenso (m)
downward hacia
abajo
dozen docena (f)
draft (n) [money]
letra (f) *o* giro (m)
**draft (n) [rough
plan]** borrador (m)
o proyecto (m)
draft (v) hacer un
borrador *o* redactar
draft a contract
redactar un
contrato
draft a letter
redactar una carta
**draft plan *or* draft
project** antepro-
yecto (m)
draw [a cheque]
girar
draw [money] sacar
draw up preparar *o*
redactar

draw up a contract
preparar *o* redactar
un contrato
drawee librado, -da
drawer librador, -ra
drawing account
cuenta (f) corriente
drive (n) [energy]
energía (f) *o*
empuje (m)
**drive (n) [part of
machine]** motor (m)
drive (v) [a car]
conducir
driver conductor
(m) *o* chófer (m)
drop (n) caída (f) *o*
baja (f)
drop (v) descender
o bajar *o* caer
drop in sales
caída (f) de las
ventas
due [awaited] que
está por llegar
due [owing]
debido, -da *o*
vencido, -da
dues [orders] pedi-
dos (mpl) por servir
dull átono, -na

duly [in time]
oportunamente
duly [legally]
debidamente
dummy producto
(m) ficticio
dummy pack
embalaje vacío *o*
ficticio
dump bin caja (f)
de artículos sueltos
para la venta
dump goods on a
market practicar el
'dumping'
dumping
'dumping' (m)
duplicate (n)
duplicado (m) *o*
copia (f)
duplicate (v)
copiar *o* duplicar
duplicate an
invoice copiar una
factura
duplicate of a
receipt duplicado
(m) de una factura
duplicate receipt
factura (f) por
duplicado

duplication
duplicación (f)
durable goods
bienes (mpl)
duraderos
duty [obligation]
obligación (f)
duty [tax]
impuestos (mpl) *o*
arancel (m)
duty-free libre de
impuestos
duty-free shop
tienda (f) libre de
impuestos
duty-paid goods
mercancías (fpl)
con impuestos
aduaneros pagados

Ee

e. & o.e. (errors
and omissions
excepted) salvo
error u omisión

early pronto o temprano

earmark funds for a project asignar fondos a un proyecto

earn (v) ganar

earn (v) [interest] devengar

earning capacity escala (f) de rendimiento

earnings ingresos (mpl)

earnings [profit] ganancias (fpl) o beneficios (mpl)

earnings per share *or* **earnings yield** dividendo (m) por acción

easy fácil

easy terms facilidades (fpl) de pago

e-commerce (n) comercio (m) electrónico

economic económico, -ca

economic cycle ciclo (m) económico

economic development desarrollo (m) económico

economic growth crecimiento (m) económico

economic indicators indicadores (mpl) económicos

economic model modelo (m) económico

economic planning planificación (f) económica

economic system sistema (m) económico

economic trends tendencias (fpl) económicas

economical económico, -ca

economics economía (f)

economies of scale economías (fpl) de escala

economist economista (mf)

economize
economizar
economy
economía (f)
economy [system]
sistema (m)
económico
economy class
clase económica o
clase turista
effect (n) efecto (m)
effect (v) efectuar
effective
efectivo, -va
effective date
fecha (f) de entrada
en vigor
effective demand
demanda (f)
efectiva
effective yield
rendimiento (m)
efectivo
effectiveness
eficiencia (f) o
eficacia (f)
efficiency eficien-
cia (f) o eficacia (f)
efficient eficaz o
eficiente
effort esfuerzo (m)

elasticity
elasticidad (f)
elect elegir
election elección (f)
electronic mail
correo (m)
electrónico
**electronic point of
sale (EPOS)** puntos
(mpl) de venta
electrónicos
elevator [goods]
montacargas (m)
elevator [grain]
elevador (m) de
granos
**email (n) [mes-
sage]** correo elec-
trónico o e-mail
email (v) mandar
por correo elec-
trónico o mandar
por e-mail
embargo (n)
embargo (m) o
prohibición (f)
embargo (v)
embargar o prohibir
embark embarcar
embark on
embarcarse en

embarkation
embarque (m)
embarkation card
tarjeta (f) de
embarque
embezzle malver-
sar *o* desfalcar
embezzlement
malversación (f) *o*
desfalco (m)
embezzler
malversador, -ra *o*
desfalcador, -ra
emergency
emergencia (f) *o*
urgencia (f)
emergency reserves
reservas (fpl)
para imprevistos
employ (v)
emplear
o dar empleo
employed [in job]
empleado, -da
employed
[used] en uso *o*
utilizado, -da
employee
empleado, -da
employer
empresario, -ria

employment
empleo (m) *o*
ocupación (f)
employment
agency *or* employ-
ment bureau ofic-
ina (f) de colocación
empty (adj)
vacío, -cía
empty (v) vaciar
EMS (= European
Monetary System)
SME (Sistema
Monetario Europeo)
encash hacer efec-
tivo *o* cobrar
encashment cobro
(m) en metálico
enclose adjuntar *o*
remitir adjunto
enclosure docu-
mento (m) adjunto
end (n) fin (m) *o*
final (m)
end (v) terminar *o*
finalizar
end of season sale
rebajas (fpl) de
fin de temporada
end product
producto (m) final

end user usuario (m) final

endorse a cheque endosar un cheque

endorsee endosatario, -ria

endorsement [action] endoso (m)

endorsement [on insurance] suplemento (m) de póliza

endorser endosante (mf)

energy [electricity] energía (f)

energy [human] energía (f) o vigor (m)

energy-saving (adj) que ahorra energía

enforce hacer cumplir o ejecutar

enforcement ejecución (f)

engaged ocupado, -da

engaged [telephone] (línea) ocupada

engaged tone señal (f) de comunicar

English inglés, -esa

enquire (= inquire)

enquiry (= inquiry)

enter [go in] entrar en

enter [write in] inscribir

enter into [discussion] entablar

entering entrada (f) o inscripción (f)

enterprise empresa (f)

entitle autorizar

entitlement derecho (m)

entrance (n) entrada (f)

entrepot port puerto (m) distribuidor

entrepreneur empresario, -ria

entrepreneurial empresarial

entrust encargar o confiar

entry [going in] ingreso (m) o entrada (f)

entry [to market] acceso (m)

entry [writing]
asiento (m) *o*
anotación (f)
entry visa visado
(m) de entrada
environmentally
friendly (adj)
ecológico
epos *or* EPOS
(= electronic point
of sale) puntos
(mpl) de venta
electrónicos
equal (adj) igual
equal (v) igualar *o*
ser igual a
equality igualdad (f)
equalization
equiparación (f)
equip equipar
equipment
equipo (m)
equities títulos
(mpl) *o* acciones
(fpl) ordinarias
equity beneficios
(mpl) *o* participación
(f) de beneficios
equity capital
capital (m) en
acciones

erode erosionar *o*
desgastar
erroneous
erróneo, -nea
error error (m) *o*
equivocación (f)
error rate
coeficiente (m) de
errores *o* tasa (f) de
errores
errors and omis-
sions excepted (e.
& o.e.) salvo error
u omisión
escalate escalar
escape clause
cláusula (f) de
excepción
escrow account
cuenta (f) de
garantía bloqueada
escudo [Portuguese
currency] escudo (m)
essential esencial
o imprescindible
establish
establecer *o*
consolidar
establishment
[business]
establecimiento (m)

establishment
[staff] personal
(m) o plantilla (f)
estimate (n)
[calculation] esti-
mación (f) o cálculo
(m) o valoración (f)
estimate (n) [quote]
presupuesto (m)
estimate (v) estimar
o calcular o valorar
estimated
estimado, -da
estimated figures
cifras (fpl) estimadas
estimated sales
ventas (fpl)
estimadas
estimation
estimación (f) o
valoración (f)
EU (= European
Union) UE (= Unión
Europea)
Eurocheque
eurocheque (m)
euro euro (m)
Eurocurrency
eurodivisa (f)
Eurodollar
eurodólar (m)

Euromarket
euromercado (m)
European europeo, -a
European
Investment Bank
(EIB) Banco
Europeo de
Inversiones (BEI)
European
Monetary System
(EMS) Sistema
Monetario Europeo
(SME)
European Union
(EU) Unión Europea
(UE)
eurozone (n) zona
(f) euro
evade evadir o eludir
evade tax evadir
impuestos
evaluate evaluar o
calcular
evaluate costs
evaluar los costes
evaluation
evaluación (f)
evasion evasión (f)
o elusión (f)
ex coupon sin
cupón de interés

ex dividend sin dividendo

ex-directory que no figura en la guía telefónica

exact exacto, -ta

exactly exactamente

examination [inspection] examen (m) *o* registro (m) *o* inspección (f)

examination [test] examen (m)

examine examinar

exceed exceder *o* sobrepasar *o* superar

excellent excelente

except excepto *o* salvo

exceptional excepcional

exceptional items partidas (fpl) excepcionales

excess exceso (m) *o* excedente (m)

excess baggage exceso (m) de equipaje

excess capacity exceso (m) de capacidad

excess profits beneficios (mpl) extraordinarios

excessive excesivo, -va

excessive costs costes (mpl) excesivos

exchange (n) cambio (m) *o* intercambio (m)

exchange (v) [currency] cambiar divisas *o* moneda extranjera

exchange (v) [one thing for another] canjear *o* intercambiar

exchange control control (m) de divisas

exchange rate tipo de cambio *o* tasa de cambio

exchangeable intercambiable *o* cambiable

Exchequer ministerio (m) de Hacienda

excise (v) [cut out] extirpar *o* suprimir

excise duty impuesto (m) sobre el consumo
Excise officer recaudador, -ra de impuestos
exclude excluir
excluding excepto *o* con excepción de
exclusion exclusión (f)
exclusion clause cláusula (f) de exclusión
exclusive agreement contrato (m) en exclusiva
exclusive of no incluido
exclusive of tax impuesto (m) no incluido
exclusivity exclusividad (f)
execute ejecutar *o* cumplir
execution ejecución (f) *o* cumplimiento (m)
executive (adj) ejecutivo, -va
executive (n) ejecutivo, -va

executive director director (m) ejecutivo
exempt (adj) exento, -ta
exempt (v) eximir
exempt from tax exento, -ta de impuestos
exemption exención (f)
exemption from tax exención fiscal
exercise (n) ejercicio (m)
exercise (v) ejercer
exercise an option ejercer derecho de opción
exercise of an option ejercicio (m) del derecho de opción
exhibit (v) exponer
exhibition exhibición (f) *o* exposición (f)
exhibition hall salón (m) *o* sala (f) de exposiciones
exhibitor expositor, -ra
expand ampliar *o* expandir
expansion expansión (f) *o* ampliación (f)

expenditure gasto (m) o desembolso (m)
expense gasto (m)
expense account cuenta (f) de gastos de representación
expenses gastos (mpl)
expensive caro, -ra o costoso, -sa
experienced experto, -ta o experimentado, -da
expertise pericia (f) o competencia (f)
expiration expiración (f) o terminación (f) o vencimiento (m)
expire caducar o expirar o vencer
expiry caducidad (f) o expiración (f) o vencimiento (m)
expiry date fecha (f) de caducidad
explain explicar
explanation explicación (f) o aclaración (f)
exploit explotar o aprovechar

explore explorar
export (n) exportación (f) o mercancía (f) exportada
export (v) exportar
export department departamento (m) de exportación
export duty derechos (mpl) de exportación
export licence or export permit licencia (f) o permiso (m) de exportación
export manager director, -ra de exportación
export trade comercio (m) de exportación
exporter exportador, -ra
exporting (adj) de exportación o exportador, -ra
exports exportaciones (fpl)
exposure exposición (f) o riesgo (m)

express (adj)
[fast] rápido, -da *o*
urgente
express (adj)
[stated clearly]
expreso, -sa
express (v) [send
fast] enviar por
correo *o* transporte
urgente
express (v) [state]
expresar
express delivery
entrega (f) urgente
express letter
carta (f) urgente
extend (v)
extender *o* ampliar
extend [grant]
conceder
extend [make
longer] prolongar *o*
prorrogar
extended credit
crédito (m) a largo
plazo
extension ampliación
(f) *o* prolongación (f)
o prórroga (f)

extension [tele-
phone] extensión (f)
external [foreign]
exterior
external [outside a
company] externo, -na
external account
cuenta (f) de no
residente
external audit
auditoría (f) externa
external auditor
auditor (m) externo
external trade com-
ercio (m) exterior
extra extra *o* no
incluido
extra charges
gastos (mpl)
adicionales y
complementarios
extraordinary
extraordinario, -ria
extraordinary items
partidas (fpl)
extraordinarias
extras gastos (mpl)
aparte *o* extras
(mpl)

Ff

face value valor (m) nominal

facilities instalaciones (fpl) *o* medios (mpl)

facility facilidad (f)

facility [building] edificio (m)

factor (n) [influence] factor (m) *o* elemento (m)

factor (n) [person, company] comisionista (mf) al por mayor

factor (v) gestionar deudas con descuento

factoring gestión (f) de deudas con descuento

factoring charges coste (m) de la gestión de deudas

factors of production factores (mpl) de producción

factory fábrica (f)

factory inspector inspector de fábrica

factory outlet tienda (f) de fábrica

factory price precio (m) de fábrica

fail [go bust] quebrar

fail [to do something] dejar de hacer algo

fail [not to succeed] fallar *o* fracasar

failing that en su defecto

failure fracaso (m)

fair (adj) justo, -ta *o* equitativo, -va

fair (n) feria (f)

fair dealing prácticas (fpl) comerciales justas

fair price precio (m) justo

fair trade política (f) comercial de reciprocidad arancelaria

fair trading
prácticas (fpl)
comerciales justas
fair wear and tear
desgaste (m) natural
fake (n)
falsificación (f) o
imitación (f)
fake (v) falsificar o
fingir
faked documents
documentos (mpl)
falsos
fall (n) caída (f) o
baja (f)
fall (v) [go lower]
bajar o caer
**fall (v) [on a
date]** caer
**fall behind [be in a
worse position]**
quedarse atrás
**fall behind [be
late]** retrasarse
fall due vencer
fall off disminuir o
bajar
fall through
venirse abajo
falling decreciente o
con tendencia a la baja

false falso, -sa o
falseado, -da
false pretences
medios (mpl)
fraudulentos
false weight peso
(m) escaso
falsification
falsificación (f)
falsify falsificar
fame fama (f)
family company
empresa (f) familiar
**FAO (for the
attention of)** a la
atención de
fare billete (m) o
pasaje (m)
farm out work man-
dar trabajo fuera
fast (adj) rápido, - da
fast (adv)
rápidamente
fast-selling items
artículos (mpl) de
fácil venta
fault [blame]
culpa (f) o falta (f)
fault [mechanical]
defecto (m) o fallo
(m) o tara (f)

faulty equipment
equipo (m)
defectuoso
favourable favor-
able o propicio, -cia
favourable balance
of trade balanza (f)
comercial favorable
fax (n) telefax (m)o
fax (m)
fax (v) enviar por fax
feasibility factibilidad (f) o viabilidad (f)
feasibility report
informe (m) de
viabilidad (de un
proyecto)
fee [admission]
cuota (f) o
derechos (mpl)
fee [for services]
honorarios (mpl) o
emolumentos (mpl)
feedback reacción
(f) o respuesta (f)
ferry transbordador
(m) o 'ferry' (m)
fiddle (n) trampa
(f) o timo (m)
fiddle (v) embaucar
o falsificar o falsear

field campo (m)
field sales manager
jefe, -fa de equipo
de ventas
field work trabajo
(m) de campo o
estudios (mpl)
sobre el terreno
FIFO (= first in
first out) primeras
entradas, primeras
salidas
figure cifra (f)
file (n) archivo (m)
o fichero (m)
file (n) [computer]
ficha (f) de ordenador
file (n) [documents]
expediente (m)
file (v) archivar
file (v) [register]
presentar
file a patent
application solicitar
una patente
file documents
archivar documentos
filing cabinet
archivador (m)
filing card ficha
(de registro)

fill a gap llenar *o* ocupar un vacío

final último, -ma *o* final

final demand último requerimiento (m) de pago

final discharge descargo (m) final

final dividend dividendo (m) final

finalize finalizar

finance (n) finanzas (fpl)

finance (v) financiar

finance an operation financiar una operación

finance company sociedad (f) financiera

finance director director, -ra de finanzas

finances finanzas (fpl)

financial financiero, -ra

financial asset activo (m) financiero

financial crisis crisis (f) financiera

financial institution institución (f) financiera

financial position situación (f) financiera

financial resources recursos (mpl) financieros

financial risk riesgo (m) financiero

financial settlement ajuste (m) financiero

financial year ejercicio (m) económico *o* año (m) fiscal

financially financieramente

financing financiación (f) *o* financiamiento (m)

find (v) encontrar

fine (adv) [very good] muy bien

fine (adv) [very small] en trozos pequeños

fine (n) multa (f)
fine (v) multar
fine tuning ajuste
(m) fino
finished acabado,
-da o terminado, -da
finished goods
productos (mpl)
acabados
fire (n) fuego (m)
o incendio (m)
fire damage daños
(mpl) causados por
incendio
fire insurance
seguro (m) contra
incendios
fire regulations
reglamento
(m)sobre incendios
fire risk peligro
(m) de incendio
**fire-damaged
goods** mercancías
(fpl) dañadas por un
incendio
firm (adj) firme
firm (n) empresa
(f) o firma (f)
firm (v)
afirmar

firm price precio
(m) en firme
first primero, -ra
**first in first out
(FIFO)** primeras
entradas, primeras
salidas
first option
primera opción
first quarter
primer trimestre
first-class de
primera clase o
excelente
fiscal fiscal
fiscal measures
medidas (fpl)
fiscales
fittings
accesorios (mpl)
fix [arrange] fijar
fix [mend] arreglar
**fix a meeting for 3
p.m.** fijar una
reunión para las 3
de la tarde
fixed fijo, -ja
fixed assets activo
(m) fijo
fixed costs costes
(mpl) fijos

fixed deposit depósito (m) a plazo fijo

fixed exchange rate cambio (m) fijo

fixed income renta (f) fija

fixed interest interés (m) fijo

fixed-interest investments inversiones (fpl) de interés fijo

fixed-price agreement acuerdo (m) a tanto alzado

fixed scale of charges lista (f) de precios fija

fixed-term contract contrato (m) de plazo fijo

fixing fijación (f)

flat (adj) [dull] átono, -na

flat (adj) [fixed] fijo, -ja o uniforme

flat (n) piso (m) o apartamento (m)

flat rate tanto (m) alzado o porcentaje (m) fijo

flexibility flexibilidad (f)

flexible flexible

flexible prices precios (mpl) flexibles

flexible pricing policy política (f) de precios flexibles

flight vuelo (m)

flight [of money] fuga (f)

flight information información (f) de vuelos

flight of capital evasión (f) o fuga (f) de capital(es)

flip chart tablero (m) de hojas sueltas

float (n) [money] fondo (m) de caja

float (n) [of company] lanzamiento (m) o flotación (f)

float (v) [a currency] (hacer) flotar una divisa

float a company fundar una compañía

floating flotante
floating exchange rates tipos (mpl) de cambio flotantes
floating of a company lanzamiento (m) de una sociedad
flood (n) inundación (f)
flood (v) inundar o desbordar
floor suelo (m)
floor [level] piso (m)
floor manager director, -ra de planta
floor plan planta (f)
floor space superficie (f) útil
flop (n) fracaso (m)
flop (v) fracasar
flotation lanzamiento (m) de una nueva compañía
flourish florecer o prosperar
flourishing floreciente o próspero, -ra
flourishing trade comercio (m) floreciente o próspero

flow (n) flujo (m)
flow (v) fluir o discurrir
flow chart organigrama (m) o diagrama (m) de flujo
flow diagram diagrama (m) de flujos o organigrama (m)
fluctuate fluctuar o oscilar
fluctuating fluctuante
fluctuation fluctuación (f) o oscilación (f)
FOB or **f.o.b. (free on board)** franco a bordo
follow seguir
follow up perseguir o investigar
follow-up letter carta (f) de reiteración
for sale en venta
forbid prohibir
force majeure fuerza (f) mayor
force prices down hacer bajar los precios

force prices up
hacer subir los
precios
forced a la fuerza
forced sale venta
(f) forzosa
forecast (n)
previsión (f) o
pronóstico (m)
forecast (v)
pronosticar o prever
o predecir
forecasting
previsión (f)
foreign extranjero, -ra
foreign currency
moneda (f) extranjera
foreign exchange
[changing money]
cambio (m) de
moneda extranjera
foreign exchange
[currency]
divisas (fpl)
foreign exchange
broker or **dealer**
operador, -ra de
cambios
foreign exchange
market mercado (m)
de divisas

foreign
investments
inversiones (fpl)
exteriores
foreign money
order giro (m)
postal internacional
foreign trade
comercio (m)
exterior
foresee prever
forfeit (n)
decomiso (m) o
confiscación (f)
forfeit (v)
decomisar o perder
el derecho a
forfeit a deposit
perder un depósito
forfeiture
decomiso (m) o
confiscación (f)
forge falsificar
forgery [action]
falsificación (f)
forgery [copy]
documento falso o
copia falsa
fork-lift truck car-
retilla (f) elevadora
de horquilla

form (n) impreso
(m) *o* formulario (m)
form (v) formar
form of words
fórmulas (fpl)
judiciales
formal formal
formality formali-
dad (f) *o* trámite (m)
forward a plazo *o*
en fecha futura
forward buying
compra (f) de
futuros
forward contract
contrato (m)
a plazo fijo
forward market
mercado (m) a
futuros
forward rate tipo
(m) de cambio para
operaciones a plazo
forward sales ven-
tas (fpl) a plazo
forwarding expedi-
ción (f) *o* envío (m)
**forwarding
address**
dirección (f) de
reenvío

forwarding agent
agente (mf)
expedidor, -ra
**forwarding instruc-
tions** instrucciones
(fpl) de envío
fourth quarter
cuarto trimestre
fragile frágil
frame marco (m)
franc
franco (m)
franchise (n)
franquicia (f) *o*
concesión (f)
franchise (v)
franquiciar
franchisee
concesionario, -ria
franchiser
franquiciador, -ra
franchising
franquicia (f) *o*
concesión (f)
franco
franco o libre
frank (v)
franquear
franking machine
máquina (f)
franqueadora

fraud fraude (m) *o* defraudación (f) *o* estafa (f)
fraudulent fraudulento, -ta
fraudulent transaction operación (f) fraudulenta
fraudulently fraudulentamente
free (adj) libre
free (adj) [no payment] gratuito, -ta *o* gratis *o* franco
free (adj) [not occupied] vacante
free (adv) [no payment] gratuitamente *o* gratis
free (v) poner en libertad *o* liberar
free delivery entrega gratuita
free gift regalo (m) *o* obsequio (m)
free market economy economía (f) de libre mercado
free of charge gratis

free of duty libre de derechos de aduana
free of tax libre de impuestos
free on board (f.o.b.) franco a bordo
free on rail franco sobre vagón *o* franco vagón FF.CC
free port puerto (m) franco
free sample muestra (f) gratuita
free trade libre cambio *o* libre comercio
free trade area zona (f) de libre cambio
free trade zone zona (f) franca
free trial prueba (f) gratuita
free zone zona (f) franca
freelance (adj) de libre dedicación

freelance (n) *or*
freelancer (n) tra-
bajador, -ra por libre
freeze (n)
congelación (f)
freeze (v) [prices]
congelar
freeze credits
bloquear
los créditos
freeze wages and
prices congelar
salarios y
precios
freight [carriage]
flete (m) *o*
transporte (m) *o*
porte (m)
freight costs
gastos (mpl) de
transporte
freight depot
estación (f) de
mercancías
freight forward
porte (m) debido
freight plane avión
(m) de carga
freight rates precio
(m) de transporte *o*
tarifas (fpl) de flete

freight train tren
(m) de mercancías
freightage
flete (m) *o*
fletamento (m)
freighter [plane]
avión (m) de carga
freighter [ship]
buque (m) de carga
freightliner tren
(m) de mercancías
de contenedores
frequent frecuente
o corriente
frozen
bloqueado, -da *o*
congelado, -da
frozen account
cuenta (f)
bloqueada
frozen assets
activo
(m) congelado
frozen
credits crédito (m)
congelado
fulfil
[carry out] cumplir
fulfil an order
despachar un
pedido

fulfilment
cumplimiento (m) *o*
realización (f)
full lleno, -na
**full discharge of a
debt** pago (m) total
de una deuda
full payment pago
(m) íntegro
full price precio
(m) sin descuento
full refund reem-
bolso (m) total
full-scale (adj)
completo,
-ta *o* general
full-time a tiempo
completo *o* en plena
dedicación
**full-time employ-
ment** trabajo (m) a
tiempo completo
fund (n) fondo (m)
fund (v) financiar *o*
asignar fondos
fundamental
fundamental
funding (financing)
financiación (f) *o*
asignación
(f) de fondos

funding [of debt]
consolidación (f) de
fondos
further to con
relación a
future delivery
entrega (f) futura
futures
futuros (mpl)

Gg

**gain (n) [becoming
bigger]**
aumento (m)
**gain (n) [increase
in value]** ganancia
(f) *o* beneficio (m)
**gain (v) [become
bigger]**
aumentar
gain (v) [get]
ganar
game fuego (m)
gap hueco (m) *o*
vacío (m)

gap in the market
hueco (m) en el
mercado
**GDP (= gross
domestic product)**
PIB (Producto
Interior Bruto)
gear ajustar
gearing
apalancamiento (m)
general general
general audit audi-
toría (f) general
general average
avería (f) gruesa
general insurance
seguro (m) general
**general
manager** director,
-ra general o
director, -ra
gerente (mf)
general meeting
junta (f) general
general office
oficina (f) general
general post offfice
oficina (f) central de
correos
general strike
huelga (f) general

**gentleman's
agreement**
acuerdo (m) entre
caballeros
genuine
genuino, -na
**genuine
purchaser** com-
prador genuino o
compradora genuina
get recibir o
obtener o conseguir
get along ir
haciendo
**get back
[something lost]**
recuperar
get into debt
endeudarse
**get rid of
something**
deshacerse
de algo
**get round [a prob-
lem]** soslayar
get the sack
ser despedido
gift regalo (m) o
obsequio (m)
gift coupon
cupón (m) de regalo

gift shop tienda (f) de regalos
gift voucher vale (m) para un regalo
gilt-edged securities títulos (mpl) del Estado
gilts bonos (mpl) del Tesoro
giro account cuenta (f) del Girobank
giro account number número (m) de cuenta del Girobank
giro system giro (m) bancario
give (v) dar
give [as gift] regalar
give away regalar
glut (n) abundancia (f)
glut (v) inundar el mercado
GNP (= gross national product) PNB (Producto Nacional Bruto)
go ir

go into business emprender un negocio
go-ahead (adj) emprendedor, -ra o activo, -va
go-slow huelga (f) de celo
going en marcha
going rate precio (m) vigente
gold card tarjeta (f) oro
good bueno, -na
good buy buena compra
good management buena gestión
good quality buena calidad
good value (for money) buen precio
goods mercancías (fpl) o bienes (mpl)
goods depot depósito (m) o almacén (m) de mercancías
goods in transit mercancías (fpl) en tránsito

goods train tren (m) de mercancías
goodwill fondo (m) de comercio
government (adj) estatal o del gobierno
government (n) gobierno (m)
government bonds títulos (mpl) del Estado
government con-tractor contratista (mf) del Estado
government stock títulos (mpl) del Estado
government-backed con apoyo estatal
government-con-trolled controlado, -da por el Estado
government-regulated regulado, -da por el Estado
government-sponsored patrocinado, -da por el Estado

graded advertising rates tarifas (fpl) publicitarias regresivas
graded hotel hotel (m) homologado
graded tax impuesto (m) progresivo
gradual gradual o progresivo, -va
graduate trainee licenciado, -da en prácticas
graduated graduado, -da o progresivo, -va
graduated income tax impuesto (m) progresivo sobre la renta
gram *or* **gramme** gramo (m)
grand total suma (f) total
grant (n) subvención (f) o beca (f)
grant (v) conceder o otorgar
graph (n) gráfico (m) o gráfica (f)

gratis gratis

grid cuadrícula (f)

grid structure estructura (f) cuadricular

gross (adj) bruto, -ta **gross (n)** (= 144) gruesa (f)

gross (v) obtener beneficios brutos

gross domestic product (GDP) Producto Interior Bruto (PIB)

gross earnings ingresos (mpl) brutos

gross income renta (f) bruta

gross margin margen (m) de beneficio bruto

gross national product (GNP) Producto Nacional Bruto (PNB)

gross profit beneficio (m) bruto

gross salary sueldo (m) bruto

gross tonnage tonelaje (m) bruto

gross weight peso (m) bruto

gross yield rendimiento (m) bruto

group [of businesses] grupo (m)

group [of people] grupo (m) o agrupación (f)

growth crecimiento (m) o desarrollo (m)

growth index índice (m) de crecimiento

growth rate tasa (f) de crecimiento

guarantee (n) garantía (f) o aval (m)

guarantee (v) avalar o garantizar o afianzar

guarantee a debt avalar una deuda

guaranteed minimum wage salario (m) mínimo interprofesional

guarantor fiador, -ra o garante (mf)

guideline directriz (f)
guild gremio (m) *o*
corporación (f)

Hh

haggle regatear
half (adj) medio, -dia
half (n) mitad (f)
**half a dozen *or* a
half-dozen** media
docena (f)
half-price sale
rebajas a mitad de
precio
half-year
semestre (m)
**half-yearly
accounts** cuentas
(fpl) semestrales
**half-yearly pay-
ment** pagos (mpl)
semestrales
**half-yearly state-
ment** estado de
cuentas semestral

hand in presentar *o*
entregar
hand luggage
equipaje (m)
de mano
hand over entregar
handle (v) [deal]
manejar *o* tratar
handle (v) [sell]
comerciar en
handling
manejo (m) *o*
manipulación (f)
handling charge
gasto (m) de
tramitación
handwriting letra
(f) *o* escritura (f)
handwritten
escrito, -ta a mano
handy útil *o*
práctico, -ca
harbour puerto (m)
harbour dues dere-
chos (mpl) portuarios
**harbour
facilities** instala-
ciones (fpl) portuarias
hard (adj) duro (-ra)
hard bargain
negocio (m) duro

hard bargaining
negocio (m) duro *o*
trato (m) difícil
hard copy copia (f)
impresa
hard currency mon-
eda (f) convertible
hard disk disco
(m) duro
hard selling venta
(f) agresiva
harmonization
armonización (f) *o*
concertación (f)
haulage acarreo (m)
haulage contractor
contratista (mf) de
transporte por
carretera
haulage costs *or*
haulage rates
gastos (mpl) de
acarreo
have tener
head jefe, -fa
head of
department
jefe, -fa de
departamento
head office oficina
(f) central

headquarters (HQ)
sede (f) *o* domicilio
(m) social
heads of agree-
ment epígafres
(mpl) de un acuerdo
health salud (f)
health insurance
seguro (m) de
enfermedad
healthy profit
beneficio (m)
considerable
heavy [important]
grande *o* importante
heavy [weight]
pesado, -da
heavy costs *or*
heavy expenditure
grandes costes (mpl)
o gran gasto (m)
heavy equipment
equipo (m) pesado
heavy goods vehi-
cle (HGV) camión
(m) de carga pesada
heavy industry
industria (f) pesada
heavy machinery
maquinaria (f)
pesada

hectare
hectárea (f)
**hedge (n) *or* hedg-
ing (n)** cobertura
(f) *o* protección (f)
help (n) ayuda (f)
help (v) ayudar
**HGV (= heavy
goods vehicle)**
camión (m) de carga
pesada
hidden asset bien
(m) encubierto
hidden reserves
reservas (fpl) ocultas
high alto, -ta
high interest
interés (m)
elevado
high quality
calidad superior *o*
alta calidad
high-quality goods
productos (mpl) de
primera calidad
high rent alquiler
(m) elevado
high taxation
imposición (f) alta
highest bidder
mejor postor

**highly motivated
sales staff** per-
sonal (m) de ventas
muy motivado
highly qualified
muy cualificado *o*
muy capacitado
**highly-geared com-
pany** sociedad con
un gran coeficiente
de endeudamiento
highly-paid muy
bien pagado
highly-priced muy
caro, -ra
hire (n) alquiler (m)
hire a car *or* a crane
alquilar un coche *o*
alquilar una grúa
hire car coche (m)
de alquiler
hire purchase (HP)
compra (f) a plazos
hire staff contratar
personal
**hire-purchase
company** compañía
(f) que financia la
compra a plazos
historic(al) cost
coste (m) inicial

historical figures cifras (fpl) históricas

hive off descentralizar

hoard (v) acaparar *o* acumular

hoarding [for posters] valla (f) publicitaria *o* cartelera (f)

hoarding [of goods] acaparamiento (m)

hold (n) [ship] bodega (f)

hold (v) [contain] contener *o* caber

hold (v) [keep] tener *o* guardar

hold a meeting *or* **a discussion** celebrar una reunión *o* tener una discusión

hold out for insistir en

hold over aplazar *o* posponer

hold the line please *or* **please hold** no cuelgue

hold up (v) [delay] retrasar

hold-up (n) [delay] retraso (m)

holder [person] poseedor, -ra *o* tenedor, -ra

holder [thing] soporte (m)

holding company sociedad (f) de cartera *o* 'holding'

holiday pay paga (f) de vacaciones

home address domicilio (m) particular

home consumption consumo (m) doméstico *o* consumo interior

home market mercado (m) interior *o* mercado nacional

home sales ventas (fpl) nacionales

homeward freight flete (m) de vuelta

homeward journey viaje (m) de regreso

homeworker trabajador, -ra a domicilio

honorarium
honorarios (mpl)
honour a bill pagar
una factura
honour a signature
aceptar o reconocer
una firma
horizontal commu-
nication comuni-
cación (f) horizontal
horizontal
integration
integración (f)
horizontal
hotel hotel (m)
hotel
accommodation
habitaciones (fpl)
de hotel o capacidad
(f) hotelera
hotel bill factura
(f) de hotel
hotel manager
director, -ra de hotel
hotel staff per-
sonal (m) del hotel
hour hora (f)
hourly por hora
hourly rate tarifa
(f) horaria

hourly wage sueldo
(m) por hora
hourly-paid
workers traba-
jadores (mpl)
pagados por horas
house casa (f)
house [company]
casa (f) comercial
house insurance
seguro (m) de la
vivienda
house magazine
boletín (m) interno
de una empresa
house-to-house a
domicilio
house-to-house
selling
venta (f) a domicilio
HP (= hire
purchase) compra
(f) a plazos
HQ (= headquar-
ters) sede (f) o
domicilio (m) social
hurry up darse
prisa
hype (n) bombo
(m) publicitario

hype (v) hacer publicidad con mucho bombo
hypermarket hipermercado (m)

Ii

illegal ilegal
illegality ilegalidad (f)
illegally ilegalmente
illicit ilícito, -ta
ILO
(= International Labour Organization) OIT (Organización Internacional del Trabajo)
IMF
(= International Monetary Fund) FMI (Fondo Monetario Internacional)

imitation imitación (f)
immediate inmediato, -ta
immediately inmediatamente
imperfect imperfecto, -ta
imperfection defecto (m) o imperfección (f) o tara (f)
implement (n) herramienta (f) o instrumento (m)
implement (v) ejecutar o realizar
implement an agreement poner en práctica un acuerdo
implementation ejecución (f) o puesta (f) en práctica
import (n) importación (f)
import (v) importar
import ban prohibición (f) de importar

import duty
derechos (mpl) de
importación
import levy grava-
men (m) sobre las
importaciones
import licence *or*
import permit
licencia (f) de
importación
import quota cuota
(f) de importación *o*
cupo (m) de
importación
import restrictions
restricción (f) a las
importaciones
import surcharge
sobretasa (f) *o*
recargo (m) de
importación
import-export (adj)
importación-
exportación
importance
importancia (f)
important
importante
importation
importación (f)
importer
importador, -ra

importing (adj)
importador, -ra
importing (n)
importación (f)
imports importa-
ciones (fpl)
impose imponer *o*
gravar
improvement
mejora (f)
impulse impulso (m)
impulse buyer
comprador (-ra)
impulsivo (-va)
impulse purchase
compra (f) impulsiva
in-house interno,
-na *o* de la casa
in-house
training formación
(f) en el puesto de
trabajo
incapable incapaz
incentive incentivo
(m) *o* estímulo (m)
incentive bonus *or*
incentive
payment prima (f)
de incentivo
incidental
expenses
gastos (mpl)

menores
include incluir
inclusive inclusive
o inclusivo, -va o
incluido, -da
inclusive charge
precio (m) todo
incluido
inclusive of tax
impuestos (mpl)
incluidos
income ingresos
(mpl) o renta (f)
income tax
impuesto (m) sobre
la renta
incoming call lla-
mada (f) de fuera
incoming mail
correspondencia (f)
recibida o correo
(m) entrante
incompetence
incompetencia (f)
incompetent
incompetente
incorporate
incorporar o incluir
incorporate
[a company]
constituir en
sociedad

incorporation
constitución (f) de
una sociedad
incorrect
incorrecto, -ta
incorrectly
incorrectamente
increase (n)
aumento (m) o
incremento (m)
increase (n)
[higher salary]
aumento (m) de
sueldo
increase (v)
aumentar o subir o
incrementar
increase (v) in
price aumentar o
subir de precio
increasing
creciente o en
aumento
increasing
profits
beneficios (mpl)
crecientes
increment
incremento (m) o
aumento (m)
incremental
incremental

incremental cost
coste (m) incremental
incremental scale
escala (f) móvil de
salarios
incur incurrir en
incur debts
contraer deudas
indebted
endeudado, -da
indebtedness
deuda (f)
indemnification
indemnización (f)
indemnify
indemnizar o
resarcir
indemnify someone
for a loss indem-
nizar a alguien por
una pérdida
indemnity
indemnidad (f) o
indemnización (f)
independent
independiente
independent com-
pany compañía (f)
independiente
index (n) [alpha-
betical] índice (m)
o repertorio (m)

index (n) [of
prices] índice (m)
index (v) catalogar
o clasificar
index card ficha (f)
index number
índice (m) o
indicador (m)
index-linked
ajustado, da al
coste de la vida
indexation
indexación (f) o
indiciación (f)
indicator
indicador (m)
indirect indirecto, -ta
indirect labour
costs costes (mpl)
laborales indirectos
indirect tax
impuesto (m)
indirecto
indirect taxation
imposición (f)
indirecta
induction
iniciación (f)
induction courses
or induction train-
ing cursos (mpl)
de iniciación

industrial
industrial
industrial accident
accidente (m)
industrial
**industrial arbitra-
tion tribunal**
tribunal (m) de
arbitraje laboral
industrial capacity
capacidad (f)
industrial
industrial centre
centro (m)
industrial
industrial design
diseño (m)
industrial
industrial disputes
conflictos (mpl)
colectivos
**industrial espi-
onage** espionaje
(m) industrial
industrial estate
zona (f) industrial
industrial expansion
expansión (f)
industrial
industrial processes
procesos (mpl)
industriales

industrial relations
relaciones (fpl)
laborales
industrial tribunal
magistratura (f) del
trabajo
industrialist
industrial (mf)
industrialization
industrialización (f)
industrialize
industrializar
**industrialized soci-
eties** sociedades
(fpl) industriales
industry industria (f)
inefficiency
ineficacia (f) *o*
incompetencia (f)
inefficient ineficaz
o incompetente
inflated currency
moneda (f)
inflacionista
inflated prices pre-
cios (mpl) exagerados
inflation inflación (f)
inflationary
inflacionario, -ria *o*
inflacionista
influence (n)
influencia (f)

influence (v)
influir *o* influenciar
inform informar
information
información (f)
information bureau
oficina (f) de
información
information officer
empleado, -da del
servicio de
información
infrastructure
infraestructura (f)
infringe infringir *o*
violar
infringe a patent
violar una patente
infringement of
customs regula-
tions infracción (f)
aduanera
infringement of
patent violación (f)
de patente
inhabitant
habitante (mf)
initial (adj) inicial
o primero, -ra
initial (v) poner las
iniciales a *o* rubricar

initial capital
capital (m) inicial
initiate iniciar
initiate discus-
sions iniciar
conversaciones
initiative
iniciativa (f)
inland interior
innovate innovar
innovation
innovación (f)
innovative
innovador, -ra
innovator (n)
innovador, -ra
input information
introducir datos
input tax IVA
(sobre los bienes y
servicios adquiridos
por una empresa)
inquire preguntar *o*
pedir información
inquiry petición (f)
de informes *o*
investigación (f)
insider iniciado (m)
insider dealing
información (f)
privilegiada

insolvency
insolvencia (f)
insolvent
insolvente
inspect
inspeccionar o
revisar
inspection inspec-
ción (f) o control (m)
inspector
inspector, ra
instalment plazo (m)
instant (adj)
[current]
del presente mes o
de los corrientes
instant (adj)
[immediate]
inmediato, -ta o
instantáneo, -nea
instant
credit
crédito (m)
instantáneo
institute (n)
instituto (m)
institute (v) instituir
institution
institución (f)
institutional
institucional

institutional
investors
inversores (mpl)
institucionales
instruction
instrucción (f)
instrument
[device]
instrumento (m)
o aparato (m)
instrument
[document] efecto
(m) o documento
(m) escrito
insufficiency
insuficiencia (f)
insufficient
funds (US) saldo
(m) insuficiente
insurable
asegurable
insurance seguro (m)
insurance agent
agente (mf) de
seguros
insurance
broker corredor
(m) de seguros
insurance claim
declaración (f) de
siniestro

insurance company compañía (f) de seguros

insurance contract contrato (m) de seguros

insurance cover cobertura (f) del seguro

insurance policy póliza (f) de seguros

insurance premium prima (f) de seguros

insurance rates tarifas (fpl) de seguros

insurance salesman vendedor, -ra de seguros

insure asegurar

insurer asegurador, ra

intangible intangible

intangible assets activo (m) intangible

interest (n) interés (m) o rédito (m)

interest (v) interesar

interest charges cargos (mpl) en concepto de interés

interest rate tipo (m) de interés o tasa (f) de interés

interest-bearing deposits depósitos (mpl) con interés

interest-free credit crédito (m) sin interés

interface (n) interfaz (m)

interface (v) conectar

interim dividend dividendo (m) provisional

interim payment pago (m) a cuenta

interim report informe (m) provisional

intermediary intermediario, -ria

internal [inside a company] interno,

internal [inside a country] interior

internal audit auditoría (f) interna

internal auditor auditor (m) interno

internal telephone
teléfono (m) interno
international
internacional
international call
llamada (f)
internacional
international direct
dialling llamadas
internacionales
directas
International
Labour
Organization (ILO)
Organización
Internacional del
Trabajo (OIT)
international law
derecho (m)
internacional
International
Monetary Fund
(IMF) Fondo
Monetario
Internacional (FMI)
international
trade comercio (m)
internacional
Internet (n)
Internet (n)

interpret interpretar
interpreter
intérprete (mf)
interruption
interrupción (f)
intervention price
precio (m) de
intervención
interview (n)
entrevista (f)
interview (v)
entrevistar
interviewee
entrevistado, -da
interviewer
entrevistador, -ra
introduce presen-
tar o introducir
introduction
[bringing into use]
presentación (f) o
introducción (f)
introduction
[letter] carta (f) de
presentación
introductory offer
oferta (f) de
lanzamiento
invalid inválido, -da
invalidate invalidar

invalidation
invalidación (f)
invalidity
invalidez (f)
inventory (n) [list of contents]
inventario (m)
inventory (n) [stock]
existencias (fpl)
inventory (v)
inventariar o hacer un inventario
inventory control
control (m) de existencias
invest invertir
investigate
investigar
investigation
investigación (f)
investment
inversión (f)
investment income renta (f) de inversiones
investor
inversor, -ra o inversionista (mf)
invisible assets
activo (m) invisible

invisible earnings
ingresos (mpl) invisibles
invisible trade comercio (m) invisible
invitation
invitación (f)
invite invitar
invoice (n)
factura (f)
invoice (v) facturar
invoice number número (m) de factura
invoice value precio (m) facturado
invoicing
facturación (f)
invoicing department
departamento (m) de facturación
IOU (= I owe you)
pagaré (m)
irrecoverable debt deuda (f) incobrable
irredeemable bond
obligación (f) perpetua

irregular irregular
irregularities
irregularidades (fpl)
irrevocable
irrevocable
**irrevocable accept-
ance** aceptación (f)
irrevocable
**irrevocable letter of
credit** carta (f) de
crédito irrevocable
**issue (n) [maga-
zine]** número (m)
**issue (n) [of
shares]** emisión (f)
issue (v) [shares]
emitir
**issue a letter of
credit** abrir una
carta de crédito
issue instructions
dar instrucciones
**issuing
bank** banco
(m) emisor
item [for sale]
artículo (m)
item [news]
noticia (f)
item [on agenda]
punto (m)

**item [on balance
sheet]** partida (f)
itemize detallar o
especificar
itemized account
cuenta (f) detallada
itemized invoice
factura (f) detallada
itinerary
itinerario (m)

Jj

job [employment]
empleo (m) o puesto
(m) de trabajo
job [piece of work]
trabajo (m) o tarea (f)
job analysis
análisis (m) de un
puesto de trabajo
job application
solicitud (f) de
empleo
job cuts reducción
(f) de empleos

job description
descripción (f) del
puesto de trabajo
job satisfaction sat-
isfacción (f) laboral
job security seguri-
dad (f) en el empleo
job specification
descripción (f) del
puesto de trabajo
job title cargo (m)
join (v) juntar o unir
**join (v) [become
part of]** ingresar en
joint común o
conjunto, -ta o
colectivo, -va
joint account
cuenta (f) conjunta
o cuenta en
participación
joint discussions
negociaciones (fpl)
conjuntas
joint management
dirección (f)
conjunta o
codirección (f)
**joint managing
director** codirector,
-ra gerente

joint owner
co-propietario, -ria
joint ownership
co-propiedad (f) o
condominio (m)
joint signatory sig-
natario (m) colectivo
joint venture
empresa (f)
conjunta
jointly
conjuntamente o
en común
**journal [accounts
book]** libro (m)
diario
**journal [maga-
zine]** revista (f) o
boletín (m)
journey order
pedido (m) cursado
al representante
(comercial)
judge (n) juez (mf)
judge (v) juzgar
**judgement or
judgment** juicio
(m) o sentencia (f)
judgment debtor
deudor, -ra
judicial

judicial processes
procedimientos (mpl)
judiciales
jump the queue
saltarse la cola
junior (adj) menor
o más joven o
subalterno, -na
junior clerk pasante
(mf) o auxiliar (mf)
administrativo, -va
junior executive *or*
junior manager
ejecutivo, -va auxiliar
junior partner
socio subalterno
o de menor
antigüedad
junk bonds bonos-
basura (mpl)
junk mail publici-
dad (f) sin interés
(por correo)
jurisdiction
jurisdicción (f)
justify justificar

Kk

keen competition
fuerte
competencia (f)
keen demand gran
demanda (f)
keen prices precios
(mpl) competitivos
keep a promise
cumplir una promesa
keep back retener
keep up sostener o
mantener
keep up with the
demand satisfacer
la demanda
key (adj) [impor-
tant] clave (f)
key (n) [on key-
board] tecla (f)
key (n) [solution]
clave (f)
key (n) [to door]
llave (f)
key industry
industria (f) clave
key money
traspaso (m)

key personnel *or*
key staff personal
(m) clave
key post puesto
(m) clave
keyboard (n)
teclado (m)
keyboard (v)
teclear
keyboarder oper-
ador, -ra de teclado
keyboarding tecleo
(m) o tecleado (m)
kilo *or* **kilogram** kilo
(m) o kilogramo (m)
knock down (v)
[price] rematar
**knock off [reduce
price]** descontar
**knock off [stop
work]** terminar de
trabajar
knock-on effect
repercusión (f) o
efecto (m) secundario
knockdown prices
precios (mpl)
mínimos o de saldo
**krona [currency
used in Sweden and
Iceland]** corona (f)

**krone [currency
used in Denmark
and Norway]**
corona (f)

Ll

label (n) etiqueta (f)
label (v) etiquetar
labelling
etiquetado (m)
labour trabajo (m)
labour costs costes
(mpl) laborales
labour disputes
conflictos (mpl)
laborales
labour force mano
(f) de obra
lack of funds falta
(f) de fondos
land (n) tierra (f)
land (v) [of plane]
aterrizar
**land (v) [passen-
gers]** desembarcar

land goods at a port descargar mercancías en un puerto

landed costs coste (m) descargado

landing card tarjeta (f) de desembarque

landing charges gastos (mpl) de descarga

landlady propietaria (f) o dueña (f)

landlord propietario (m) o dueño (m)

lapse (v) caducar

large (adj) grande

laser printer impresora (f) láser

last (adj) último, ma

last in first out (LIFO) últimos en entrar, primeros en salir

last quarter último trimestre

late (adj) atrasado, -da

late (adv) tarde o con retraso

late: to be late retrasarse

late-night opening abierto por la noche

latest último, -ma

launch (n) lanzamiento (m)

launch (v) lanzar

launching lanzamiento (m)

launching costs costes (mpl) de lanzamiento

launching date fecha (f) de lanzamiento

launder (money) blanquear (dinero negro)

law ley (f)

law [rule] regla (f) o norma (f)

law [study] derecho (m)

law courts tribunales (mpl) de justicia

law of diminishing returns ley (f) de rendimientos decrecientes

law of supply and demand ley (f) de la oferta y la demanda

lawful legal o lícito, -ta

lawful trade comercio (m) legal

lawsuit pleito (m) o juicio (m) o proceso (m)

lawyer abogado, -da

lay off workers despedir por falta de trabajo

LBO (= leveraged buyout) compra (f) o adquisición (f) apalancada

L/C (= letter of credit) carta (f) de crédito

lead time plazo (m) de espera

leaflet folleto (m) o prospecto (m)

leakage pérdidas (fpl) o mermas (fpl)

lease (n) arrendamiento (m) o arriendo (m)

lease (v) [of landlord] arrendar (ceder en arriendo)

lease (v) [of tenant] arrendar (tomar en arriendo)

lease back realizar una operación de cesión-arrendamiento

lease-back cesión-arrendamiento (f)

lease equipment arrendar equipo

leasing arrendamiento (m) financiero o 'leasing' (m)

leave (n) permiso (m)

leave (v) [go away] irse o marcharse

leave (v) [resign] abandonar o dejar

leave of absence excedencia (f)

ledger libro (m) mayor

left [not right] izquierdo, -da

left: be left
quedar
left luggage office
consigna (f)
**legal [according to
law]** legal o lícito, -ta
**legal [referring to
law]** jurídico, -ca o
judicial
legal action acción
(f) legal
legal advice
asesoramiento (m)
jurídico
legal adviser
asesor (m) jurídico
**legal costs *or* legal
charges** costas
(fpl) judiciales
legal currency
moneda (f) de curso
legal
legal department
asesoría (f) jurídica
legal expenses
costas (fpl)
judiciales
**legal
proceedings**
proceso (m) judicial

legal status condi-
ción (f) jurídica o per-
sonalidad (f) jurídica
legal tender
moneda (f) de
curso legal
legislation
legislación (f)
lend prestar
lender
prestamista (mf)
lending concesión
(f) de un préstamo
lending limit
límite (m) de
crédito
less menos
lessee arren-
datario, -ria o
inquilino, -na
lessor
arrendador, -ra
let (v) alquilar o
arrendar
let an office
alquilar una oficina
letter carta (f)
**letter of applica-
tion** carta (f) de
solicitud

**letter of appoint-
ment** carta (f) de
nombramiento
letter of complaint
carta (f) de
reclamación
**letter of credit
(L/C)** carta (f) de
crédito
letter of intent
carta (f) de
intención
**letter of
reference** carta (f)
de recomendación
**letters of
administration**
nombramiento (m)
de administrador
judicial
letters patent
patente (f) de
invención
letting agency
agencia (f) de
alquiler de
viviendas
level nivel (m)
level off or **level
out** nivelarse o
estabilizarse

leverage
apalancamiento (m)
financiero
**leveraged buyout
(LBO)** compra (f)
o adquisición (f)
apalancada
levy (n)
recaudación (f)
de impuestos
levy (v) recaudar o
gravar
liabilities deudas
(fpl) o pasivo (m)
liability respons-
abilidad (f)
liable for
responsable de
liable to sujeto, -ta a
licence licencia (f)
license conceder
una licencia
o autorizar
licensee persona
(f) autorizada o
concesionario, -ria
licensing
licencia (f)
lien gravamen (m)
o derecho (m) de
retención

life assurance *or* **life insurance** seguro (m) de vida
life interest renta (f) vitalicia *o* usufructo (m) vitalicio
LIFO (= last in first out) últimos en entrar, primeros en salir
lift (n) ascensor (m)
lift (v) levantar *o* suprimir
lift an embargo levantar un embargo
limit (n) límite (m) *o* acotación (f)
limit (v) limitar
limitation limitación (f)
limited limitado, -da
limited (liability) company (Ltd) sociedad (f) de responsabilidad limitada (S.R.L.)
limited liability responsabilidad (f) limitada

limited market mercado (m) limitado
limited partnership sociedad (f) en comandita
line (n) línea (f) *o* raya (f)
line management gestión (f) lineal
line organization organización (f) lineal
line printer impresora (f) de líneas
link (n) vínculo (m)
liquid assets activo (m) líquido
liquidate a company liquidar una compañía
liquidate stock liquidar existencias
liquidation liquidación (f)
liquidator síndico (m)
liquidity liquidez (f)
liquidity crisis crisis (f) de liquidez
lira [currency used in Turkey] lira (f)

list (n) lista (f) *o* relación (f)

list (n) [catalogue] catálogo (m) *o* repertorio (m)

list (v) hacer una lista *o* enumerar

list price precio (m) de catálogo

litre litro (m)

Lloyd's register Registro (m) Marítimo de Lloyd

load (n) cargamento (m)

load (v) cargar

load a lorry *or* a ship cargar un camión *o* un barco

load factor coeficiente (m) de ocupación

load line línea (f) de carga *o* línea de flotación

loading bay nave (f) de carga

loading ramp rampa (f) de carga

loan (n) préstamo (m)

loan (v) prestar

loan capital empréstito (m)

loan stock obligaciones (fpl)

local local

local call llamada (f) local

local government administración (f) local

local labour mano (f) de obra local

lock (n) cerradura (f)

lock (v) cerrar con llave

lock up a shop *or* an office cerrar una tienda *o* una oficina

lock up capital inmovilizar capital

lock-up premises local (m) sin vivienda incorporada

log (v) anotar *o* apuntar

log calls anotar las llamadas recibidas

logo logotipo (m)

long largo, -ga

long credit crédito (m) a largo plazo
long-dated bill letra (f) a largo plazo
long-distance flight *or* **long-haul flight** vuelo (m) de larga distancia
long-range a largo plazo
long-standing de hace tiempo *o* de muchos años
long-standing agreement acuerdo (m) de muchos años
long-term largo plazo
long-term debts deudas (fpl) a largo plazo
long-term forecast previsión (f) a largo plazo
long-term liabili-ties pasivo (m) a largo plazo
long-term loan préstamo (m) a largo plazo

long-term objectives objetivos (mpl) a largo plazo
long-term planning planificación (f) a largo plazo
loose (adj) suelto, -ta *o* a granel
loose (adj) [slack] flojo, -ja
lorry camión (m)
lorry driver camionero, -ra
lorry-load carga (f) de un camión
lose perder
lose an order perder un pedido
lose money perder dinero
lose value perder valor
loss [not a profit] pérdida (f)
loss of an order pérdida (f) de un pedido
loss of customers pérdida (f) de clientela

loss of value pér-
dida (f) de valor
loss adjustment
ajuste (m) de
pérdidas
loss-leader artículo
(m) de reclamo
lot lote (m)
low (adj) bajo, -ja
low (n) mínimo (m)
low sales ventas
(fpl) bajas
low-grade de baja
calidad
low-level de bajo
nivel o de grado
inferior
low-quality de
poca calidad o
mediocre
lower (adj) más
bajo, -ja o inferior
lower (v) bajar
lower prices
reducir los precios
lowering disminución
(f) o reducción (f)
**Ltd (= limited com-
pany)** S.(R.) L. (=
sociedad (de respon-
sabilidad) limitada)

luggage equipaje
(m) o maletas (fpl)
lump sum pago
(m) único o suma
(f) global
luxury goods artícu-
los (mpl) de lujo

Mm

machine máquina
(f) o aparato (m)
machinery
maquinaria (f)
macro-economics
macroeconomía (f)
magazine revista (f)
magazine insert
encarte (m) publici-
tario (de una revista)
magazine mailing
envío (m) de revis-
tas por correo
**magnetic tape or
mag tape** cinta (f)
magnética

mail (n) correo (m) o correspondencia (f)
mail (v) mandar por correo o echar al correo
mail shot publicidad (f) por correo
mail-order pedido (m) por correo
mail-order business or mail-order firm empresa (f) de ventas por correo
mail-order catalogue catálogo (m) de ventas por correo
mailing envío (m) por correo
mailing list lista (f) de destinatarios
mailing piece folleto (m) publicitario enviado por correo
mailing shot envío (m) de publicidad por correo
main principal o mayor
main building edificio (m) principal

main office oficina (f) principal
maintain [keep at same level] mantener o conservar
maintain [keep going] mantener o sostener
maintenance mantenimiento (m) o conservación (f)
maintenance of contacts mantenimiento (m) de relaciones
maintenance of supplies mantenimiento (m) de suministros
major mayor o importante
major shareholder accionista (mf) importante
majority mayoría (f)
majority shareholder accionista (mf) mayoritario
make (v) hacer

make good [a defect or loss] indemnizar o compensar

make money ganar dinero

make out [invoice] confeccionar o extender

make provision for tomar medidas

make up for compensar

make-ready time tiempo (m) de preparación (de una máquina)

maladministration mala administración (f)

man (n) hombre (m)

man (v) asignar personal

man-hour horahombre (f)

manage dirigir o gestionar o administrar

manage to arreglárselas o conseguir

manageable manejable

management [action] dirección (f) o gestión (f)

management [managers] junta (f) de directores

management accounts cuentas (fpl) de gestión

management buyout (MBO) compra (f) de una empresa por sus ejecutivos

management consultant asesor, -ra de empresas

management course curso (m) de gestión empresarial

management team equipo (m) directivo

management techniques técnicas (fpl) de dirección de empresas

management trainee ejecutivo, - va en formación

management training formación (f) de mandos

manager [of branch or shop] gerente (mf) *o* encargado, -da

manager [of department] director, -ra *o* jefe, -fa

managerial directivo, -va

managerial posts órganos (mpl) de gestión

managerial staff personal (m) administrativo

managing director (MD) director, -ra gerente

mandate mandato (m)

manifest manifiesto (m)

manned asistido, da *o* atendido, -da

manning dotación (f) de personal

manning levels niveles (mpl) de dotación de personal

manpower mano (f) de obra

manpower forecasting previsión (f) de mano de obra

manpower planning planificación (f) de la mano de obra

manpower shortage escasez (f) de mano de obra

manual (adj) manual

manual (n) manual (m)

manual work trabajo (m) manual

manual worker obrero, -ra

manufacture (n) fabricación (f)

manufacture (v) manufacturar *o* fabricar *o* elaborar

manufactured goods productos (mpl) manufacturados

manufacturer fabricante (m)

manufacturer's recommended price (MRP) precio (m) de venta recomendado

manufacturing fabricación (f)

manufacturing capacity capacidad (f) de fabricación

manufacturing costs costes (mpl) de fabricación

manufacturing overheads gastos (mpl) generales de fabricación

margin [profit] margen (m)

margin of error margen (m) de error

marginal marginal

marginal cost coste (m) marginal o coste incremental

marginal pricing fijación (f) de precios marginal

marine marino, -na

marine insurance seguro (m) marítimo

marine underwriter asegurador, -ra de riesgos marinos

maritime marítimo, -ma

maritime law derecho (m) marítimo

maritime lawyer abogado (m) especializado en derecho marítimo

maritime trade comercio (m) marítimo

mark (n) marca (f) o señal (f)

mark (v) marcar o señalar

mark down rebajar

mark up recargar

mark-up [profit margin] margen (m) de beneficio

marker pen rotulador (m) o marcador (m)

market (n) mercado (m) o plaza (f)

market (v) vender

market analysis análisis (m) de mercado

market analyst analista (mf) de mercado

market capitalization capitalización (f) bursátil

market economist economista (mf) de mercado

market forces fuerzas (fpl) del mercado

market forecast previsión (f) de mercado

market leader líder (m) del mercado

market opportunities oportunidades (fpl) de mercado

market penetration penetración (f) en el mercado

market price precio (m) de mercado

market rate precio (m) o tarifa (f) de mercado

market research estudio (m) o investigación (f) de mercado

market share cuota (f) de mercado

market trends tendencias (fpl) del mercado

market value valor (m) de mercado

marketable vendible o comerciable

marketing mercadotecnia (f) o 'marketing' (m)

marketing agreement acuerdo (m) de comercialización

marketing department departamento (m) de 'marketing'

marketing division sección (f) de 'marketing'

marketing manager director, -ra de 'marketing'

marketing strategy estrategia (f) de 'marketing'

marketing techniques técnicas (fpl) de 'marketing'

marketplace mercado (m) o plaza (f) del mercado

mass masa (f)

mass market product producto destinado a un mercado de masas
mass marketing comercialización (f) a gran escala
mass media medios (mpl) de comunicación
mass production producción (f) en serie
mass-produce fabricar en serie
mass-produce cars fabricar coches en serie
Master's degree in Business Administration (MBA) master (m) en administración de empresas
materials control control (m) de materiales
materials handling manejo (m) de materiales
maternity leave licencia (f) por maternidad

matter (n) cuestión (f) o asunto (m)
matter (v) importar
mature (v) vencer
mature economy economía (f) madura
maturity date fecha (f) de vencimiento
maximization maximización (f)
maximize maximizar
maximum (adj) máximo, -ma
maximum (n) máximo (m)
maximum price precio (m) máximo
MBA (= Master in Business Administration) master (m) en administración de empresas
MBO (= management buyout) compra (f) de una empresa por sus ejecutivos
MD (= managing director) director, -ra gerente

mean (adj)
medio, -dia
mean (n) promedio
(m) *o* media (f)
mean annual
increase aumento
(m) anual medio
means [money]
recursos (mpl) *o*
medios (mpl)
means [ways] medio
(m) *o* manera (f)
means test
comprobación (f)
de los recursos
económicos
measurement
of profitability
evaluación (f) *o*
medición (f) de la
rentabilidad
measurements
medidas (fpl) *o*
dimensiones (fpl)
media coverage
cobertura (f)
periodística
median
mediana (f)
mediate mediar
mediation
mediación (f)

mediator
mediador, -ra *o*
intermediario, -ria
mediocre mediocre
medium (adj)
medio, -dia *o*
mediano, -na
medium (n)
medio (m) *o*
instrumento (m)
medium-sized
mediano, -na
medium-term
plazo (m) medio
meet [be satisfac-
tory] cumplir *o*
satisfacer
meet [someone]
encontrar *o*
encontrarse (con)
o reunirse
meet a deadline
cumplir un plazo
establecido
meet a demand
satisfacer *o* atender
una demanda
meet a
target cumplir un
objetivo
meet expenses
cubrir gastos

meeting reunión (f) *o* asamblea (f)
meeting place lugar (m) de reunión
member [of a group] miembro (m) *o* socio, -cia
membership afiliación (f) *o* ingreso (m)
membership [all members] los socios *o* los miembros
memo *or* **memorandum** memorandum (m)
memory [computer] memoria (f)
mend (v) arreglar
mention (v) mencionar
merchandise (n) mercancías (fpl) *o* género (m)
merchandize (v) comercializar
merchandize a product comercializar un producto
merchandizer comerciante (mf)

merchandizing comercialización (f) *o* mercadeo (m)
merchant comerciante (mf) *o* mercader (m)
merchant bank banco (m) mercantil
merchant navy marina (f) mercante
merchant ship *or* **merchant vessel** buque (m) mercante
merge fusionar
merger fusión (f)
merit mérito (m)
merit award *or* **merit bonus** gratificación (f) por méritos
message mensaje (m) *o* recado (m)
messenger mensajero, -ra
micro-economics microeconomía (f)
microcomputer microordenador (m)
mid-month accounts cuentas (fpl) de mediados de mes

mid-week a media-
dos de semana
**middle manage-
ment** mandos
(mpl) intermedios
**middle-sized
company** empresa
mediana
middleman
intermediario, -ria
mileage allowance
kilometraje (m)
million millón (m)
millionaire
millonario, -ria
minimum (adj)
mínimo, -ma
minimum (n)
mínimo (m)
minimum dividend
dividendo (m) mínimo
**minimum
payment** pago (m)
mínimo
minimum wage
salario (m) mínimo
minor shareholders
pequeños
accio-nistas (mpl)
minority
minoría (f)

**minority share-
holder** accionista
(m) minoritario
minus menos
minus factor
factor (m) negativo
minute (n) [time]
minuto (m)
minute (v) tomar
nota o levantar acta
**minutes (n) [of
meeting]** acta (f)
de la reunión
misappropriate
malversar
misappropriation
malversación (f)
miscalculate
calcular mal
miscalculation
error (m) de
cálculo
miscellaneous
misceláneo, -nea
o diverso, -sa
miscellaneous items
artículos mpl) varios
mismanage
administrar mal
mismanagement
mala administración

miss [not to hit]
errar *o* fallar
miss [not to meet]
no encontrar
miss [train, plane]
perder (el tren *o* avión)
miss a target no
cumplir un objetivo
miss an instalment
saltarse un plazo
missing (adj)
desaparecido, -da
mistake equivo-
cación (f) *o* error (m)
misunderstanding
malentendido (m)
mixed mixto, -ta *o*
mezclado, -da
mixed economy
economía (f) mixta
mobile phone
teléfono móvil
mobility
movilidad (f)
mobilize movilizar
mobilize capital
movilizar capital
mock-up maqueta
(f) *o* modelo (m) a
escala
mode modo (m)

mode of payment
modo (m) de pago
model (n)
modelo (mf)
**model (n) [small
copy]** maqueta (f) *o*
modelo (m) a escala
model (v) [clothes]
pasar modelos
model agreement
prototipo (m) de
contrato
modem modem (m)
moderate (adj)
moderado, -da
moderate (v)
moderar
moderate price
precio módico
modern
moderno, -na
monetary
monetario, -ria
monetary base
base (f) monetaria
monetary unit
unidad (f)
monetaria
money dinero (m)
money changer
cambista (mf)

money markets mercados (mpl) monetarios

money order giro (m) postal

money rates tipos (mpl) de interés

money supply oferta (f) monetaria

money up front pago (m) por adelantado

money-making lucrativo, -va o remunerativo, -va

money-making plan plan (m) remunerativo

money-lender prestamista (mf)

monitor (v) controlar o comprobar

monopolization monopolización (f)

monopolize monopolizar

monopoly monopolio (m)

month mes (m)

month end fin (m) de mes

month-end accounts cuentas (fpl) de fin de mes

monthly (adj) mensual

monthly (adv) mensualmente

monthly payments pagos (mpl) mensuales

monthly statement estado (m) de cuenta mensual

moonlighter pluriempleado, -da

moonlighting pluriempleo (m)

moratorium moratoria (f)

more más

mortgage (n) hipoteca (f)

mortgage (v) hipotecar

mortgage payments pagos (mpl) de la hipoteca

mortgagee acreedor (-ra) hipotecario (-ria)

mortgager or mortgagor deudor (-ra) hipotecario (-ria)

most-favoured nation nación (f) más favorecida

motivated motivado, -da

motivation motivación (f)

motor insurance seguro (m) de automóviles

mount up aumentar *o* subir

mounting creciente

move (v) trasladar(se) *o* mudar(se)

movement movimiento (m)

movements of capital movimientos (mpl) de capital

MRP (= manufacturer's recommended price) precio (m) de venta recomendado

multicurrency operation operación (f) en multiples divisas

multilateral multilateral

multilateral agreement acuerdo (m) multilateral

multilateral trade comercio (m) multilateral

multinational (n) multinacional (f)

multiple (adj) múltiple

multiple entry visa visado (m) de entradas múltiples

multiple ownership propiedad (f) conjunta

multiple store cadena (f) de grandes almacenes

multiplication multiplicación (f)

multiply multiplicar

multitude multitud (f)

mutual (adj)
mutuo, -tua
mutual (insurance)
company mutua (f)
de seguros

Nn

national (adj)
nacional
national advertising
publicidad (f) a
escala nacional
nationalization
nacionalización (f)
nationalized industry
industria (f)
nacionalizada
nationwide de
ámbito nacional
natural resources
recursos (mpl)
naturales
natural wastage
pérdida (f) de
trabajadores por
jubilación

**near letter-quality
(NLQ)** calidad (f) de
semicorrespondencia
necessary
necesario, -ria
need (n) necesidad (f)
need (v) necesitar
negative cash flow
flujo (m) de caja
negativo
neglected business
negocio (m)
descuidado
neglected shares
acciones (fpl) poco
buscadas en la bolsa
negligence
negligencia (f)
negligent
descuidado, -da
negligible
insignificante
negotiable
negociable
**negotiable
instrument**
instrumento (m)
negociable
negotiate negociar o
gestionar
negotiation
negociación (f)

negotiator
negociador, -ra
net (adj) neto, -ta
net (v) obtener
beneficios netos
net assets or
net worth activo (m)
neto o patrimonio (m)
net earnings or net
income ganancias
(fpl) netas o
ingresos (mpl)
netos
net income or net
salary salario (m)
neto o sueldo
(m) neto
net loss pérdida
(f) neta
net margin margen
(m) neto
net price precio
(m) neto
net profit beneficio
(m) neto
net receipts ingresos
(mpl) netos
net sales ventas
(fpl) netas
net weight peso
(m) neto

net worth valor
(m) neto
net yield
rendimiento
(m) neto
network (n)
red (f)
network (v)
difundir a través de
la red de emisoras
networking (n)
[making business
contracts]
establecimiento de
contactos en el
mundo de negocios
news (n) noticia (f)
news agency agen-
cia (f) de prensa
newspaper
periódico (m)
niche hueco (m) de
un mercado
night noche (f)
night rate tarifa (f)
nocturna
night shift
turno (m) de
noche
nil nada (f)
o cero (m)

nil return
declaración (f) de
ingresos nulos
**NLQ (= near letter
quality)** calidad de
semicorrespon
dencia
no-claims bonus
prima (f) por ausen-
cia de siniestralidad
**no-strike agree-
ment** *or* **no-strike
clause** cláusula (f)
que prohibe la
huelga
nominal capital
capital (m) nominal
nominal ledger
libro (m) mayor de
resultados
nominal rent renta
(f) nominal
nominal value
valor (m) nominal
nominee
candidato (-ta)
propuesto (-ta)
nominee account
cuenta (f)
administrada por
un apoderado

non profit-making
sin fines lucrativos
non-delivery falta
(f) de entrega
**non-executive
director** director
(m) no ejecutivo
**non-negotiable
instrument**
documento (m)
no negociable
**non-payment [of a
debt]** impago (m)
de una deuda
**non-recurring
items** partidas (fpl)
extraordinarias
**non-refundable
deposit** depósito
(m) no reem-
bolsable
**non-returnable
packing** envase (m)
no retornable
non-stop sin parar
o sin escalas
non-taxable income
ingresos (mpl)
libres de impuestos
nonfeasance delito
(m) por omisión

norm norma (f)
normal normal
notary public
notario (m)
note (n) nota (f)
note (v) [details]
apuntar *o* anotar
note of hand
pagaré (m) *o* letra
(f) al propio cargo
nothing nada
**notice [piece of
information]**
letrero (m) *o* anun-
cio (m) *o* aviso (m)
**notice [leaving a
job]** notificación (f)
de despido *o* de
dimisión
**notice [period of
time]** plazo (m)
**notice [legal docu-
ment]** aviso (m) *o*
notificación (f)
notification
notificación (f)
notify notificar *o*
avisar
null nulo, -la
number (n)
número (m)

number (v)
numerar
**numbered
account** cuenta (f)
numerada
numeric or numerical
numérico, -ca
numeric keypad
teclado (m)
numérico

Oo

obey (v) obedecer
o acatar
objective (adj)
objetivo, -va
objective (n)
objetivo (m)
obligation [debt]
deuda (f)
obligation [duty]
obligación (f) *o*
compromiso (m)
obsolescence
obsolescencia (f)

obsolescent obsolescente
obsolete obsoleto, ta
obtain obtener *o* conseguir
obtainable asequible
occupancy ocupación (f)
occupancy rate índice (m) de ocupación
occupant ocupante (mf) *o* habitante (mf) *o* inquilino, -na
occupation ocupación (f)
occupational laboral
occupational accident accidente (m) laboral
odd [not a pair] suelto, -ta *o* desparejado, -da
odd [number] impar
odd numbers números (mpl) impares
off [away from work] ausente del trabajo
off [cancelled] cancelado, -da *o* suspendido, -da
off [reduced by] con descuento
off the record extraoficialmente *o* fuera de actas
off-peak fuera de horas punta
off-season temporada (f) baja
off-the-job training formación (f) profesional fuera del trabajo
offer (n) oferta (f)
offer (v) ofrecer
offer for sale oferta (f) de venta
offer price precio (m) de oferta
office oficina (f) *o* despacho (m)
office equipment equipo (m) de oficina
office furniture muebles (mpl) de oficina
office hours horario (m) de oficina

office security medidas (fpl) de seguridad (en una oficina)
office space espacio (m) para oficinas
office staff personal (m) administrativo
office stationery artículos (mpl) de papelería para oficina
offices to let oficinas (fpl) de alquiler
official (adj) oficial
official (n) funcionario, -ria
official receiver administrador, -ra judicial o síndico (m)
official return declaración (f) oficial
officialese lenguaje (m) burocrático
offload descargar o deshacerse de
offshore en aguas territoriales
oil aceite (m)

oil [petroleum] petróleo (m)
oil price precio (m) del crudo o del petróleo
oil-exporting countries países (mpl) exportadores de petróleo
oil-producing countries países (mpl) productores de petróleo
old viejo, -ja o antiguo, -gua
old-established antiguo, -gua
old-fashioned anticuado, -da o pasado, -da de moda
ombudsman defensor (m) del pueblo
omission omisión (f)
omit omitir
on a short-term basis a corto plazo
on account a cuenta
on agreed terms en las condiciones acor dadas

on an annual basis anualmente
on an average por término medio
on approval a prueba
on behalf of en nombre de
on board a bordo
on business por asuntos de negocios
on condition that a condición de que
on credit a crédito
on favourable terms en condi-ciones favorables
on line *or* **online** en línea
on order pedido, -da
on request a petición
on sale a la venta
on the increase en aumento
on time a tiempo
on-the-job training formación (f) profe-sional en el trabajo
one-off único, -ca

one-off item artículo (m) único
one-sided unilateral
one-sided agreement acuerdo (m) unilateral
one-way fare billete (m) de ida o pasaje (m) sencillo
one-way trade comercio (m) unilateral
OPEC (= Organization of Petroleum Expor ting Countries) OPEP (Organización de los Países Exportadores de Pet-róleo)
open (adj) abierto, -ta
open (v) abrir
open an account abrir una cuenta
open a bank account abrir una cuenta bancaria

open a line of credit
abrir una línea de
crédito

open a meeting
abrir la sesión

open a new business
abrir un negocio

open account
cuenta (f) abierta

open cheque
cheque (m) abierto
o cheque sin cruzar

open credit crédito
(m) abierto

open market
mercado (m) libre

open negotiations
entablar
negociaciones

open ticket billete
(m) abierto

open to offers se
admiten ofertas

**open-ended agree-
ment** acuerdo (m)
modificable

open-plan office
oficina (f) de dis-
tribución modificable

opening (adj)
inaugural o inicial

opening (n)
apertura (f) o
inauguración (f)

opening balance
saldo (m) inicial

opening bid oferta
(f) inicial

opening hours hor
ario (m) comercial

opening price pre-
cio (m) o cotización
(f) de apertura

opening stock
existencias (fpl)
iniciales

opening time hora
(f) de apertura

operate (v) operar
o manejar

operate (v) [work]
entrar en vigor

operating (n) fun-
cionamiento (m) o
operación (f)

operating budget
presupuesto (m) de
explotación

**operating costs or
operating expenses**
gastos (mpl) de
explotación

operating manual
manual (m) de
funcionamiento
operating profit
beneficio (m) de
explotación
operating system
sistema (m) operativo
operation
operación (f)
operational
operacional
operational budget
presupuesto (m) de
explotación
operational costs
gastos (mpl) de
explotación
operative (adj)
operativo, -va
operative (n) *or*
operator (n)
operario, -ria *o*
maquinista (mf)
opinion poll
encuesta (f) *o* son-
deo (m) de opinión
oppor tunity opor
tunidad (f)
option to purchase
opción (f) de compra

optional opcional *o*
optativo, -va
optional extras
extras (mpl)
opcionales
order (n) orden (m)
order (n) [for
goods] pedido (m)
order (n) [money]
libramiento (m) *o or*
den (f) de pago
order (v) ordenar
order (v) [goods]
hacer un pedido *o*
encargar
order book libro
(m)de pedidos
order fulfilment
despacho (m) de
pedidos
order number
número (m) de
pedido
order picking selec-
ción (f) de artículos
para un pedido
order processing
preparación (f) de
pedidos
order: on order
pedido, -da

ordinary ordinario, -ria o corriente
ordinary shares acciones (fpl) ordinarias
organization organización (f)
organization [institution] organismo (m) o asociación (f)
organization and methods organización y métodos
organization chart organigrama (m)
Organization of Petroleum Exporting Countries (OPEC) Organización de los Países Exportadores de Petróleo (OPEP)
organizational organizativo, -va
organize organizar
origin origen (m)
original (adj) original
original (n) original (m) **OS (= outsize)** talla (f) muy grande

out of control fuera de control
out of date antic uado, da o caducado, -da
out of stock agotado, -da
out of work sin empleo o sin trabajo
out-of-pocket expenses gastos (mpl) reembor sables
outbid pujar más alto o sobrepujar
outgoing saliente
outgoing mail correspondencia (f) de salida
outgoings desembolsos (mpl)
outlay desembolso (m) o gasto (m)
outlet mercado (m)
outline (n) bosq-uejo (m)
output (n) producción (f)o rendimie -nto (m)
output (n) [computer] datos (mpl) de salida

output (v) producir
output tax impuesto
(m) sobre las ventas
de bienes o servicios
outright en su
totalidad
outside exterior o
externo, -na
outside director
director externo,
directora externa
outside line línea
(f) exterior
**outside office
hours** fuera de hor
as de oficina
outsize (OS) talla
(f) muy grande
**outstanding
[exceptional]**
notable o destacado,
-da o sobresaliente
**outstanding
[unpaid]** pendiente
outstanding debts
deudas (fpl)
pendientes
outstanding orders
pedidos (mpl)
pendientes
overall global o en
conjunto o general

overall plan plan
(m) general
overbook reservar
con exceso
overbooking sobre-
contratación (m)
overcapacity
sobrecapacidad (f)
overcharge (n)
precio (m) excesivo
o recargo (m)
overcharge (v)
cargar en exceso o
cobrar de más
overdraft
sobregiro (m) o
descubierto (m)
overdraft facility
límite (m) de descu-
bierto bancario
overdraw
girar en
descubierto
overdrawn account
cuenta (f) en
descubierto
overdue
vencido, da o
atrasado, -da
overestimate (v)
sobrevalor ar
o so brestimar

overhead budget
presupuesto (m) de
gastos generales
overhead costs *or*
expenses gastos
(mpl) generales o
de producción
overheads gastos
(mpl) generales o
de producción
overmanning
exceso (m) de per-
sonal o excedente
(m) laboral
overpayment pago
(m) en exceso
overproduce pro-
ducir en exceso
overproduction so
breproducción (f)
overseas (adj)
extranjero, -ra
overseas (adv) en
el extranjero
overseas (n)
extranjero (m)
overseas markets
mercados (mpl)
extranjeros
overseas trade com-
ercio (m) exterior

overspend gastar
excesivamente
overspend one's
budget gastar más
de lo presupuestado
overstock (v)
acumular en exceso
o abarrotar
overstocks exceso
(m) de existencias
overtime horas
(fpl) extraor dinarias
overtime ban
prohibición (f) de
hacer horas extras
overtime pay tarifa
(f) de hor as extras
overvalue sobre-
valor ar o sobrestimar
overweight: to be
overweight pesar
en exceso
owe deber
owing debido, -da
owing to debido a o
a causa de
own (v) poseer o
tener
own brand goods
productos (mpl) de
marca propia

own label goods
productos (mpl) de
marca propia
owner amo (m) o
propietario, -ria o
dueño, -ña
ownership
propiedad (f) o
posesión (f)

Pp

**p & p (= postage
and packing)**
franqueo y embalaje
**PA (= personal
assistant)** ayu-
dante (mf) personal
pack (n) paquete
(m) o envase (m)
pack (v) embalar o
envasar o empaquetar
**pack goods into
cartons** embalar
mercancías en cajas
de cartón

pack of envelopes
paquete (m) de
sobres
package [of goods]
paquete (m) o
embalaje (m) o
envase (m)
**package [of eco-
nomic measures]**
conjunto (m) de
medidas económicas
package deal
acuerdo (m) o
transacción (f)
global
packaging
embalaje (m) o
envase (m)
packaging material
material (m) de
embalaje
packer embalador,
-ra o empaque-
tador, -ra
packet paquete (m)
o cajetilla (f) o
bulto (m)
**packet of ciga-
rettes** paquete (m)
o cajetilla (f) de
cigarrillos

packing embalaje (m) *o* envase (m)
packing case caja (f) de embalar
packing charges gastos (mpl) de embalaje
packing list *or* **packing slip** lista (f) de bultos *o* de contenidos
paid pagado, -da
pallet paleta (f)
palletize empaletar
panel panel (m) *o* tablero (m)
panic buying compra (f) febril
paper bag bolsa (f) de papel
paper feed alimen-tador (m) del papel
paper loss pérdida (f) sobre el papel
paper profit ben-eficio (m) ficticio *o* beneficio sobre el papel
paperclip sujetapapeles (m) *o* clip (m)

papers papeles (mpl) *o* documentos (mpl)
paperwork papeleo (m)
par par
par value valor (m) a la par
parcel (n) paquete (m)
parcel (v) empaquetar *o* envolver
parcel post servicio (m) de paquetes postales
parent company sociedad (f) matriz *o* casa (f) matriz
parity paridad (f) *o* igualdad (f)
part (n) parte (m)
part exchange canje (m) parcial
part-owner copropietario, -ria
part-ownership copropiedad (f)
part-time a tiempo parcial

part-time work *or* **part-time employ-ment** trabajo por horas *o* empleo a tiempo parcial

part-timer trabajador, -ra a tiempo parcial

partial loss pérdida (f) parcial

partial payment pago (m) parcial

particulars detalles (mpl) *o* pormenores (mpl)

partner socio, -cia

partnership sociedad (f) *o* asociación (f)

party parte (f)

patent patente (f)

patent agent agente (mf) de patentes y marcas

patent an invention patentar un invento

patent applied for *or* **patent pending** patente (f) solici-tada *o* patente en tramitación

patented patentado, -da

pay (n) paga (f)

pay (v) pagar *o* abonar

pay a bill pagar una cuenta

pay a dividend dis-tribuir un dividendo

pay an invoice pagar una factura

pay back devolver *o* reembolsar

pay by cheque pagar con cheque

pay by credit card pagar con tarjeta de crédito

pay cash pagar al contado *o* en efectivo

pay cheque cheque (m) de sueldo *o* cheque de salario

pay desk caja (f)

pay in advance pagar por adelantado

pay in instalments pagar a plazos

pay interest pagar intereses

pay money down
hacer un depósito *o*
dar una entrada
pay off [debt] red-
imir *o* reembolsar
pay off [worker]
despedir
pay out pagar *o*
desembolsar *o*
abonar
pay phone teléfono
(m) público
pay rise aumento
(m) de sueldo
pay slip hoja (f) de
sueldo *o* de salario
pay up pagar una
deuda
payable
pagadero, -ra
**payable at sixty
days** pagadero a
sesenta días
payable in advance
pagadero por
adelantado
payable on delivery
pagadero a la
entrega
payable on demand
pagadero a la vista

payback clause
cláusula (f) de
reembolso
payback period
periodo (m) de
reembolso
payee portador, -ra
payer pagador, -ra
paying (adj)
rentable
paying-in slip
recibo (m) (de
depósito)
payload carga (f) útil
payment pago (m)
o remuneración (f)
payment by cheque
pago (m) mediante
cheque
**payment by
results**
pago (m) a destajo
payment in cash
pago (m) en metálico
o en efectivo
**payment in
kind** pago (m) en
especie
**payment
on account**
pago (m) a cuenta

PC (= personal computer) orde-nador (m) personal
P/E ratio (= price/ earnings ratio) relación (f) preciobeneficios
peak (n) cumbre (f) o punto (m) máximo o cima (f)
peak (v) llegar al máximo o alcanzar el punto más alto
peak output rendimiento (m) máximo
peak period horas (fpl) punta
peg prices estabi-lizar los precios
penalize penalizar o sancionar
penalty pena (f) o multa (f)
penalty clause cláusula (f) penal
pending pendiente
penetrate a market penetrar un mercado
pension pensión (f) o retiro (m)

pension fund fondo (m) de pensiones
pension scheme plan (m) de pensiones
per per o a o por
per annum al año
per capita per cápita
per cent por ciento
per day al día
per head por persona
per hour por hora
per week por semana
per year al año
percentage por-centaje (m) o tanto (m) por ciento
percentage dis-count porcentaje (m) de descuento
percentage increase porcentaje (m) de aumento
percentage point punto (m) porcentual
perform (v) actuar o ejercer

performance
actuación (f) o fun-
cionamiento (m) o
rendimiento (m)
performance rating
valoración (f) de
resultados
period periodo (m)
o plazo (m)
period of notice
periodo (m) de
preaviso
period of validity
periodo (m) de
validez
periodic *or* **periodical (adj)**
periódico, -ca
periodical (n)
publicación (f) per-
iódica o revista (f)
peripherals
periféricos (mpl)
perishable
perecedero, -ra
perishable goods
artículos (mpl)
perecederos
perishables
productos (mpl)
perecederos

permanent contract
contrato (m)
permanente
permission permiso
(m) o licencia (f)
permit (n)
permiso (m)
permit (v) permitir
personal personal
**personal
allowances**
deducciones (fpl)
personales
personal assets
bienes (mpl)
personales
**personal
assistant (PA)**
ayudante (mf)
personal
**personal
computer (PC)**
ordenador (m)
personal
personal income
renta (f) personal
personalized con
las iniciales
**personalized
briefcase** cartera
con las iniciales

personalized cheques cheques con el nombre impreso

personnel personal (m)

personnel department departamento (m) de personal

personnel management dirección (f) de personal

personnel manager jefe, -fa de personal

peso [South American currency] peso (m)

petty insignificante

petty cash fondos (mpl) o dinero (m) para gastos menores

petty cash box caja (f) para gastos menores

petty expenses gastos (mpl) menores

phase (n) fase (f)

phase in introducir gradualmente

phase out reducir o retirar gradualmente

phoenix syndrome síndrome del fénix

phone (n) teléfono (m)

phone (v) telefonear o llamar (porteléfono)

phone back volver a telefonear o llamar

phone call llamada (f) telefónica

phone card teletarjeta (f)

phone number número (m) de teléfono

photocopier foto-copiadora (f)

photocopy (n) fotocopia (f)

photocopy (v) fotocopiar

photocopying fotocopiaje (m) o fotocopia (f)

photocopying bureau servicio (m) de fotocopias

picking list inventario (m) de posición (en almacén)
pie chart gráfico (m) circular o gráfico sectorial
piece pieza (f)
piece rate precio (m) a destajo
piecework trabajo (m) a destajo
pilferage *or* **pilfering** (pequeño) hurto (m)
pilot (adj) piloto
pilot (n) [person] piloto (mf)
pilot scheme programa (m) piloto
pioneer (n) pionero, -ra
pioneer (v) iniciar o abrir camino
place (n) lugar (m) o posición (f) o sitio (m)
place (n) [job] puesto (m)
place (v) colocar o poner o situar
place an order cursar un pedido

place of work lugar (m) de trabajo
plaintiff demandante (mf) o querellante (mf)
plan (n) [drawing] plano (m)
plan (n) [project] plan (m) o proyecto (m)
plan (v) planear o planificar o proyectar
plan investments planificar las inversiones
plane avión (m)
planner planificador, -ra
planning planificación (f)
plant (n) [factory] planta (f) o fábrica (f)
plant (n) [machinery] maquinaria (f)
plant-hire firm empresa (f) de alquiler de maquinaria
platform [railway station] andén (m)

PLC *or* plc (= Public Limited Company) Sociedad Anónima (S.A.)
plug (n) enchufe (m)
plug (v) [block] detener *o* frenar
plug (v) [publicize] dar publicidad
plummet caer
plus más
plus factor factor (m) positivo
pocket (n) bolsillo (m) *o* bolsa (f)
pocket (v) embolsar
pocket calculator *or* pocket diary calculadora (f) de bolsillo *o* diario (m) de bolsillo
point punto (m)
point of sale (p.o.s. *or* POS) punto (m) de venta
point of sale material (POS material) publicidad (f) en el punto de venta

policy política (f)
pool resources reunir recursos
poor quality mala calidad (f)
poor service servicio (m) deficiente
popular popular
popular prices precios (mpl) populares
port puerto (m)
port [computer] conexión (f)
port authority autoridades (fpl) portuarias
port charges *or* port dues derechos (mpl) de dársena *o* portuarios
port of call puerto (m) de escala
port of embarkation puerto (m) de embarque
port of registry puerto (m) de registro
portable portátil
portfolio cartera (f) (de valores)

**portfolio manage-
ment** gestión (f) *o*
administración (f)
de cartera
POS *or* **p.o.s.**
(= point of sale)
punto (m) de venta
**POS material
(point of sale
material)** publici-
dad (f) en el punto
de venta
position [job]
puesto (m) *o* cargo
(m) *o* plaza (f)
**position [state of
affairs]** posición
(f) *o* situación (f) *o*
postura (f)
positive positivo, -va
positive cash flow
flujo (m) de caja
positivo
possess (v) poseer
possession (n)
posesión (f)
possibility
posibilidad (f)
possible posible
post (n) [job]
puesto (m)

post (n) [letters]
correo (m)
post (n) [system]
correos (mpl)
post (v) enviar *o*
mandar por correo *o*
echar al correo
post an entry
hacer un asiento
post free sin gas-
tos de franqueo
postage franqueo
(m) *o* tarifa (f)
postal
**postage and pack-
ing** (p & p)
(gastos de) fran-
queo y embalaje
postage paid fran-
queo (m) concer-
tado *o* por te pagado
postal postal
postal charges *or*
postal rates
gastos (mpl) de
franqueo *o* tarifas
(fpl) postales
postal order giro
(m) postal
postcard
(tarjeta) postal

postcode código (m) postal
postdate posfechar
poste restante lista (f) de correos
postpaid porte (m) pagado o franqueo (m) concertado
postpone aplazar o posponer
postponed aplazado, -da
postponement aplazamiento (m)
potential (adj) potencial
potential (n) potencial (m)
potential customers clientes (mpl) eventuales
potential market mercado (m) potencial
pound libra (f)
pound sterling libra (f) esterlina
power (n) poder (m)
power of attorney poder (m) notarial o poderes (mpl)

PR (= public relations) relaciones (fpl) públicas
pre-empt prevenir
pre-financing prefinanciación (f)
prefer preferir
preference preferencia (f)
preference shares acciones (fpl) preferentes
preferential preferente o preferencial
preferential creditor acreedor, -ra preferente
preferential duty or **preferential tariff** tarifa (f) preferente o tarifa preferencial
preferred creditor acreedor, -ra preferente
premises local (m) o edificio (m)
premium [extra charge] agio (m)

**premium [insur-
ance]** prima (f) de
seguros
premium [on lease]
traspaso (m)
premium offer
obsequio (m)
publicitario
premium quality
alta calidad
prepack *or*
prepackage
preempaquetar
prepaid pagado,
-da por adelantado
prepay pagar por
adelantado
prepayment pago
(m) por adelantado
prescribe prescribir
present (adj)
[being there]
presente
present (adj)
[now] actual
present (n) [gift]
regalo (m) *o*
obsequio (m)
present (v)
[give] regalar *o*
obsequiar

**present (v) [show
a document]**
presentar
**present a bill for
acceptance** presen-
tar una letra a la
aceptación
**present a bill for
payment** presentar
una letra al pago
present value valor
(m) actual
presentation
presentación (f)
press prensa (f)
press conference
conferencia (f) de
prensa
press release
comunicado (m) de
prensa
prestige
prestigio (m)
prestige product
producto (m)
prestigioso
pretax profit benefi-
cio (m) antes de
deducir los impuestos
prevent impedir *o*
evitar *o* prevenir

prevention
prevención (f)
preventive
preventivo, -va
previous previo,
-via o anterior
price (n) precio (m)
price (v) poner
precio a
price ceiling límite
(m) de precios
price control con-
trol (m) de precios
price controls con-
trol (m) de precios
price differential
coeficiente (m) de
ajuste de precios
price ex quay
franco en muelle
price ex warehouse
franco en almacén
price ex works pre-
cio (m) en fábrica o
franco en fábrica
price label etiqueta
(f) de precio
price list lista (f)
de precios
price range gama
(f) de precios

price reductions
rebajas (fpl) de
precios
price stability
estabilidad (f) de
los precios
**price tag or price
ticket** etiqueta (f)
de precio
price(-cutting) war
guerra (f) de precios
**price-sensitive
product** producto
(m) sensible a los
cambios de precio
**price/earnings
ratio (P/E ratio)**
relación (f) precio-
ganancias
pricing fijación (f)
de los precios
pricing policy
política (f) de precios
primary
primario, -ria
primary industry
sector (m) primario
prime principal o
primero, -ra
prime cost coste
(m) de producción

prime rate tipo (m)
preferencial de
interés bancario
principal (adj)
principal
principal (n)
[money]
principal (m)
principal (n) [per-
son] mandante (m)
principle
principio (m)
print out imprimir
printer [company]
imprenta (f)
printer [machine]
impresora (f)
printout
impresión (f)
prior anterior o
previo, -via
private privado, -da
o particular
private enterprise
empresa (f) privada
private limited
company sociedad
(f) limitada (S.L.)
private ownership
propiedad (f)
privada

private property
propiedad (f) privada
private sector sec-
tor (m) privado
privatization
privatización (f)
privatize privatizar
pro forma (invoice)
factura (f) pro
forma
pro rata prorrata
probation periodo
(m) de prueba
probationary de
prueba o
probatorio, -ria
problem
problema (m)
problem area
asunto (m)
problemático
problem solver
mediador (m) de
conflictos
problem solving
investigación (f) de
conflictos
procedure proced-
imiento (m) o
tramitación (f) o
trámite (m)

proceed proceder *o* seguir *o* continuar
process (n) pro-cedimiento (m)
process (v) preparar *o* elaborar *o* tramitar
process (v) [raw materials] elaborar
process figures elaborar cifras
produce (n) productos (mpl)
produce (v) pro-ducir *o* fabricar
produce (v) [bring out] presentar
produce (v) [yield] producir *o* dar
producer productor, -ra *o* fabricante (m)
product producto (m)
product advertising anuncio (m) del producto
product cycle ciclo (m) del producto
product design diseño (m) de productos

product develop-ment desarrollo (m) de productos
product engineer ingeniero, -ra de producto
product line gama (f) de productos *o* línea (f) de productos
product mix gama (f) de productos de una compañía
production producción (f)
production [show-ing] presentación (f)
production cost coste (m) de producción
production department departamento (m) de producción
production line cadena (f) de montaje
production man-ager director, -ra de producción
production standards normas (fpl) de producción

production target
objetivo (m) de
producción
production unit
unidad (f) de
producción
productive
productivo, -va
productive
discussions con-
versaciones (fpl)
fructíferas
productivity
productividad (f)
productivity agree-
ment acuerdo (m)
de productividad
productivity bonus
prima (f) de
productividad
professional (adj)
[expert]
profesional
professional (n)
[expert]
profesional (mf)
professional quali-
fications títulos
(mpl) profesionales
profit ganancia (f)
o beneficio (m)

profit after tax
beneficio (m) neto
de impuestos
profit and loss
account cuenta (f)
de pérdidas y
ganancias
profit before tax
beneficio (m) antes
de deducir los
impuestos
profit centre centro
(m) de beneficios
profit margin mar-
gen (m) de beneficio
profit-making
rentable o
lucrativo, -va
profit-oriented
company empresa
(f) con fines de lucro
profit-sharing
participación (f) en
los beneficios
profitability
[making a profit]
rentabilidad (f)
profitability [ratio
of profit to cost]
coeficiente (m) de
rentabilidad

profitable rentable *o* productivo, -va *o* lucrativo, -va

program a computer programar un ordenador

programme *or* **program** programa (m)

programming language lenguaje (m) de programación

progress (n) progreso (m) *o* marcha (f) *o* avance (m)

progress (v) progresar *o* avanzar

progress chaser responsable (mf) del progreso de un trabajo

progress payments pagos (mpl) a cuenta

progress report informe (m) sobre la marcha de un trabajo

progressive progresivo, -va

progressive taxation tributación (f) progresiva

prohibitive prohibitivo, -va

project (n) proyecto (m) *o* plan (m)

project (v) proyectar

project analysis análisis (m) de proyectos

project manager director, -ra de proyecto

projected proyectado, -da *o* previsto, -ta

projected sales ventas (fpl) previstas

promise (n) promesa (f)

promise (v) prometer

promissory note pagaré (m) *o* letra (f) al propio cargo

promote [advertise] promocionar

promote [give better job] ascender

promote a corporate image promocionar la imagen pública de una empresa

promote a new product promocionar un nuevo producto

promotion [publicity] promoción (f)

promotion [to better job] ascenso (m)

promotion(al) budget presupuesto (m) de promoción

promotion of a product promoción (f) de un producto

promotional de promoción o en promoción

prompt pronto, -ta o rápido, -da o inmediato, -ta

prompt payment pronto pago (m)

prompt service servicio (m) rápido

proof (n) prueba (f)

property (n) propiedad (f)

proportion (n) parte (f) o proporción (f)

proportional proporcional

proposal proposición (f) o propuesta (f)

propose [a motion] proponer

propose to [do something] proponer(se)

proposition propuesta (f) o proposición (f)

proprietary company (US) sociedad (f) de cartera

proprietor propietario (m) o dueño (m)

proprietress propietaria (f) o dueña (f)

prosecute procesar o enjuiciar

prosecution [legal action] procesamiento (m)

prosecution [party in legal action] parte (f) acusadora o acusación (f)

prosecution counsel fiscal (m)

prospective eventual
prospective buyer posible
comprador, -ra
prospects
perspectivas (fpl)
prospectus
prospecto (m) *o*
folleto (m)
protect proteger
protection
protección (f)
protectionist
proteccionista
protective
protector, -ra *o*
proteccionista
protective tariff
arancel (m)
proteccionista
protest (n)
protesta (f)
protest (n) [offi-cial document]
protesto (m)
protest (v) protes-tar contra algo
protest a bill
protestar una letra
protest strike
huelga (f) de protesta

provide proveer
provide for prever
provided that *or*
providing a condi-ción de que
provision [condi-tion] disposición
(f) *o* estipulación (f)
provision [money put aside] pro-visión (f) de fondos
o reserva (f)
provisional
provisional
provisional budget
presupuesto (m)
provisional
provisional forecast of sales previsión
(f) provisional de ventas
proviso condición
(f) *o* salvedad (f)
proxy [deed]
procuración (f) *o*
poder (m)
proxy [person]
poderhabiente (mf)
o apoderado, -da
proxy vote voto
(m) por poderes

public (adj)   166

public (adj)
público, -ca
public finance finan-
zas (fpl) públicas
public funds fon-
dos (mpl) públicos
public holiday
fiesta (f) nacional
public image
imagen (f) pública
**Public Limited
Company (Plc)**
sociedad (f)
anónima (S.A.)
public opinion
opinión (f) pública
**public relations
(PR)** relaciones
(fpl) públicas
**public relations
department** depar-
tamento (m) de
relaciones públicas
**public relations
man** persona
dedicada a las
relaciones públicas
**public relations
officer** responsable
(mf) de relaciones
públicas

public sector
sector (m) público
public transport
transporte (m)
público
publicity publicidad (f)
publicity budget
presupuesto (m)
publicitario
publicity campaign
campaña (f)
publicitaria
**publicity depart-
ment** departamento
(m) de publicidad
**publicity expendi-
ture** gastos (mpl)
de publicidad
publicity manager
director, -ra de
publicidad
publicize dar publi-
cidad o divulgar
purchase (n)
compra (f)
purchase (v) comprar
purchase ledger
libro (m) mayor de
compras
purchase order
orden (f) de compra

purchase price precio (m) de compra
purchase tax impuesto (m) de venta
purchaser comprador, -ra
purchasing compra (f)
purchasing department departamento (m) o sección (f) de compras
purchasing manager jefe, -fa de compras
purchasing power poder (m) adquisitivo
put (v) [place] poner
put back [later] aplazar
put in order ordenar
put in writing poner por escrito
put money down dar una entrada

Qq

qty (= quantity) cantidad (f)
qualified cualificado, -da o capacitado, -da
qualified [with reservations] con reservas o condicionado, -da
qualify capacitar
qualify as obtener o sacar el título de
quality calidad (f)
quality control control (m) de calidad
quality controller inspector, -ra de calidad
quality label signo (m) de calidad
quango organismo (m) paraestatal
quantity cantidad (f)
quantity discount descuento (m) por cantidad

quarter [25%]
cuarto (m) o cuarta
parte (f)
**quarter [three
months]**
trimestre (m)
quarter day día
(m) de ajuste
quarterly (adj)
trimestral
quarterly (adv)
trimestralmente o
cada tres meses
quay muelle (m)
question (n)
pregunta (f) o
cuestión (f)
question (v)
preguntar o
cuestionar
questionnaire
cuestionario
(m) o encuesta (f)
quorum
quórum (m)
quota
cupo (m) o cuota (f)
quotation (n) *or*
quote (n)
cotización (f) o
presupuesto (m)

**quote (v) [esti-
mate costs]** cotizar
o ofrecer un precio
**quote (v) [refer-
ence]** citar o
indicar
quoted company
sociedad (f) coti-
zada en bolsa
quoted shares
acciones (fpl) que
se cotizan en bolsa

Rr

**R&D (= research
and development)**
investigación y
desarrollo (I+D)
racketeer
estafador, -ra o
timador, -ra
racketeering
negocio (m)
ilícito
rail ferrocarril (m)

rail transport
transporte (m) por
ferrocarril
railroad (US)
ferrocarril (m)
railway (GB)
ferrocarril (m)
railway station
estación (f) de
ferrocarril
raise (v)
aumentar o subir
**raise (v) [a ques-
tion]** plantear
**raise (v) [obtain
money]** conseguir
raise an invoice
preparar una factura
rally (n)
recuperación (f)
rally (v)
recuperarse
random al azar o
aleatorio, -ria
random check
chequeo (m) al azar
random error error
aleatorio
random sample
muestra (f)
aleatoria

random sampling
muestreo (m)
aleatorio
**range (n) [series of
items]** gama (f) o
surtido (m)
**range (n) [varia-
tion]** escala (f)
range (v) oscilar
rapid rápido, -da
rate (n) [amount]
tasa (f) o coefi-
ciente (m)
rate (n) [price]
precio (m) o tarifa (f)
rate of exchange
tipo (m) de cambio
rate of inflation
tasa (f) de inflación
rate of interest
rédito (m) o tipo
(m) de interés
rate of production
ritmo (m) de
producción
rate of return
tasa (f) de
rendimiento
ratification
ratificación (f)
ratify ratificar

rating
clasificación (f)
ratio razón (f) o
relación (f)
rationalization
racionalización (f)
rationalize
racionalizar
raw materials mate-
rias (fpl) primas
reach llegar o
alcanzar
reach a decision
tomar una decisión
reach an agreement
llegar a un
acuerdo
readjust
reajustar
readjustment
reajuste (m)
ready listo, -ta o
preparado, -da
ready cash
efectivo (m)
real real o
verdadero, -ra
real estate bienes
(mpl) raíces o
propiedad (f)
inmobiliaria

real income *or* **real
wages** renta (f)
real
real-time system
sistema (m) de
ordenador a
tiempo real
realizable assets
activo (m) realizable
realization (n)
realización (f)
**realization of
assets** liquidación
(f) de activo
realize realizar
**realize
[understand]** darse
cuenta
realize a project *or*
a plan realizar un
proyecto o un plan
realize property *or*
assets liquidar
propiedades o
realizar activos
reapplication
segunda solicitud (f)
reapply volver a
presentarse
reappoint
volver a nombrar

reappointment
nuevo nom-
bramiento (m)
reason razón (f)
reassess revaluar
reassessment
revaluación (f)
rebate [money back]
reembolso (m)
**rebate [price reduc-
tion]** rebaja (f) o
descuento (m)
receipt [paper]
recibo (m) o
resguardo (m)
receipt [receiving]
recepción (f)
receipt book
talonario (m) de
recibos
receipts ingresos
(mpl) o entradas (fpl)
receivable a cobrar
o por cobrar
receivables efectos
(mpl) a cobrar
receive recibir
**receiver (who
receives)**
destinatario, -ria
o receptor (m)

**receiver [liquida-
tor]** síndico (m)
reception recepción
(f) o acogida (f)
reception clerk
recepcionista (mf)
reception desk
recepción (f)
receptionist
recepcionista (mf)
recession recesión (f)
reciprocal
recíproco, -ca o
bilateral
**reciprocal agree-
ment** acuerdo (m)
recíproco o acuerdo
bilateral
reciprocal trade
comercio (m)
recí-proco
reciprocity
reciprocidad (f)
recognition
reconocimiento (m)
**recognize a
union** reconocer a
un sindicato
recommend
recomendar
o aconsejar

recommendation
recomendación (f)
reconcile cuadrar o
ajustar
reconciliation
reconciliación (f) o
concertación (f)
**reconciliation of
accounts** concil-
iación (f) de cuentas
record (n)
récord (m)
**record (n) [for per-
sonnel]** historial
(m) o expediente (m)
**record (n) [of what
has happened]**
acta (f) o registro
(m) o informe (m)
record (v) registrar
o anotar
record-breaking
récord
recorded delivery
entrega (f) con
acuse de recibo
records
archivos (mpl)
recoup one's losses
resarcirse de las
pérdidas

**recover [get bet-
ter]** recuperarse o
mejorar
**recover [get some-
thing back]** recu-
perar o recobrar
recoverable
recuperable
**recovery [getting
better]**
reactivación (f)
**recovery [getting
something back]**
recuperación (f) o
rescate (m)
rectification
rectificación (f)
rectify corregir o
rectificar
recurrent
que se repite o
constante
recycle reciclar
recycled paper
papel (m)
reciclado
red tape
burocracia (f) o
papeleo (m)
redeem amortizar o
redimir

redeem a bond
vender un bono o
amortizar una
obligación
redeem a debt
pagar una deuda
redeem a pledge
rescatar una prenda
redeemable rescat-
able o amortizable
**redemption [of a
loan]** amortización
(f) o rescate (m)
redemption date
fecha (f) de amorti-
zación o fecha de
rescate
redevelop renovar
redevelopment
renovación (f)
urbana
redistribute
redistribuir
reduce (a price)
rebajar o reducir (un
precio)
reduce expenditure
reducir gastos
reduced rate precio
(m) reducido o
tarifa (f) reducida

reduction reduc-
ción (f) o rebaja (f)
redundancy exce-
dente (m) de plan-
tilla o despido (m)
redundant
redundante
re-elect reelegir
re-election
reelección (f)
re-employ emplear
de nuevo
re-employment
reempleo (m)
re-export (n)
reexportación (f)
re-export (v)
reexportar
**refer [pass to
someone]** remitir
refer [to item]
referirse o
mencionar
reference
referencia (f)
reference number
número (m) de
referencia
**refinancing of a
loan** refinanciación
(f) de un préstamo

refresher course
curso (m) de
reciclaje o curso de
actualización
refund (n)
devolución (f)
o reembolso (m)
refund (v) reem-
bolsar o devolver
refundable
reembolsable
refundable deposit
depósito (m)
reembolsable
refunding of a loan
conversión (f) de un
préstamo
refusal negativa (f)
o rechazo (m)
refuse (v) rehusar
o negar(se) o
rechazar
regarding relativo
a o en cuanto a
regardless of sin
tener en cuenta
region región (f)
regional regional
**register (n) [large
book]** libro (m) de
registro

**register (n) [official
list]** registro (m)
**register (v) [at
hotel]** registrarse o
inscribirse
**register (v) [in
official list]** regis-
trar o inscribir (en
un registro)
**register (v) [let-
ter]** certificar
register a company
inscribir una com-
pañía en un registro
register a property
registrar una
propiedad
**register a trade-
mark** registrar una
marca comercial
**register of direc-
tors** relación (f) de
directivos de una
empresa
**register of share-
holders** libro (m)
registro de
accionistas
registered (adj)
registrado, -da o
certificado, -da

registered design
diseño (m) reg-
istrado
registered letter
carta (f) certificada
registered office
domicilio (m) social
**registered trade-
mark** marca (f)
registrada
registrar registrador,
-ra o secretario, -ria
(general)
**Registrar of
Companies**
Registro (m)
Mercantil
registration
registro (m) o
inscripción (f) o
matrícula (f)
registration fee
cuota (f) de inscrip-
ción o matrícula (f)
registration form
boletín (m) de
inscripción
**registration num-
ber** número (m) de
registro o número
de matrícula

registry registro (m)
registry office
oficina (f) del
registro civil
**regular [always at
same time]** regular
regular [ordinary]
normal o ordinario,
-ria o corriente
regular customer
cliente (mf) habitual
**regular
income**
ingreso (m) fijo
**regular
route** ruta (f)
habitual
regular size
tamaño (m) normal
regular staff per-
sonal (m) fijo
regulate [adjust]
regular
regulate [by law]
reglamentar
regulation
regulación (f) o
reglamentación (f)
regulations
normas (fpl) o
reglamento (m)

reimbursement
reembolso (m) *o*
reintegro (m)
reimbursement of
expenses reem-
bolso (m) de gastos
reimport (n) reim-
portación (f)
reimport (v)
reimportar
reimportation
reimportación (f)
reinsurance
reaseguro (m)
reinsure reasegurar
reinsurer reasegu-
rador, -ra
reinvest reinvertir
reinvestment
reinversión (f)
reject (n) producto
(m) defectuoso
reject (v) rechazar
rejection
rechazo (m)
relating to refer-
ente *o* relativo a
relation
relación (f)
relations
relaciones (fpl)

release (n)
liberación (f)
release (v) [free]
liberar
release (v) [make
public] divulgar *o*
publicar
release (v) [put on
the market] poner
a la venta *o* lanzar
al mercado
release dues
despachar pedidos
atrasados
relevant apropiado,
-da *o* pertinente
reliability fiabili-
dad (f)
reliable fiable *o* de
confianza *o* cumpli-
dor, -ra
remain [be left]
quedar *o* sobrar
remain [stay]
quedarse
remainder [things
left] resto (m)
remember
recordar
o acordarse (de)
remind recordar

reminder recorda-
torio (m) *o* adver-
tencia (f)
remit (v) remitir
remit by cheque
remitir por cheque
remittance envío
(m) *o* giro (m)
remote control
mando (m) a
distancia
removal mudanza
(f) *o* traslado (m)
**removal [sacking
someone]**
destitución (f) *o*
despido (m)
remove (v)
quitar *o* destituir *o*
suprimir
**remove [to new
house]** trasladar *o*
mudar
remunerate
remunerar
remuneration
remuneración (f)
**render an
account** presentar
una cuenta *o* una
factura

renew renovar *o*
prorrogar
renew a lease
prorrogar un
arrendiamiento
**renew a subscrip-
tion** renovar una
suscripción *o* un
abono
renewal renovación
(f) *o* prórroga (f)
renewal notice
notificación (f) de
renovación
renewal premium
prima (f) de reno-
vación
rent (n) alquiler
(m) *o* renta (f)
**rent (v) [pay
money for]** alquilar
o arrendar
rent collector
cobrador (m) de
alquileres
rent control control
(m) de rentas *o* con-
trol de alquileres
rent tribunal
tribunal (m) de
rentas

rent-free exento de alquiler

rental alquiler (m)

rental income ingresos (mpl) o renta (f) por alquiler

renunciation renuncia (f)

reorder (n) nuevo pedido (m)

reorder (v) renovar un pedido

reorganization reorganización (f)

reorganize reorganizar

rep (= representative) representante (mf)

repair (n) reparación (f)

repair (v) reparar o componer

repay pagar o reembolsar o resarcir

repayable reembolsable

repayment reembolso (m) o pago (m)

repeat repetir

repeat an order renovar un pedido

repeat order pedido (m) suplementario

replace reemplazar o sustituir o reponer

replacement [item] reemplazo (m) o repuesto (m)

replacement [person] sustituto, -ta

replacement value valor (m) de reposición

reply (n) respuesta (f) o contestación (f)

reply (v) responder o contestar

reply coupon boletín (m) de respuesta

report (n) informe (m) o memoria (f)

report (v) informar

report (v) [go to a place] presentarse

report a loss anunciar un déficit

report for an inter-view presentarse a una entrevista
report (v) [on progress] informar sobre la marcha
report to someone rendir cuentas a alguien
repossess recuperar *o* recobrar
represent representar
representative (adj) representativo, -va
representative (n) representante (mf)
repudiate repudiar
repudiate an agreement negarse a cumplir un acuerdo
reputation reputación (f)
request (n) ruego (m) *o* petición (f) *o* solicitud (f)
request (v) pedir *o* solicitar
request: on request a petición

require requerir
require [demand] exigir
requirements requisitos (mpl)
resale reventa (f)
resale price precio (m) de reventa
rescind rescindir *o* anular
research (n) investigación (f)
research (v) investigar
research and development (R & D) investigación y desarrollo (I+D)
research programme programa (m) de investigación
research worker *or* researcher investigador, -ra
reservation reserva (f)
reserve (n) reserva (f)
reserve (n) [supplies] reservas (fpl)

reserve (v)
reservar
reserve currency
divisas (fpl) de
reserva
reserve price
precio (m) mínimo
aceptable
reserves
reservas (fpl)
residence
residencia (f)
residence permit
permiso (m) de
residencia
resident (adj)
residente
resident (n)
residente (mf) *o*
habitante (mf)
resign resignar *o*
dimitir
resignation
dimisión (f) *o*
renuncia (f)
resolution
resolución (f)
resolve resolver *o*
decidir
resources
recursos (mpl)

respect (v)
respetar *o* acatar
respond responder
response respuesta
(f) *o* reacción (f)
responsibilities
responsabilidades
(fpl) *o* obligaciones
(fpl)
responsibility
responsabilidad (f)
responsible (for)
responsable
**responsible to some-
one** ser responsable
ante alguien
rest (n)
descanso (m)
**rest (n) [remain-
der]** resto (m)
restock renovar
existencias *o*
repostar
restocking
renovación (f) de
existencias
restraint
restricción (f)
restraint of trade
restricción (f)
comercial

restrict restringir o limitar
restrict credit limitar el crédito
restriction restricción (f) o limitación (f)
restrictive restrictivo, -va
restrictive practices prácticas (fpl) restrictivas
restructure reestructurar
restructuring reestructuración (f)
restructuring of a loan consolidación (f) de un préstamo
restructuring of the company reestructuración (f) de la compañía
result [general] resultado (m)
result from resultar de o derivar de
result in resultar o dar por resultado

results [company's profit or loss] resultados (mpl)
resume reanudar
resume negotiations reanudar las negociaciones
retail (n) venta (f) al por menor o venta al detalle
retail (v) vender o venderse al por menor
retail dealer comerciante (mf) al por menor o minorista (mf)
retail goods vender al por menor
retail outlets tiendas (fpl) al detall
retail price precio (m) al por menor
retail price index índice (m) de precios al comsumo
retailer detallista (mf) o minorista (mf)
retailing comercio (m) al por menor

retire [from one's job] jubilarse *o* retirarse

retirement jubilación (f) *o* retiro (m)

retirement age edad (f) de jubilación

retiring saliente

retrain reciclar

retraining reciclaje (m) profesional

retrenchment reducción (f) de gastos

retrieval recuperación (f) *o* rescate (m)

retrieval system sistema (m) de recuperación

retrieve recuperar *o* rescatar

retroactive retroactivo, -va

retroactive pay rise aumento (m) retroactivo de salarios

return (n) vuelta (f) *o* regreso (m)

return (n) [profit] ganancia (f) *o* rendimiento (m)

return (n) [sending back] devolución (f)

return (v) [send back] devolver

return a letter to sender devolver una carta al remitente

return address remite (m)

return on investment (ROI) rendimiento (m) de la inversión

returnable retornable

returned empties envases (mpl) devueltos

returns [profits] beneficios (mpl)

returns [unsold goods] productos (mpl) devueltos sin vender

revaluation revaluación (f)

revalue revaluar

revenue ingreso (m)

revenue accounts contabilidad (f) de ingresos

revenue from advertising ingresos (mpl) por publicidad

reversal inversión (f) o revocación (f)

reverse (adj) revertido, -da

reverse (v) revocar

reverse charge call llamada (f) a cobro revertido

reverse takeover contra OPA (f)

reverse the charges llamar a cobro revertido

revise revisar o corregir

revoke revocar

revolving credit crédito (m) renovable

rider cláusula (f) adicional

right (adj) [not left] derecho, a

right (adj) [not wrong] correcto, ta

right (n) [legal title] derecho (m)

right of veto derecho (m) de veto

right of way derecho (m) de paso

right-hand man brazo (m) derecho o hombre (m) de confianza

rightful legítimo, -ma

rightful claimant derechohabiente (m)

rightful owner propietario legítimo, propietaria legítima

rights issue emisión (f) de derechos

rise (n) [increase] alza (f) o subida (f) o aumento (m)

rise (n) [salary] aumento (m) de salario

rise (v) subir

risk (n) riesgo (m)

risk (v) [money] arriesgar

risk capital capitalriesgo (m)

risk premium prima (f) de riesgo

risk-free investment inversión (f) sin riesgo

risky arriesgado, -da
rival company empresa (f) competidora
road carretera (f)
road haulage
transporte (m)
por carretera
road haulier
transportista (mf)
road tax impuesto
(m) de circulación
road transport
transporte (m) por
carretera
rock-bottom prices
precios (mpl)
reventados
**ROI (= return on
investment)**
rendimiento (m) de
la inversión
**roll on/roll off
ferry** ferry roll-on
roll-off
rollout (n) [of product] lanzamiento (m)
**roll over credit or a
debt** refinanciar un
crédito o una deuda
rolling plan plan
(m) periódicamente
actualizado

room [general]
sala (f)
room [hotel]
habitación (f)
room [space]
espacio (m)
room reservations
departamento (m)
de reservas
room service servicio (m) de habitaciones de un hotel
rough [estimate]
aproximado, -da
rough calculation
cálculo (m)
aproximado
rough draft borrador
(m) o bosquejo (m)
rough estimate cálculo (m) aproximado
round down
redondear por
defecto
round up redondear
por exceso
routine (adj) rutinario, -ria o habitual
routine (n) rutina
(f) o costumbre (f)
routine call
llamada (f) rutinaria

routine work trabajo (m) rutinario
royalty canon (m) o derechos (mpl) de autor
rubber check (US) cheque (m) sin fondos
rule (n) norma (f) o regla (f)
rule (v) [be in force] regir
rule (v) [give decision] decretar
ruling (adj) vigente
ruling (n) decisión (f) o fallo (m)
run (n) [regular route] ruta (f) habitual
run (n) [rush to buy] demanda (f) excesiva
run (n) [work routine] ciclo (m) de trabajo
run (v) [be in force] ser válido o regir
run (v) [buses, trains] circular (v)

run (v) [manage] dirigir o llevar
run (v) [work machine] utilizar o hacer funcionar
run a risk correr un riesgo
run into debt endeudarse o adeudarse
run out agotar las existencias
run to ascender
running (n) [of machine] funcionamiento (m)
running costs or **running expenses** gastos (mpl) corrientes o gastos de mantenimiento
running total total (m) acumulado
rush (n) prisa (f)
rush (v) precipitarse
rush hour horas punta
rush job trabajo (m) urgente
rush order pedido (m) urgente

Ss

sack (v) someone
despedir a alguien
safe (adj)
seguro, -ra
safe (n) caja (f)
fuerte o caja de
caudales
safe deposit caja (f)
de seguridad
safe investment
inversión (f) segura
safeguard proteger
safety seguridad (f)
safety measures
medidas (fpl) de
seguridad
safety precautions
precauciones (fpl) o
medidas (fpl) de
precaución
safety regulations
normas (fpl) de
seguridad
salaried
asalariado, -da
salary salario (m)
o sueldo (m)

salary cheque
cheque (m) de sueldo
salary review
revisión (f) de sueldos
**sale (n) [at a low
price]** liquidación
(f) o saldo (m) o
rebajas (fpl)
sale (n) [selling]
venta (f)
sale by auction
venta (f) en subasta
sale or return
venta (f) a prueba o
venta en depósito
saleability facili-
dad (f) de venta
saleable vendible
sales ventas (fpl)
sales analysis análi-
sis (m) de ventas
sales book libro
(m) de ventas
sales budget
presupuesto (m) de
ventas
sales campaign
campaña (f) de
ventas
sales chart gráfico
(m) de ventas

sales clerk
vendedor, -ra
sales conference
reunión (f) de ventas
sales curve curva
(f) de ventas
sales department
sección (f) de ventas
sales drive cam-
paña (f) *o* promo-
ción (f) de ventas
sales executive ejec-
utivo (m) de ventas
sales figures cifras
(fpl) de ventas
sales force per-
sonal (m) de ventas
sales forecast pre-
visión (f) de ventas
sales ledger libro
(m) mayor de ventas
sales ledger clerk
encargado, -da del
libro de ventas
sales literature
información (f)
publicitaria
sales manager
director, -ra comercial
sales people per-
sonal (m) de ventas

sales pitch rollo
(m) publicitario
sales promotion pro-
moción (f) de ventas
sales receipt com-
probante (m) de caja
sales representative
representante (mf)
sales revenue ingre-
sos (mpl) de ventas *o*
facturación (f)
sales target obje-
tivo (m) de ventas
sales tax impuesto
(m) sobre la venta
sales team equipo
(m) de ventas
sales volume volu-
men (m) de ventas
salesman [in shop]
dependiente (m) *o*
vendedor (m)
**salesman [repre-
sentative]** repre-
sentante (mf)
salvage (n) [action]
salvamento (m) *o*
rescate (m)
**salvage (n) [things
saved]** objetos
(mpl) salvados

salvage (v) salvar
salvage vessel buque
(m) de salvamento
sample (n) [group]
muestra (f) *o*
muestreo (m)
**sample (v) [ask
questions]** hacer
un muestreo
sample (v) [test]
probar
**sampling [statis-
tics]** muestreo (m)
por áreas
satisfaction
satisfacción (f)
satisfy [customer]
satisfacer
satisfy a demand
satisfacer una
demanda
saturate saturar
saturate the market
saturar el mercado
saturation
saturación (f)
save (v) ahorrar *o*
economizar
**save (v) [on com-
puter]** archivar *o*
guardar

save on ahorrar *o*
economizar
save up ahorrar
savings
ahorros (mpl)
savings account
cuenta (f) de ahorro
scale [system]
escala (f)
**scale down or
scale up** reducir *o*
aumentar a escala
scale of charges
lista (f) de precios
scarcity value
valor (m) de escasez
scheduled flight
vuelo (m) regular
scheduling
programación (f)
screen (n)
pantalla (f)
screen candidates
seleccionar can-
didatos, -tas *o* pasar
por la criba
scrip certificado (m)
provisional de acciones
scrip issue
emisión (f) de
acciones gratuitas

seal (n) precinto (m)
**seal (v) [attach a
seal]** sellar *o*
precintar
seal (v) [envelope]
cerrar
sealed envelope
sobre (m) cerrado
sealed tenders
ofertas (fpl) lacradas
**season [time for
something]**
temporada (f)
**season [time of
year]** estación (f)
season ticket
abono (m) *o* billete
(m) de abono
seasonal estacional
**seasonal adjust-
ments** ajustes
(mpl) estacionales
seasonal demand
demanda (f) estacional
seasonal variations
variaciones (fpl)
estacionales
**seasonally adjusted
figures** cifras (fpl)
ajustadas esta-
cionalmente

second (adj)
segundo, -da
**second (v) [mem-
ber of staff]**
trasladar
temporalmente
second quarter
segundo trimestre
second-class de
segunda clase *o* de
segunda categoría
secondary
secundario, -ria
secondary industry
industria (f)
secundaria
secondhand usado,
-da *o* de segunda
mano
seconds artículos
(mpl) con
desperfectos
secret (adj)
secreto, -ta
secret (n)
secreto (m)
secretarial college
escuela (f) de
secretariado
secretary
secretario, -ria

**secretary [govern-
ment minister]** min-
istro (m) del gobierno
section (n)
sección (f) *o* depar-
tamento (m)
sector sector (m)
secure funds
conseguir fondos
secure investment
inversión (f) segura
secure job empleo
(m) seguro
secured creditor
acreedor, -ora con
garantía
secured debts deu-
das (fpl) garantizadas
secured loan prés-
tamo (m) garantizado
securities títulos
(mpl) *o* valores (mpl)
**security [being
safe]** seguridad (f)
**security [guaran-
tee]** fianza (f) *o*
garantía (f)
security guard
guardia (m) de
seguridad *o*
vigilante (m)

**security of employ-
ment** seguridad (f)
de empleo
security of tenure
derecho (m) de
ocupación
see-safe venta (f)
a prueba *o* venta en
depósito
seize embargar *o*
confiscar *o* incautar
o secuestrar
seizure embargo
(m) *o* incautación
(f) *o* secuestro (m)
selection selección
(f) *o* surtido (m)
selection procedure
procedimiento (m)
de selección
self-employed
(trabajador, -ra)
autónomo, -ma
self-financing (adj)
autofinanciado, -da
self-financing (n)
autofinanciación (f)
self-regulation
autoregulación (f)
self-regulatory
autoregulado, -da

sell vender
sell forward
vender con entrega
aplazada *o* vender a
futuros
sell off liquidar
sell out [all stock]
agotar las existencias
**sell out [sell one's
business]** vender
un negocio
sell-by date fecha
(f) de caducidad
seller vendedor, -ra
seller's market
mercado (m) de
vendedores
selling (n) venta (f)
selling price precio
(m) de venta
**semi-finished prod-
ucts** productos
(mpl) semiacabados
**semi-skilled work-
ers** obreros (mpl)
semicualificados
send enviar
**send a package by
airmail** enviar un
paquete por correo
aéreo

**send a package by
surface mail** enviar
un paquete por vía
terrestre o marítima
**send a shipment by
sea** enviar una carga
por vía marítima
**send an invoice by
post** enviar una
factura por correo
sender
remitente (mf)
senior mayor *o* más
antiguo *o* superior
**senior manager *or*
senior executive**
director, -ra principal
senior partner
socio, -cia principal
sentence
sentencia (f)
separate (adj)
separado, -da
separate (v)
separar *o* dividir
**separate: under
separate cover** por
separado
**sequester *or*
sequestrate** secues-
trar *o* embargar

sequestration embargo (m)
sequestrator embargador, -ra
serial number número (m) de serie
serve servir o atender
serve a customer atender a un cliente
service (n) servicio (m)
service (n) [of machine] revisión (f)
service (v) [a machine] revisar
service a debt pagar los intereses de una deuda
service centre centro (m) de reparaciones
service charge suplemento (m) por el servicio
service department servicio (m) de mantenimiento
service industry industria (f) de servicios
service manual manual (m) de mantenimiento
set (adj) fijo, -ja
set (n) juego (m)
set (v) establecer o fijar
set against compensar o deducir
set price precio (m) fijo
set targets fijar objetivos
set up a company crear o fundar una compañía
set up in business poner un negocio o establecerse
setback revés (m)
settle [an invoice] saldar o pagar una factura
settle [arrange things] establecerse
settle a claim pagar una reclamación
settle an account liquidar o saldar una cuenta

settlement [agree-
ment] acuerdo (m)
(después de un
conflicto)
settlement [pay-
ment] finiquito (m)
o pago (m)
setup [company]
empresa (f)
setup [organiza-
tion] sistema (m)
share (n) partici-
pación (f)
share (n) [in a com-
pany] acción (f)
share (v) [divide
among] dividir o
repartir
share (v) [use with
someone] compartir
share an office
compartir una oficina
share capital capi-
tal (m) en acciones
share certificate
título (m) o
certificado (m) de
una acción
share issue
emisión (f) de
acciones

shareholder
accionista (mf)
shareholding
tenencia (f) de
acciones
sharp practice
negocio (m) deshon-
esto (pero no ilegal)
sheet of paper hoja
(f) de papel
shelf estantería (f)
o anaquel (m)
shelf filler
empleado, -da para
mantener llenos los
estantes
shelf life of a prod-
uct periodo (m) de
conservación de un
producto
shell company
sociedad (f) ficticia
(para la compra de
acciones)
shelter refugio (m)
shelve dar car-
petazo o arrinconar
shelving [shelves]
estantería (f)
shift (n) [change]
cambio (m)

shift (n) [team of workers] turno (m)

shift key tecla (f) de mayúsculas

shift work trabajo (m) por turnos

ship (n) barco (m) o buque (m)

ship (v) expedir

ship broker agente (m) marítimo

shipment envío (m) o carga (f)

shipper expedidor, -ra o transportista (mf)

shipping envío (m) o expedición (f)

shipping agent agente (m) marítimo o agencia (f) de transportes

shipping charges *or* **shipping costs** costes (mpl) de envío

shipping clerk agente (mf) expedidor, -ra

shipping company compañía (f) naviera o compañía marítima

shipping instructions instrucciones (fpl) de envío

shipping line compañía (f) naviera

shipping note nota (f) de envío

shop tienda (f)

shop around comparar precios

shop assistant dependiente, -ta

shop window escaparate (m)

shop-soiled deteriorado, -da

shopkeeper tendero, -ra o comerciante (mf)

shoplifter ratero, -ra de tiendas o mechera (f)

shoplifting hurto (m) en las tiendas

shopper comprador, -ra

shopping [action] ir de compras o ir de tiendas

shopping [goods bought] compras (fpl)

shopping arcade galería (f) comercial

shopping centre centro (m) comercial

shopping mall galería (f) comercial

shopping precinct zona (f) comercial peatonal

short credit crédito (m) a corto plazo

short of menos de lo necesario *o* escaso, -sa

short-dated bills letras (fpl) a corto vencimiento

short-term (adj) a corto plazo

short-term contract contrato (m) de corta duración

short-term credit crédito (m) a corto plazo

short-term debts deudas (fpl) a corto plazo

short-term loan préstamo (m) a corto plazo

shortage escasez (f) *o* falta (f)

shortfall déficit (m) *o* insuficiencia (f)

shortlist (n) prese-lección (f) *o* terna (f)

shortlist (v) preseleccionar

show (n) [exhibi-tion] exposición (f) *o* feria (f)

show (v) mostrar *o* indicar *o* enseñar

show a profit mostrar un beneficio

showcase vitrina (f)

showroom sala (f) de exposición

shrink-wrapped envasado, -da al vacío

shrink-wrapping envase (m) al vacío

shrinkage contracción (f) *o* encogimiento (m) *o* reducción (f)

shut (adj) cerrado, -da

shut (v) cerrar

side lado (m)

sideline negocio (m) suplementario

sight vista (f)

sight draft giro (m) a la vista

sign (n) señal (f) o letrero (m) o rótulo (m)

sign (v) firmar

sign a cheque firmar un cheque

sign a contract firmar un contrato

signatory signatario, -ria o firmante (mf)

signature firma (f)

simple interest interés (m) simple

single único, -ca o sencillo, -lla

Single European Market Mercado Unico Europeo **sink (v)** hundirse

sister company compañía (f) asociada

sister ship buque (m) gemelo (de la misma flota)

sit-down protest sentada (f)

sit-down strike huelga (f) de brazos caídos

site sitio (m) o lugar (m) o solar (m)

site engineer ingeniero, -ra de obra

sitting tenant inquilino, -na en posesión

situated situado, -da

situation situación (f)

situations vacant ofertas (fpl) de trabajo

size tamaño (m) o dimensiones (fpl)

skeleton staff personal (m) reducido al mínimo

skill habilidad (f) o técnica (f) o destreza (f)

skilled cualificado, -da o especializado, -da

skilled labour
mano (f) de obra
cualificada
skilled workers
obreros (mpl)
cualificados
slack flojo, -ja *o*
débil
slash prices *or*
credit terms
reducir drástica-
mente (los precios *o*
las condiciones)
sleeping partner
socio (m) comandi-
tario *o* socio en
comandita
slip (n) [mistake]
error (m)
slip (n) [piece of
paper] resguardo (m)
slow lento, -ta *o*
atrasado, -da
slow down desacel-
erar *o* reducir
slow payer
moroso, -sa
slowdown
desaceleración (f)
o reducción (f)

slump (n)
[depression]
depresión (f) *o* cri-
sis (f) económica
slump (n) [rapid
fall] baja (f) *o*
caída (f) repentina
slump (v) caer en
picado *o* hundirse
slump in sales
caída (f) de las
ventas
small pequeño, -ña
small ads anuncios
(mpl) breves
small businesses
pequeñas (fpl)
empresas
small businessman
pequeño (m)
empresario
small change
moneda (f) suelta
small-scale a
pequeña escala
small-scale enter-
prise empresa (f) a
pequeña escala
smart card tarjeta
(f) inteligente

SME (small and medium-sized businesses) PYME (pequeñas y medianas empresas)

soar dispararse *o* remontarse

social social

social costs costes (mpl) sociales

social security seguridad (f) social

society sociedad (f) *o* club (m)

socio-economic groups grupos (mpl) socio-económicos

soft currency moneda (f) débil

soft loan préstamo (m) sin interés *o* crédito (m) blando

soft sell venta (f) sin presionar al cliente

software programa (m) informático *o* 'software' (m)

sole único, -ca *o* exclusivo, -va

sole agency representación (f) exclusiva

sole agent representante (m) exclusivo

sole owner propietario único, propietaria única

sole right exclusiva (f)

sole trader comerciante (m) exclusivo

solicit orders solicitar pedidos

solicitor abogado, -da

solution solución (f)

solve a problem resolver *o* solucionar un problema

solvency solvencia (f)

solvent (adj) solvente

soon pronto

source of income fuente (f) de ingresos

space espacio (m)

spare part pieza (f) de recambio *o* de repuesto

spare time tiempo (m) libre
special especial
special drawing rights (SDRs) dere-chos (mpl) especiales de giro (DEG)
special offer oferta (f) especial
specialist especialista (mf)
specialization especialización (f)
specialize especializar
specification especificación (f)
specify especificar o precisar o indicar
speech of thanks palabras (fpl) de agradecimiento
spend [money] gastar
spend [time] pasar
spending money dinero (m) para gastos personales
spending power poder (m) adquisitivo

spinoff efecto (m) indirecto
spoil estropear
sponsor (n) patrocinador, -ra o padrino (m)
sponsor (v) patrocinar
sponsorship patrocinio (m)
spot [place] lugar (m)
spot cash pago (m) al contado o dinero (m) en mano
spot price precio (m) de entrega inmediata
spot purchase com-pra (f) al contado
spread a risk repartir un riesgo
spreadsheet hoja (f) de cálculo
square (n) plaza (f)
stability estabilidad (f)
stabilization estabilización (f)
stabilize estabilizar(se)

stable estable
stable currency
moneda (f) estable
stable economy
economía (f)
estable
**stable exchange
rate** tipo (m) de
cambio estable
stable prices pre-
cios (mpl) estables
staff (n) personal
(m) o plantilla (f)
staff (v) contratar
personal
staff appointment
empleo (m) fijo
staff meeting
reunión (f) o asam-
blea (f) de personal
stage (n) fase (m)
o etapa (f)
**stage (v) [organ-
ize]** presentar
stage a recovery
experimentar una
recuperación
staged payments
pagos (mpl) por
etapas
stagger escalonar

stagnant
estancado, -da
stagnation
estancamiento (m)
stamp (n) sello (m)
**stamp (n) [on doc-
ument]** estampilla
(f) o timbre (m)
stamp (v) [letter]
franquear o poner el
sello
stamp (v) [mark]
sellar o timbrar
stamp duty
impuesto (m) del
timbre
stand (n) local (m)
de exposición o
'stand' (m)
stand down retirarse
(de una elección)
stand security for
avalar a
**stand surety for
someone** avalar o
afianzar
standard (adj)
normal o estándar
standard (n)
norma (f) o modelo
(m) o patrón (m)

standard letter
carta (f) tipo o carta
estándar
standard rate (of
tax) tasa (f) de
impuestos normal
standardization
normalización (f) o
estandarización (f)
standardize
normalizar o
estandarizar
standby arrange-
ments planes (mpl)
de contingencia
standby credit
crédito (m) de
apoyo o crédito
'stand by'
standby ticket bil-
lete (m) en lista de
espera
standing repu-
tación (f)
standing order
domiciliación (f)
bancaria
staple (n) grapa (f)
staple (v) grapar
staple industry
industria (f) principal

staple papers
together grapar
papeles
staple product pro-
ducto (m) principal
stapler grapadora (f)
start (n) comienzo
(m) o principio (m)
o inicio (m)
start (v) comenzar
o empezar
start-up puesta (f)
en marcha (de un
negocio)
start-up costs
costes (mpl) o gas-
tos (mpl) iniciales
starting (adj) inicial
starting date fecha
(f) inicial
starting point
punto (m) de partida
starting salary
salario (m) inicial
state (n) estado (m)
state (v) declarar o
afirmar
state-of-the-art
muy moderno
statement declaración
(f) o informe (m)

statement of account estado (m) de cuentas

statement of expenses relación (f) de gastos

station [train] estación (f)

statistical estadístico, -ca

statistical analysis análisis (m) estadístico

statistician estadístico, -ca

statistics estadísticas (fpl)

status status (m) o posición (f)

status inquiry petición (f) de informes sobre crédito

status symbol símbolo (m) de prestigio

statute of limitations ley (f) de prescripción

statutory statutario, -ria o reglamentario, -ria o legal

statutory holiday fiesta (f) oficial o vacaciones (fpl) reglamentarias

stay (n) [time] estancia (f) o permanencia (f)

stay (v) permanecer o quedarse o alojarse

stay of execution aplazamiento (m) de una sentencia

steadiness estabilidad (f)

sterling libra (f) esterlina

stevedore estibador (m)

stiff competition competencia (f) dura

stimulate the economy estimular la economía

stimulus estímulo (m)

stipulate estipular

stipulation estipulación (f)

stock (n) [goods] existencias (fpl)

stock (v) [goods] almacenar *o* tener existencias
stock code código (m) de almacenamiento
stock control control (m) de existencias
stock controller jefe, -fa de almacén
stock exchange bolsa (f)
stock level nivel (m) de existencias
stock list inventario (m) *o* lista (f) de existencias
stock market mercado (m) de valores *o* bolsa (f)
stock market valuation tasación (f) de acciones
stock movements movimientos (mpl) de existencias
stock of raw materials reservas (fpl) de materias primas
stock size talla (f) *o* tamaño (m) corriente

stock turnover rotación (f) de existencias
stock up acumular
stock valuation valoración (f) de existencias
stockbroker corredor, -ra *o* agente (mf) de bolsa
stockbroking corredería (f) de bolsa
stockist distribuidor, -ra
stockpile (n) reservas (fpl)
stockpile (v) acumular
stockroom almacén (m) *o* depósito (m)
stocktaking inventario (m)
stocktaking sale liquidación (f) de inventario
stop (n) parada (f) *o* alto (m)
stop (v) parar *o* frenar *o* detener
stop a cheque detener el pago de un cheque

stop an account suspender una cuenta

stop payments suspender pagos

stoppage suspensión (f) o paro (m)

stoppage of payments suspensión (f) de pagos

storage (n) almacenaje (m)

storage (n) [cost] coste (m) de almacenaje

storage (n) [in warehouse] depósito (m) o almacenamiento (m)

storage capacity capacidad (f) de almacenaje

storage facilities instalaciones (fpl) de almacenaje

storage unit unidad (f) de almacenaje

store (n) almacén (m) o depósito (m)

store (n) [items kept] reserva (f)

store (n) [large shop] grandes almacenes (mpl)

store (v) almacenar o guardar

storeroom almacén (m) o depósito (m)

storm damage daños (mpl) por tormenta

straight line depreciation amortización (f) anual uniforme o lineal

strategic estratégico, -ca

strategic planning planificación (f) estratégica

strategy estrategia (f)

street directory guía (f) urbana o callejero (m)

strength fuerza (f) o vitalidad (f)

strike (n) huelga (f)

strike: go on strike ir a la huelga

strike (v) ir a la huelga o declararse en huelga

striker
huelguista (mf)
strong fuerte o vigoroso, -sa o firme
strong currency
moneda (f) fuerte
structural estructural
structural adjustment
ajuste (m) estructural
structural unemployment paro (m) estructural
structure (n)
estructura (f)
structure (v)
[arrange] estucturar
study (n) estudio (m)
study (v) estudiar
sub judice sub judice o en manos de los tribunales
subcontract (n)
subcontrato (m)
subcontract (v)
subcontratar
subcontractor subcontratista (mf)
subject (n) asunto (m) o tema (f)
subject to
sujeto, -ta a

sublease (n)
subarriendo (m)
sublease (v)
subarrendar
sublessee subarrendatario, -ria
sublessor subarrendador, -ra
sublet subarrendar
subsidiary (adj)
subsidiario, -ria o secundario, -ria
subsidiary (n)
filial (f)
subsidiary company compañía (f) filial o compañía subsidiaria
subsidize
subvencionar
subsidy subsidio (m) o subvención (f)
subtotal total (m) parcial
subvention
subvención (f)
succeed [do well]
tener éxito o prosperar
succeed [follow someone] suceder

succeed in conseguir hacer algo
success éxito (m)
successful afortunado, -da o próspero, -ra
successful bidder adjudicatario, -ria
sue demandar
suffer damage sufrir daños
sufficient suficiente
sum suma (f) o total (m)
summons citación (f) judicial o emplazamiento (m)
sundries *or* **sundry items** artículos (mpl) varios
superior (adj) [better quality] superior
supermarket supermercado (m)
superstore hipermercado (m)
supervise supervisar
supervision supervisión (f)
supervisor supervisor, -ra

supervisory de supervisión o de control
supplement suplemento (m)
supplementary suplementario, -ria
supplier suministrador, -ra o proveedor, -ra o abastecedor, -ra
supply (n) [action] oferta (f) o abastecimiento (m) o suministro (m)
supply (n) [stock of goods] reserva (f) o provisión (f)
supply (v) suministrar o abastecer o proveer
supply and demand oferta (f) y demanda
supply price precio (m) de oferta
supply side economics economía (f) de oferta
support (v) respaldar o apoyar

support price
precio (m) de
subvención
surcharge sobretasa
(f) *o* recargo (m)
surety (n) [person]
garante (mf) *o*
fiador, -ra
**surety (n) [secu-
rity]** fianza (f) *o*
garantía (f)
surface (n)
superficie (f)
surface mail correo
(m) por via terrestre
o marítima
surface transport
transporte (m) por
carretera o por via
marítima
surplus excedente
(m) *o* exceso (m) *o*
superávit (m)
surplus dividend
dividendo (m) por
superávit
**surrender (n)
[insurance policy]**
rescate (m)
surrender a policy
rescatar una póliza

surrender value
valor (m) de rescate
**survey (n)
[examination]**
inspección (f)
**survey (n) [general
report]** estudio (m)
o informe (m)
survey (v) [inspect]
inspeccionar
surveyor inspector,
-ra de obra
suspend suspender
suspension
suspensión (f)
**suspension of
deliveries** suspen-
sión (f) de entregas
**suspension of pay-
ments** suspensión
(f) de pagos
swap (n)
intercambio (m)
swap (v) cambiar *o*
intercambiar
swatch muestra (f)
pequeña
**switch (v)
[change]** cambiar
switch over to cam-
biarse a *o* pasarse a

switchboard
centralita (f)
swop (= swap)
intercambio (m)
symbol (n)
símbolo (m)
sympathy strike
huelga (f) de
solidaridad
synergy sinergia (f)
system sistema (m)
systems analysis
análisis (m) de
sistemas
systems analyst
analista (mf) de
sistemas

Tt

tabulate
tabular
tabulation
tabulación (f)
tabulator
tabulador, -ra

tachograph
tacógrafo (m)
tacit agreement
acuerdo (m) tácito
tacit approval
aprobación (f) tácita
take (n) [money received]
ingresos (mpl) o recaudación (f)
take (v) tomar
take (v) [need]
llevar o hacer falta
take (v) [receive money] ingresar en caja o recibir
take a call recibir una llamada
take a risk arriesgarse
take action tomar medidas
take legal action entablar un pleito
take legal advice consultar a un abogado
take note tomar nota
take off [deduct] rebajar o quitar

take off [plane] despegar

take on freight fletar

take on more staff emplear más personal

take out a policy hacerse un seguro

take over tomar posesión *o* hacerse cargo *o* sustituir

take place tener lugar

take someone to court llevar a alguien ante los tribunales

take stock hacer un inventario

take the initiative tomar la iniciativa

take the soft option decidirse por la opción más fácil

take time off work tomarse tiempo libre (durante el trabajo)

take up an option suscribir una opción

takeover adquisición (f)

takeover bid oferta (f) pública de adquisición (OPA)

takeover target objeto (m) de una OPA

takings ingresos (mpl) *o* recaudación (f) (de un negocio)

tangible tangible

tangible assets activo (m) tangible

tanker buque (m) cisterna *o* petrolero (m)

tare tara (f)

target (n) objetivo (m) *o* meta (f)

target (v) tener como objetivo

target market mercado (m) previsto

tariff [price] tarifa (f) *o* precio (m)

tariff barriers barreras (fpl) arancelarias

task tarea (f)

tax (n) impuesto (m)

tax (v) gravar con un impuesto

tax adjustment
ajuste (m) impositivo
tax allowance des-
gravación (f) fiscal
tax assessment
cálculo (m) de la
base impositiva
tax avoidance
evasión (f) o elusión
(f) de impuestos
tax code código
(m) impositivo o
código fiscal
tax collection
recaudación (f) de
impuestos
tax collector
recaudador, -ra de
impuestos
tax concession
desgravación (f)
fiscal o privilegio
(m) fiscal
tax consultant
asesor, -ra fiscal **tax
credit** crédito (m) por
impuestos pagados
**tax deducted at
source** impuestos
(mpl) retenidos en
el origen

tax deductions
retención (f) fiscal o
deducción (f) de
impuestos
tax evasion
evasión (f) de
impuestos o fraude
(m) fiscal
tax exemption
exención (f) fiscal
tax form formulario
(m) de declaración
de la renta
tax haven paraíso
(m) fiscal
tax inspector inspec-
tor, -ra de Hacienda
tax loophole
laguna (f) fiscal
tax offence infrac-
ción (f) fiscal
tax paid impuesto
(m) pagado
tax rate tipo (m)
impositivo o tipo de
gravamen
tax reductions
reducción (f) de los
impuestos
tax relief des-
gravación (f) fiscal

tax return *or*
tax declaration
declaración (f)
de renta
tax shelter amparo
(m) fiscal
tax system sistema
(m) tributario
tax year año (m)
fiscal *o* ejercicio (m)
fiscal
tax-deductible
desgravable
tax-exempt exento,
-ta de impuestos
tax-free libre de
impuestos
taxable sujeto, -ta a
impuesto *o* imponible
taxable income
renta (f) imponible
taxation imposición
(f) *o* impuesto (m)
taxpayer con-
tribuyente (mf)
teach (v) enseñar
technique técnica (f)
telephone (n)
teléfono (m)
telephone (v) tele-
fonear *o* llamar

telephone book
guía (f) telefónica
telephone call lla-
mada (f) telefónica
telephone directory
guía (f) telefónica
telephone
exchange central
(f) telefónica
telephone line
línea (f) telefónica
telephone number
número (m) de
teléfono
telephone sub-
scriber abonado
(m) telefónico
telephone switch-
board centralita (f)
telefónica
telephonist
telefonista (mf)
telesales ventas
(fpl) por teléfono
teleworking (n)
teletrabajo (m)
telex (n) télex (m)
telex (v) enviar
por télex
teller cajero, -ra de
un banco

temp (n) secre-
tario, -ria eventual *o*
interino, -ina
temp (v) hacer
trabajo eventual
temp agency
agencia (f) de
trabajo temporal
**temporary employ-
ment** ocupación (f)
temporal *o* empleo
(m) eventual
temporary staff per-
sonal (m) eventual
**tenancy
[agreement]**
contrato (m) de
arrendamiento (m)
tenancy [period]
periodo (m) de
arrendamiento (m)
tenant inquilino, -na
o arrendatario, -ria
**tender (n) [offer to
work]** oferta (f)
**tender for a
contract** licitar para
un contrato
tenderer postor
(m) *o* licitador (m)
tendering oferta (f)

tenure [right]
tenencia (f) *o*
ocupación (f) *o*
posesión (f)
tenure [time]
mandato (m)
**term [part of
academic year]**
trimestre (m)
**term [time of
validity]** plazo (m)
o término (m)
term insurance
seguro (m) temporal
term loan préstamo
(m) a plazo fijo
terminal (adj)
terminal
terminal bonus
bonificación (f)
recibida al concluir
un seguro
terminate terminar
**terminate an agree-
ment** poner término
a un acuerdo
termination
terminación (f)
termination clause
cláusula (f)
resolutoria

terms condiciones (fpl) *o* términos (mpl)

terms of employment condiciones (fpl) de servicio

terms of payment condiciones (fpl) de pago

terms of reference mandato (m) *o* campo (m) de aplicación

terms of sale condiciones (fpl) de venta

territory territorio (m)

tertiary industry industria (f) terciaria *o* industria de los servicios

tertiary sector sector (m) terciario *o* sector de los servicios

test (n) examen (m) *o* ensayo (m) *o* prueba (f)

test (v) probar *o* someter a prueba

text texto (m)

theft robo (m)

third party tercero (m)

third quarter tercer trimestre (m)

third-party insurance seguro (m) contra terceros

threshold umbral (m)

threshold price precio (m) umbral

throughput rendimiento (m)

ticket (n) billete (m) *o* entrada (f)

tie-up [link] enlace (m) *o* conexión (f)

tight money dinero (m) escaso

tighten up on intensificar (el control)

till (n) caja (f)

time and motion study estudio (m) de desplazamientos y tiempos

time deposit depósito (m) *o* imposición (f) a plazo

time limit plazo (m) *o* término (m)

time limitation
plazo (m) de tiempo
límite
time rate tarifa (f)
horaria o tarifa por
horas
time scale
calendario (m)
time: on time a
tiempo
timetable (n)
horario (m) o
calendario (m)
timetable (v)
preparar un horario
timing medida (f)
de tiempo
tip (n) [advice]
confidencia (f)
tip (n) [money]
propina (f)
tip (v) [give money]
dar una propina
**tip (v) [say what
might happen]**
pronosticar o prevenir
**TIR (= Transports
Internationaux
Routiers)** Transporte
Internacional por
Carretera

token símbolo (m)
token charge pre-
cio (m) simbólico
token payment
pago (m) simbólico
toll peaje (m)
toll free (US) a
cobro revertido
**toll free number
(US)** número
(m) de llamada
gratuita
ton tonelada (f)
tonnage tonelaje (m)
tonne tonelada (f)
métrica
tool (n)
herramienta (f)
tool up instalar la
maquinaria en una
fábrica
top (adj) superior o
principal
**top (n) [highest
point]** cima (f) o
cumbre (f)
**top (n) [upper
surface]** parte (f)
superior
**top (v) [go higher
than]** superar

top management alta dirección (f)
top quality alta calidad (f) o calidad superior
top-selling más vendido, -da
total (adj) total
total (n) total (m) o totalidad (f)
total (v) totalizar o sumar
total amount cantidad (f) total
total assets activos (mpl) totales
total cost coste (m) total
total expenditure gastos (mpl) totales
total income renta (f) total
total invoice value valor (m) total de factura
total output producción (f) total
total revenue ingreso (m) total
track record antecedentes (mpl)

trade (n) [business] comercio (m)
trade (v) comerciar
trade agreement acuerdo (m) o tratado (m) comercial
trade association agrupación (f) sectorial
trade cycle ciclo (m) económico
trade deficit or
trade gap déficit (m) comercial
trade description descripción (f) comercial
trade directory guía (f) comercial
trade discount descuento (m) para comerciantes del sector
trade fair feria (f) comercial
trade in [buy and sell] comerciar
trade-in canje (m) parcial
trade-in price precio (m) con entrega de artículo usado

trade journal *or*
trade magazine
revista (f) profe-
sional especializada
trade mission mis-
ión (f) comercial
trade price precio
(m) al detallista
trade terms des-
cuento (m) para
comerciantes del
sector
trade union
sindicato (m)
trade unionist
sindicalista (mf)
trademark *or* **trade**
name marca (f)
comercial *o* nombre
(m) comercial
trader
comerciante (mf)
trading comercio (m)
trading company
sociedad (f)
comercial
trading loss pér-
dida (f) de ejercicio
trading partner
empresa (f) que
comercia con otra

trading profit ben-
eficios (mpl) de
explotación
train (n) tren (m)
train (v) [learn]
prepararse *o* for-
marse *o* aprender
train (v) [teach]
preparar *o* capacitar
o formar
trainee aprendiz, -za
traineeship
aprendizaje (m)
training aprendizaje
(m) *o* capacitación
(f) *o* formación (f)
training levy
impuesto (m) para
financiar la forma-
ción profesional
training officer
responsable (mf) de
la capacitación
transact business
hacer negocios
transaction
transacción (f) *o*
operación (f)
transfer (n)
traslado (m) *o*
transferencia (f)

transfer (n) [travel]
transbordo (m)
transfer (v)
[move to new
place] trasladar o
transferir
transfer fee
traspaso (m)
transfer of funds
transferencia (f)
de fondos
transferable
transferible
transferred charge
call llamada (f) a
cobro revertido
transit tránsito (m)
transit lounge sala
(f) de tránsito
transit visa visado
(m) de tránsito
translate traducir
translation
traducción (f)
translation bureau
agencia (f) de
traducciones
translator
traductor, -ra
transport (n)
transporte (m)

transport (v)
transportar o llevar
transport facilities
medios (mpl) de
transporte
treasury Tesoro
(m) o Hacienda (f)
Pública
treble triplicar
trend tendencia (f)
trial [court case]
proceso (m) o
juicio (m)
trial [test of prod-
uct] prueba (f) o
ensayo (m)
trial and error
tanteo (m)
trial balance
balance (m) de
comprobación
trial period periodo
(m) de prueba
trial sample
muestra (f)
triple (adj) triple
triple (v) triplicar
triplicate: in tripli-
cate por triplicado
troubleshooter
mediador, -ra

troubleshooting (n)
investigación (f) de
conflictos
truck [lorry]
camión (m)
**truck [railway
wagon]** vagón (m)
(de ferrocarril)
trucker
camionero, -ra
trucking acarreo
(m) o transporte
(m) por carretera
true (adj)
verdadero, -ra
true copy
compulsa (f) o
copia (f) exacta
trust company
compañía
(f) fiduciaria
turn down rechazar
turn over (v)
[make sales] girar
(volumen de ventas)
turnkey operation
operación (f) llaves
en mano

turnkey operator
agente (mf) de
operaciones llaves
en mano
turnover [of staff]
rotación (f) de
personal
turnover [of stock]
rotación (f) (de
mercancias)
turnover [sales]
volumen (m) de
ventas o cifra (f) de
negocios
turnover tax
impuesto (m) sobre
el volumen de
ventas
**turnround [goods
sold]** rotación
(f) de existencias
**turnround [making
profitable]**
reactivación (f)
turnround [of plane]
descarga (f) y carga
de un avión

Uu

unaccounted for
inexplicado, -da *o*
desaparecido, -da *o*
sin figurar
unaudited no
verificado, -da
unaudited accounts
cuentas (fpl) sin
verificar
unauthorized
expenditure gastos
(mpl) no autorizados
unavailability
indisponibilidad (f)
unavailable
inasequible
unchanged
inalterado, -da *o*
invariable
unchecked figures
cifras (fpl) sin
comprobar
unclaimed baggage
equipaje (m) no
reclamado
unconditional
incondicional *o* sin
condiciones

unconfirmed sin
confirmar
undated sin fecha
undelivered no
entregado, -da
under [according
to] conforme a *o*
según
under [down] abajo
under [less than]
por debajo de *o*
menos de
under construction
en construcción
under contract
bajo contrato
under control bajo
control
under new manage-
ment cambio (m)
de dirección
undercharge
cobrar de menos
undercut a rival
vender a precio más
bajo que un rival
underdeveloped
countries países
(mpl) sub-
desarrollados
underequipped mal
equipado, -da

underpaid mal pagado, -da
undersell vender más barato
undersigned abajo firmante (mf)
underspend gastar menos
understand entender o comprender
understanding acuerdo (m)
undertake emprender o encargarse de o comprometerse
undertaking [company] empresa (f)
undertaking [promise] compromiso (m) o promesa (f)
underwrite [guarantee] avalar
underwrite [pay costs] garantizar el pago
underwriting syndicate consorcio (m) asegurador o emisor
undischarged bankrupt quebrado (m) no rehabilitado

uneconomic rent renta (f) que no llega a cubrir los costes
unemployed parado, -da o desempleado, -da
unemployment paro (m) o desempleo (m)
unemployment pay subsidio (m) de paro
unexplained inexplicado, -da
unfair injusto, -ta
unfair competition competencia (f) desleal
unfair dismissal despido (m) injusto
unfavourable desfavorable o adverso, -sa
unfavourable exchange rate tipo (m) de cambio desfavorable
unfulfilled order pedido (m) no servido o pedido por servir

unilateral unilateral
union sindicato (m)
union recognition
reconocimiento (m)
de un sindicato
unique selling
point *or* **proposition**
(USP) argumento
(m) de venta
unit unidad (f)
unit [in unit trust]
título (m)
unit cost coste (m)
unitario *o* coste por
unidad
unit price precio
(m) por unidad
unit trust fondos
(mpl) mutuos *o*
fondos de inversión
unite (v) unir
unlimited liability
responsabilidad (f)
ilimitada
unload (v) descargar
unload [get rid of]
deshacerse de
unobtainable
inalcanzable *o*
imposible de
conseguir

unofficial extraofi-
cial *o* no oficial *o*
oficioso, -sa
unpaid impagado,
-da *o* sin pagar
unpaid invoices
facturas (fpl)
impagadas
unsealed envelope
sobre (m) abierto
unsecured creditor
acreedor, -ra común
o sin garantía
unskilled no
cualificado, -da
unsold no vendido,
-da *o* sin vender
unsubsidized no
subvencionado, -da
unsuccessful
fracasado, -da *o* sin
éxito
up front por
adelantado
up to hasta
up to date actual *o*
moderno, -na *o* al día
up-market de
primera calidad
update (n)
actualización (f)

update (v) actualizar *o* poner al día
updating (n) actualización (f) *o* puesta (f) al día
upset price precio (m) inicial
upturn mejora (f) *o* reactivación (f)
upward trend tendencia (f) alcista
urgent urgente
use (n) uso (m)
use (v) emplear *o* usar *o* utilizar
use up spare capacity utilizar capacidad ociosa
useful útil
user usuario, -ria
user-friendly de fácil uso *o* de fácil manejo
USP (= unique selling point *or* proposition) argumento (m) de venta
usual normal *o* usual *o* habitual
utilization utilización (f) *o* uso (m)

Vv

vacancy [for job] plaza (f) *o* vacante (f)
vacant vacante *o* libre *o* disponible
vacate desocupar
valid válido, -da *o* valedero, -ra
validity validez (f)
valuation valoración (f) *o* evaluación (f) *o* tasación (f)
value (n) valor (m)
value (v) valorar *o* tasar *o* evaluar
value added tax (VAT) impuesto (m) sobre el valor añadido (IVA)
valuer tasador, -ra
van camioneta (f)
variable costs costes (mpl) variables
variance variación (f) *o* discrepancia (f)
variation variación (f)
VAT (= value added tax) IVA (impuesto sobre el valor añadido)

VAT declaration declaración (f) del IVA
VAT inspector inspector, -ra del IVA
VAT invoice factura (f) con el IVA
vehicle vehículo (m)
vendor vendedor, -ra
venture (n) [business] empresa (f)
venture (v) [risk] arriesgar
venture capital capital-riesgo (m)
venue lugar (m) o punto (m) de reunión
verbal verbal
verbal agreement acuerdo (m) verbal
verification verificación (f)
verify verificar
vertical communication comunicación (f) vertical
vertical integration integración (f) vertical
vested interest interés (m) personal o intereses (mpl) creados

veto a decision vetar una decisión
via por o vía
viable viable
videoconference (n) videoconferencia (f)
violate (v) violar
VIP lounge salón (m) VIP (salón de personalidades)
visa visado (m)
visible imports importaciones (fpl) visibles
visible trade comercio (m) de visibles
visit (n) visita (f)
visit (v) visitar
voicemail (n) audiomensajería (f)
void (adj) [not valid] nulo, -la o inválido, -da
void (v) invalidar
volume volumen (m)
volume discount descuento (m) por volumen
volume of sales volumen (m) de ventas

volume of trade *or*
volume of business
volumen (m) comer-
cial o volumen de
negocios
**voluntary liquida-
tion** liquidación (f)
voluntaria
**voluntary redun-
dancy** baja (f) incen-
tivada o voluntaria
vote of thanks
voto (m) de gracias
voucher bono (m)
o vale (m)
**voucher [document
from an auditor]**
comprobante (m)

Ww

wage sueldo (m) o
salario (m)
wage claim
reivindicación (f)
salarial

wage freeze con-
gelación (f) de salarios
wage levels niveles
(mpl) de salarios
wage negotiations
negociaciones (fpl)
salariales
wage scale escala
(f) salarial o escala
de salarios
waive a payment
renunciar a un pago
waiver [of right]
renuncia (f)
waiver clause
cláusula (f) de
renuncia
warehouse (n)
almacén (m)
warehouse (v)
almacenar
warehouseman
almacenista (mf)
warehousing
almacenaje (m)
warn (v) avisar
warning (n) aviso
(m) o advertencia (f)
**warrant (n) [docu-
ment]** autorización
(f) o orden (f)

warrant (v) [guar-antee] garantizar
warrant (v) [justify] justificar
warranty (n) garantía (f)
wastage pérdida (f) o desperdicio (m)
waste (n) desperdicio (m) o desecho (m) o residuos (mpl)
waste (v) [use too much] desperdiciar o malgastar
waybill carta (f) de porte
weak (adj) débil o flojo, -ja
weak market mercado (m) débil
wear and tear desgaste (m) natural o normal
web (n): the web la Web o la Red
website (n) sitio (m) web o website (f)
week semana (f)
weekly semanalmente
weigh pesar

weighbridge báscula (f) puente o puente-báscula (m)
weight peso (m)
weight limit peso (m) máximo
weighted average promedio (m) ponderado o media (f) ponderada
weighted index índice (m) ponderado
weighting ponderación (f)
welcome (n) acogida (f)
welfare (n) bienestar (m)
well-paid job trabajo (m) bien remunerado
wharf muelle (m) o embarcadero (m)
white knight rescatador, -ra de empresas
whole-life insurance seguro (m) corriente de vida
wholesale (adv) al por mayor

wholesale dealer
mayorista (mf) *o*
comerciante (mf) al
por mayor
wholesale discount
descuento (m) al
por mayor
wholesale price
precio (m) al por
mayor
**wholesale price
index** índice (m) de
precios al por mayor
wholesaler
mayorista (mf) *o*
comerciante (mf) al
por mayor
wide (adj)
amplio, -plia
wildcat strike
huelga (f) salvaje
win a contract con-
seguir un contrato
**wind up [a com-
pany]** liquidar una
sociedad
wind up [a meeting]
terminar *o* concluir
winding up
liquidación (f)
window ventana (f)

window display
escaparate (m)
withdraw retirar
(una oferta) *o* sacar
(dinero)
**withdraw a takeover
bid** retirar una
oferta de adquisición
**withdrawal [of
money]** retirada (f)
o retiro (m) *o*
reintegro (m)
withholding tax
retención (f) de
impuestos en origen
witness (n) testimo-
nio (m) *o* testigo (mf)
**witness (v) [a doc-
ument]** firmar
como testigo
**witness an
agreement** actuar
de testigo
word-processing
tratamiento (m) de
textos
wording texto (m)
work (n) trabajo (m)
work (v) trabajar
work in progress
trabajo (m) en curso

work permit permiso (m) de trabajo
work-to-rule huelga (f) de celo o paro (m) técnico
worker trabajador, -ra o obrero, -ra o operario, -ria
worker director delegado, -da del personal
workforce mano (f) de obra
working capital capital (m) operativo o capital circulante
working conditions condiciones (fpl) de trabajo
working party grupo (m) de trabajo
workman obrero (m)
workshop taller (m)
workstation [at computer] estación (f) o puesto (m) de trabajo
world mundo (m)
world market mercado (m) mundial
worldwide (adj) mundial o global

worldwide (adv) mundialmente
World Wide Web Teleraña (f) mundial
worry (n) inquietud (f) o preocupación (f)
worth (n) [value] valor (m)
worth: be worth valer
worthless sin valor
wrap up [goods] envolver
wrapper or wrapping envoltorio (m)
wrapping paper papel (m) de envolver
wreck (n) [company] empresa (f) en ruinas
wreck (n) [ship] naufragio (m)
wreck (v) [ruin] naufragar o fracasar
writ orden (f) o mandato (m) **write** escribir
write down [assets] depreciar el valor de un activo
writedown [of asset] depreciación (f) de un activo

write off [debt]
anular *o* cancelar
write-off [loss]
deuda (f) incobrable
o pérdida (f) total
write out copiar *o*
escribir sin abreviar
write out a cheque
extender un cheque
writing escrito (m) *o*
escritura (f) *o* letra (f)
written agreement
acuerdo por escrito
wrong erróneo, -nea
o equivocado, -da
wrongful dismissal
despido (m) injusto

yellow pages pági-
nas (fpl) amarillas
**yield (n) [on
investment]**
rendimiento (m) *o*
producción (f) *o*
renta (f)
yield (v) [interest]
rendir *o* devengar
young joven
younger más joven
o menor

Xx Yy

year año (m)
year end cierre (m)
del ejercicio
yearly payment
pago (m) anual

Zz

zero cero (m)
zero-rated con un
IVA del 0%
zip code (US)
código (m) postal

Español-Inglés
Spanish-English

Aa

abajo down *or* under *or* below
abajo firmante (mf) undersigned (n)
abandonar leave (v) *or* abandon (v)
abandono (m) de responsabilidad disclaimer (n)
abarrotar overstock (v)
abastecedor (-ra) supplier
abastecer supply (v) *or* cater for (v)
abastecimiento (m) supply (n)
abierto (-ta) open (adj)
abierto por la noche late-night opening
abogado (-da) lawyer (n) *or* solicitor (n) *or* counsel (n)
abogado defensor defence counsel

abogado especializado en derecho marítimo maritime lawyer
abonado (-da) telefónico (-ca) telephone subscriber
abonar pay (v) *or* pay out (v)
abonar [acreditar] credit (v)
abono (m) [billete] season ticket (n)
abono (m) [crédito] credit entry (n)
abordar [embarcarse] board (v)
abrir open (v)
abrir la sesión open a meeting
abrir un negocio open (v) *or* start (v) new business
abrir una carta de crédito issue a letter of credit
abrir una cuenta open an account
abrir una cuenta bancaria open a bank account

abrir una línea de crédito open a line of credit

abundancia (f) abundance (n) *or* glut (n)

acabado (-da) finished (adj)

acaparamiento (m) hoarding

acaparar [acumular] hoard (v)

acaparar [capturar] capture (v)

acaparar el mercado corner (v) the market *or* monopolize (v)

acarreo (m) haulage (n)

acarreo [transporte] trucking (n)

acarreo: gastos de acarreo haulage costs *or* haulage rates

acatar respect (v) *or* obey (v)

accesible accessible (adj)

acceso (m) access (n)

acceso [mercado] entry (n)

accesorios (mpl) fittings (n)

accidente (m) accident (m)

accidente industrial industrial accident

accidente laboral occupational accident

acción (f) action (n)

acción (f) [finanzas] share (n)

acción de primera categoría blue chip (n)

acción legal (legal) action

acción preferente acumulativa cumulative preference share

acciones (fpl) ordinarias ordinary shares *or* equities (n)

acciones poco buscadas en la bolsa neglected shares

acciones preferentes preference shares

acciones que se cotizan en bolsa quoted shares

accionista (mf)
shareholder (n)
accionista
importante major
shareholder
accionista mayori-
tario majority
shareholder
accionista minori-
tario minority
shareholder
aceite (m) oil (n)
aceptable
acceptable (adj)
aceptación (f)
acceptance (n)
aceptación de una
oferta acceptance
of an offer
aceptación irrevo-
cable irrevocable
acceptance
aceptar accept (v) *or*
allow (v) *or* agree (v)
aceptar hacer
algo agree to do
something
aceptar la entrega
de mercancías
accept delivery of a
shipment

aceptar la respons-
abilidad de algo
accept liability for
something
aceptar una letra
accept a bill
aclaración (f)
explanation (n)
aclarar clear (v) *or*
clarify (v)
acogida (f)
reception (n) *or*
welcome (n)
acomodamiento
(m) composition
(n) (with creditors)
acomodo (m)
[acuerdo]
arrangement (n)
aconsejar advise (v)
or recommend (v)
acordado (-da)
agreed (adj)
acordar agree (v)
acordarse (de)
remember (v)
acotación (f)
[límite] limit (n)
acreditar credit (v)
acreedor (-ra)
creditor (n)

**acreedor común o
sin garantía** unse-
cured creditor
**acreedor con garan-
tía** secured creditor
acreedor diferido
deferred creditor
**acreedor hipote-
cario** mortgagee (n)
**acreedor prefer-
ente** preferential
creditor *or* preferred
creditor
acta (f) [registro]
record (n)
**acta (f) de la
reunión** minutes (n)
acta (f) notarial
affidavit (n)
Acta Unica Europea
Single European Act
actividad (f)
activity (n)
activo (m) asset (n)
activo (-va)
active (adj) *or* go-
ahead (adj)
activo circulante
current assets
activo congelado
frozen assets

activo fijo fixed
assets
activo financiero
financial asset
activo intangible
intangible assets
activo invisible
invisible assets
activo líquido
liquid assets
activo neto net
assets *or* net worth
activo realizable
realizable assets
activo tangible
tangible assets
activo y pasivo (m)
assets and liabilities
**activos (mpl)
totales** total assets
actuación (f)
performance (n)
actual present (adj)
or current (adj)
actual [moderno]
up to date (adj)
actualización (f)
update (n) *or*
updating (n)
actualizar
update (v)

actuar act (v) *or* perform (v)

actuar de testigo en la firma de un contrato witness an agreement

actuario (-ria) actuary (n)

acuerdo (m) agreement (n) *or* compromise (n)

acuerdo: negarse a cumplir un acuerdo repudiate an agreement

acuerdo [arreglo] arrangement (n) *or* understanding (n)

acuerdo [después de un conflicto] settlement (n)

acuerdo a tanto alzado fixed-price agreement

acuerdo bilateral o reciproco reciprocal agreement

acuerdo comercial trade agreement

acuerdo de doble imposición double taxation agreement

acuerdo (m) de comercialización marketing agreement

acuerdo de muchos años long-standing agreement

acuerdo de productividad productivity agreement

acuerdo entre caballeros gentleman's agreement

acuerdo global package deal (n)

acuerdo modificable open-ended agreement

acuerdo multilateral multilateral agreement

acuerdo por escrito written agreement

acuerdo tácito tacit agreement

acuerdo unilateral one-sided agreement

acuerdo verbal verbal agreement

acumulación (f) accrual (n)

acumulación de interés accrual of interest

acumulación de trabajo atrasado backlog (n)

acumular accumulate (v) *or* hoard (v)

acumular [existencias] stockpile (v) *or* stock up (v)

acumular en exceso overstock (v)

acumularse accumulate (v) *or* accrue (v)

acumulativo (-va) cumulative (adj)

acusación (f) accusation (n) *or* charge (n)

acusación [parte acusadora] prosecution (n)

acusado (-da) defendant (n)

acusar accuse (v) *or* charge (v)

acusar recibo de una carta acknowledge (v) receipt of a letter

acuse (m) de recibo acknowledgement (n)

ad valorem ad valorem

adecuado (-da) adequate (adj)

adelantado (-da) advanced (adj)

adelantado: por adelantado up front

adeudar debit (v)

adeudarse run (v) into debt

adeudo (m) debit entry (n)

adicional additional (adj)

adjudicación (f) adjudication (n)

adjudicar award (v)

adjudicar un contrato (a alguien) award a contract (to someone)

adjudicar un derecho (a alguien) assign (v) a right (to someone)

adjudicatario (-ria) successful bidder (n)

adjuntar attach (v) *or* enclose (v)

adjunto (m) attachment (n) *[email]*

adjunto (-ta)
deputy (n)
administración (f)
administration (n)
**administración de
cartera** portfolio
management
**administración
local** local
government
**administrador (-ra)
judicial** official
receiver (n)
administrar
manage (v)
administrar mal
mismanage (v)
**administrar una
propiedad** manage
property
**administrativo
(-va)** administra-
tive (adj)
admisible
acceptable (adj)
admitir admit (v)
adquirir acquire (v)
or buy (v)
**adquirir una
compañía** acquire a
company

adquisición (f)
acquisition (n) or
takeover (n)
**adquisición apalan-
cada** leveraged
buyout (LBO)
aduana (f)
customs (n)
**Aduanas y
Arbitrios** Customs
and Excise
aduanero (-ra)
customs officer or
customs official
adverso (-sa)
unfavourable (adj)
advertencia (f)
reminder (n) or
warning (n)
aerograma (m) air
letter (n)
aeropuerto (m)
airport (n)
afianzar guarantee
(v) or stand surety (v)
afiliación (f)
affiliation (n) or
membership (n)
afiliado (-da)
affiliated (adj) or
associate (adj)

afirmar firm (v)
afirmar [declarar]
state (v)
afirmativo (-va)
affirmative (adj)
afortunado (-da)
successful (adj)
agencia (f)
agency (n)
**agencia de alquiler
de viviendas**
letting agency
agencia de cambio
bureau de change
**agencia de cobro de
morosos** debt col-
lection agency
**agencia de
informes comer-
ciales** credit agency
agencia de prensa
news agency
**agencia de
publicidad**
advertising agency
**agencia de trabajo
temporal** temp
agency
**agencia de
traducciones**
translation bureau

**agencia de
transportes**
shipping agent
agencia exclusiva
concession (n)
agenda (f)
appointments book
(n) *or* diary (n)
agenda de mesa
desk diary
agente (mf) agent
(n) *or* broker (n)
agente de aduanas
customs broker
**agente de operacio-
nes llaves en mano**
turnkey operator
**agente de patentes y
marcas** patent agent
agente de seguros
insurance agent
agente del credere
del credere agent
agente en exclusiva
sole agent
agente expedidor
forwarding agent *or*
shipping clerk
agente marítimo
shipping agent *or*
ship broker

agio (m) [especu-lación] premium (n)
agotado (-da)
out of stock
agotar las existen-cias sell out (v) *or*
run out (v)
agrario (-ria)
agricultural
agregado (-da)
comercial
commercial attaché
agrícola agricultural
agropecuario (-ria)
agricultural
agrupación (f)
group (n) *or*
consolidation (n)
agrupación
sectorial trade
association
agrupar batch (v)
or bracket together
or consolidate (v)
agua: en aguas ter-ritoriales offshore
ahorrar save (v) *or*
save up *or* save on
ahorrar: que
ahorra energía
energy-saving (adj)

ahorros (mpl)
savings (n)
aire (m) air (n)
ajustado (-da) al
coste de la vida
index-linked
ajustar adjust (v)
or gear (v)
ajustar [cuadrar]
reconcile (v)
ajuste (m)
adjustment (n)
ajuste estructural
structural adjustment
ajuste financiero
financial settlement
ajuste impositivo
tax adjustment
ajuste fino fine tuning
ajustes (mpl)
estacionales sea-sonal adjustments
albarán (m)
delivery note (n)
alcanzar reach (v)
alcanzar el punto
más alto peak (v)
alcista (mf)
[bolsa] bull (n)
aleatorio (-ria)
random (adj)

alegar claim (v)
**alimentación (f) con-
tinua** continuous feed
**alimentador (m) del
papel** paper feed
almacén (m) ware-
house (n) *or* store
(n) *or* storeroom (n)
almacén [depósito]
depository (n) *or*
stockroom (n)
almacén central
depot (n)
**almacén de
mercancías** goods
depot
almacén frigorífico
cold store
almacenaje (m)
storage (n) *or*
warehousing (n)
**almacenaje frigorí-
fico** cold storage
**almacenamiento
(m)** storage (n)
almacenar store (v)
or warehouse (v)
**almacenar [tener
existencias]** stock (v)
almacenista (m)
warehouseman

**almuerzo (m) de
negocios** business
lunch
alojarse stay (v)
alquilar
rent (v) *or* let (v)
alquilar [fletar]
charter (v)
**alquilar un coche o
una grúa** hire (v) a
car or a crane
alquilar una oficina
let an office
alquiler (m) rental
(n) *or* hire (n) *or*
rent (n)
**alquiler (m)
[medio de trans-
porte]** charter (n)
or chartering (n)
**alquiler (m) ele-
vado** high rent
alternativa (f)
alternative (n)
alternativo (-va)
alternative (adj)
alta calidad high
quality *or* premium
quality *or* top quality
alta dirección top
management

alto (-ta) high (adj)
alto (m)[freno]
stop (n)
alza (f) rise (n)
amarradero (m)
berth (n)
ámbito: de
ámbito nacional
nationwide (adj)
americano (-na)
American (n & adj)
amo (m) owner (n)
amo [jefe] boss (n)
amortizable
redeemable (adj)
amortización (f)
amortization (n) *or*
depreciation (n)
amortización
[rescate]
redemption (n)
amortización acel-
erada accelerated
depreciation
amortización anual
uniforme o lineal
straight line
depreciation
amortizar
amortize (v) *or*
depreciate (v)

amortizar [redimir]
redeem (v)
amortizar una
obligación redeem
a bond
amparo (m) fiscal
tax shelter (n)
ampliación (f)
expansion (n) *or*
extension (n)
ampliar expand (v)
or extend (v)
amplio (-plia)
wide (adj)
análisis (m)
analysis
análisis coste-ben-
eficio cost-benefit
analysis
análisis de costes
cost analysis
análisis de mercado
market analysis
análisis de proyec-
tos project analysis
análisis de sis-
temas systems
analysis
análisis de un
puesto de trabajo
job analysis

análisis de ventas
sales analysis
análisis estadístico
statistical analysis
analista (mf) de
mercado market
analyst (n)
analista de
sistemas systems
analyst
analizar analyse
(v) *or* analyze (v)
analizar las posibil-
idades del mercado
analyse the market
potential
anaquel (m)
shelf (n)
andén (m)
platform (n)
anexo (m) annex
(n) *or* appendix (n)
anotación (f)
entry (n)
anotar log (v) *or*
note (v)
anotar [registrar]
minute (v) *or*
record (v)
anotar las llamadas
recibidas log calls

anotar una contra-
partida o un con-
traasiento contra
an entry
antecedentes (mpl)
track record
antedatar backdate
(v) *or* antedate (v)
anteproyecto (m)
draft plan *or* draft
project
anterior prior (adj)
or previous (adj)
antes: lo antes
posible as soon as
possible (a.s.a.p.)
anticipado (-da)
advance (adj)
anticipar advance (v)
anticipar [prever]
anticipate (v)
anticipo (m)
advance (n)
anticipo a cuenta
advance on account
anticipo de caja a
cuenta cash advance
anticuado (-da)
dated (adj) *or*
out of date *or*
old-fashioned

antiguo (-gua) old (adj) *or* old-established
antiguo: más antiguo senior
anual annual (adj)
anualmente annually (adv) *or* on an annual basis
anulación (f) cancellation (n)
anular cancel (v)
anular [deuda] write off (v)
anular un acuerdo call off a deal
anular un cheque cancel a cheque
anular un contrato cancel a contract
anunciante (mf) advertiser (n)
anunciar announce (v) *or* advertise (v)
anunciar un nuevo producto advertise a new product
anunciar una vacante advertise a vacancy
anuncio [aviso] announcement (n) *or* notice (n)
anuncio (m) [publicitario] advertisement (n) *or* commercial (n)
anuncio del producto product advertising
anuncios (mpl) breves small ads
anuncios por palabras classified ads or advertisements
añadir add (v)
añadir el 10% por el servicio add on 10% for service
año (m) year (n)
año base base year
año civil calendar year
año fiscal financial year *or* tax year
año: al año per annum *or* per year
año: de muchos años long-standing
apalancamiento (m) gearing (n)
apalancamiento financiero leverage (n)

aparato (m) device (n) *or* instrument (n) *or* machine (n)

apartamento (m) apartment (n) *or* flat (n)

apelación (f) appeal (n)

apelar appeal (v)

apéndice (m) appendix (n)

apertura (f) opening (n)

aplazado (-da) deferred (adj) *or* postponed (adj)

aplazamiento (m) deferment (n) *or* postponement (n)

aplazamiento de pago deferment of payment

aplazamiento de una sentencia stay of execution

aplazar defer (v) *or* postpone (v) *or* put back (v) *or* hold over (v)

aplazar una reunión adjourn a meeting

aplicación (f) application (n) *or* enforcement (n)

aplicar apply (v)

apoderado (-da) attorney (n) *or* proxy (n)

apoyar back up (v) *or* support (v)

apoyo (m) financiero backing (n)

apoyo: con apoyo estatal government- backed

apreciación (f) appreciation (n)

apreciar appreciate (v)

aprecio (m) appreciation (n)

apremiar chase (v)

aprendiz (-za) apprentice (n) *or* trainee (n)

aprendizaje (m) training (n) *or* traineeship (n)

aprobación (f) approval (n)

aprobación tácita tacit approval

aprobar approve (v)
**aprobar los térmi-
nos de un contrato**
approve the terms
of a contract
**apropiación (f)
indebida de fondos**
conversion of funds
apropiado (-da)
appropriate (adj) *or*
relevant (adj)
aprovechar capitalize
on (v) *or* exploit (v)
aproximadamente
approximately (adv)
aproximado (-da)
approximate (adj)
**aproximado (-da)
[cálculo]** rough (adj)
aptitud (f) capacity
(n) *or* ability (n)
apuntar note (v)
or log (v)
arancel (m) duty (n)
arancel aduanero
customs tariff
**arancel protec-
cionista** protective
tariff
arbitraje (m)
arbitration (n)

arbitrar arbitrate
(v) *or* moderate (v)
arbitrar un litigio
adjudicate or arbi-
trate in a dispute
árbitro (mf) arbitra-
tor (n) *or* adjudicator
archivador (m)
filing cabinet
archivar save (v) *or*
back up (v) *or* file (v)
archivar documentos
file (v) documents
archivo (m) file (n)
or computer file
archivos (mpl)
records (n)
área (f) area (n)
argumento (m)
argument (n)
**argumento (m) de
venta** unique
selling point or
proposition (USP)
armonización (f)
harmonization (n)
arreglar fix (v) *or*
mend (v)
arreglárselas
cope (v) *or*
manage to (v)

arreglo (m)
arrangement (n)
arrendador (-ra)
lessor (n)
arrendamiento (m)
lease (n)
**arrendamiento
financiero**
leasing (n)
arrendar lease (v)
or let (v)
arrendar equipo
lease equipment
arrendatario (-ria)
lessee (n) *or* tenant
arriendo (m)
lease (n)
arriesgado (-da)
risky
arriesgar risk (v)
or venture (v)
arriesgarse
take a risk
arrinconar shelve (v)
arruinado (-da)
broke (adj)
arruinar bankrupt (v)
artículo (m) article
(n) *or* item (n)
artículo de reclamo
loss-leader

artículo único one-
off item
**artículos (mpl) con
desperfectos**
seconds (n)
**artículos de fácil
venta** fast-selling
items
artículos de lujo
luxury goods
**artículos de papel-
ería para oficina**
office stationery
artículos varios
sundries (n) *or*
sundry items *or*
miscellaneous items
**artículos pere-
cederos** perishable
goods
asalariado (-da)
salaried
asamblea (f)
assembly (n) *or*
meeting (n)
**asamblea (f) de per-
sonal)** staff meeting
**ascender [promo-
ción]** promote (v)
ascender [total] run
to (v) *or* amount to (v)

ascenso (m)
promotion (n)
ascensor (m) lift (n)
asegurable
insurable (adj)
asegurador (-ra)
insurer (n)
**asegurador de ries-
gos marinos**
marine underwriter
asegurar insure (v)
**asegurar la vida de
alguien** assure
someone's life
asequible
available (adj) *or*
obtainable (adj)
asesor (-ra) adviser
(n) *or* advisor (n) *or*
consultant (n)
**asesor de
empresas** manage-
ment consultant
asesor fiscal tax
consultant
asesor jurídico
legal adviser
**asesoramiento (m)
jurídico** legal advice
asesoría (f) con-
sultancy (firm)

asesoría jurídica
legal department
asiento (m) entry (n)
asiento de débito
debit entry
asignación (f)
assignment (n)
**asignación (f) de
fondos** funding
asignar allocate (v)
or assign (v)
asignar [fondos]
appropriate (v) *or*
fund (v)
**asignar fondos a un
proyecto** commit or
earmark funds to a
project
asignar personal
man (v)
asistencia (f) [ayuda]
assistance (n)
**asistencia (f)
[reunión]**
attendance (n)
**asistido (-da) [aten-
dido]** attended (adj)
or manned (adj)
**asistido por
ordenador**
computer-assisted

asistir [ayudar]
assist (v)
asistir [reunión]
attend (v)
asociación (f)
association (n) *or*
partnership (n)
asociado (-da)
associate (adj)
aspirante (mf)
candidate (n)
aspirar a aim (v)
asunto (m) matter
(n) *or* subject (n)
**asunto [de nego-
cios]** business (n)
asunto problemático
problem area
atacar attack (v)
atasco (m)
bottleneck (n)
atención (f)
attention (n)
atención al cliente
customer service
**atención: a la aten-
ción de** FAO (for
the attention of)
atender serve (v)
atender a un cliente
serve a customer

**atender una
demanda** meet a
demand
atendido (-da)
manned (adj)
aterrizar land (v)
átono (-na) flat
(adj) *or* dull (adj)
atracar berth (v) *or*
dock (v)
atractivo (m) appeal
(n) *or* attraction (n)
**atractivo para los
clientes** customer
appeal
atraer attract (v)
or appeal to (v)
atrasado (-da)
slow (adj)
atrasado [pago]
late (adj) *or*
overdue (adj)
atrasos (mpl)
arrears (n)
**audiomensajería
(f)** voicemail (n)
auditar audit (v)
auditor (m) externo
external auditor
auditor interno
internal auditor

auditoría (f) audit (n) *or* auditing (n)
auditoría externa external audit
auditoría general general audit
auditoría interna internal audit
auge (m) boom (n)
aumentar [subir] raise (v) *or* increase (v) *or* climb (v) *or* mount up
aumentar [ganar] gain (v)
aumentar [prosperar] boom (v)
aumentar a escala scale up (v)
aumentar de precio increase in price
aumento (m) increase (n) *or* increment (n)
aumento: en aumento on the increase *or* increasing (adj)
aumento [valor] appreciation (n)
aumento anual medio mean annual increase

aumento de salario o de sueldo rise (n) *or* increase (n) *or* pay rise
aumento de sueldo por coste de vida cost-of-living increase
aumento retroactivo de salarios retroactive pay rise
ausencia (f) absence (n)
ausente absent (adj)
ausente del trabajo off [away from work]
autentificar authenticate (v)
autobús (m) bus (n)
autobús del aeropuerto airport bus
autoedición (f) desktop publishing (DTP)
autofinanciación (f) self-financing (n)
autofinanciado (-da) self-financing (adj)
autónomo (-ma) self-employed
autoregulación (f) self-regulation
autoregulado (-da) self-regulatory

autoridad (f)
authority (n)
autoridades (fpl)
portuarias port
authority
autorización (f)
authorization (n) *or*
warrant (n)
autorizado (-da)
authorized (adj)
autorizar authorize
(v) *or* entitle (v)
autorizar [licencia]
license (v)
autorizar el pago
authorize payment
autoservicio (m)
mayorista cash
and carry
auxiliar (mf)
assistant (n)
auxiliar (mf)
administrativo (-va)
junior clerk
aval (m)
guarantee (n)
avalar guarantee
(v) *or* underwrite (v)
avalar a stand secu-
rity or surety for
avalar una deuda
guarantee a debt

avance (m) advance
(n) *or* progress (n)
avanzar advance
(v) *or* progress (v)
avería (f) [máquina]
breakdown (n)
avería (f) [seguro]
average (n)
avería gruesa
general average
averiarse break
down (v)
avión (m) plane (n)
avión charter
charter plane
avión de carga
freighter (n) *or*
freight plane
avisar notify (v)
or warn (v)
aviso (m) notice
(n) *or* warning (n)
ayuda (f) assis-
tance (n) *or* help (n)
ayudante (mf)
assistant (n)
ayudante personal
personal assistant (PA)
ayudar assist (v) *or*
help (v)
azar: al azar
random (adj)

Bb

baja (f)
decline (n) *or* fall
(n) *or* drop (n)
**baja: con tendencia
a la baja** falling
baja incentivada *o*
voluntaria volun-
tary redundancy
bajada (f) de precio
decrease in price
bajar lower (v) *or*
drop (v)
bajar [disminuir]
decline (v) *or* fall
or fall off
bajista (mf) bear (n)
bajo contrato
under contract
bajo control under
control
bajo (-ja) low (adj)
bajo: más bajo
lower (adj)
**balance (m) de
comprobación** trial
balance

balance general *o*
de situación
balance sheet
**balanza (f) comer-
cial** balance of trade
**balanza comercial
favorable** favourable
balance of trade
balanza de pagos
balance of payments
banca (f) banking
**bancarrota: en
bancarrota**
bankrupt (adj)
banco (m) bank (n)
banco central
central bank
banco comercial
clearing bank
banco de crédito
credit bank
banco de descuento
discount house *or*
discounter
banco emisor
issuing bank
**Banco Europeo de
Inversiones (BEI)**
European Investment
Bank (EIB)

banco mercantil
merchant bank
banquero (-ra)
banker
barato (-ta) cheap
barco (m) ship (n)
barco de carga
cargo ship
barrera (f) barrier
**barreras (fpl) arance-
larias** customs barri-
ers *or* tariff barriers
basar base (v)
báscula (f) puente
weighbridge
base (f) base (n)
or basis
base de datos
database
base monetaria
monetary base
básico (-ca) basic
(adj) *or* simple
beca (f) grant (n)
beneficiario (-ria)
beneficiary
beneficiarse de
benefit from (v)
beneficio (m) bene-
fit (n) *or* profit *or* gain

**beneficio antes de
deducir los
impuestos** pretax
profit *or* profit
before tax
beneficio bruto
gross profit
**beneficio consider-
able** healthy profit
**beneficio de
explotación**
operating profit
beneficio ficticio
paper profit
beneficio neto
net profit
**beneficio neto de
impuestos** profit
after-tax
**beneficio sobre el
papel** paper profit
beneficios (mpl)
returns *or* profits
**beneficios (mpl)
[participación]** equity
beneficios crecientes
increasing profits
**beneficios de
explotación**
trading profit

beneficios de la empresa corporate profits
beneficios distribuibles distributable profit
beneficios extraordinarios excess profits
beneficios netos de impuestos aftertax profit
bien: muy bien fine (adv) *or* very good
bien (m) encubierto hidden asset
bienes (mpl) goods (n)
bienes (mpl) de capital [activo fijo] capital assets
bienes de capital [equipo] capital goods
bienes de consumo consumer goods
bienes de consumo duraderos consumer durables
bienes de equipo capital equipment
bienes duraderos durable goods
bienes personales personal assets
bienes raíces real estate
bienestar (m) welfare (n)
bilateral bilateral *or* reciprocal
billete (m) banknote *or* bill (n) (US)
billete (m) [pasaje] fare (n) *or* ticket (n)
billete abierto open ticket
billete de abono season ticket
billete de banco banknote *or* currency note *or* (US) bill
billete en lista de espera standby ticket
billete de ida o pasaje sencillo one-way fare
blanco (m) blank (n)
blanco: en blanco blank (adj)
blanquear (dinero negro) launder (money)

bloqueado (-da)
frozen
bloquear block (v)
**bloquear los crédi-
tos** freeze credits
bodega (f) [buque]
hold (n)
boicot (m)
boycott (n)
boicotear boycott (v)
boletín (m)
bulletin *or* journal
boletín de inscripción
registration form
boletín de respuesta
reply coupon
**boletín interno de
una empresa** house
magazine
bolsa (f) stock
exchange *or* stock
market
bolsa (f) [bolsillo]
pocket (n)
bolsa (f) [saco] bag
**bolsa de contrat-
ación** commodity
market *or* commod-
ity exchange
bolsa de papel
paper bag

bolsillo (m)
pocket (n)
**bombo (m) publici-
tario** hype (n)
bonificación (f)
bonus
**bonificación
recibida al concluir
un seguro** terminal
bonus
bono (m) bond *or*
debenture
bono (m) [vale]
voucher
**bono (m) de interés
fijo** debenture
**bonos (mpl) del
Tesoro** gilts
bonos-basura (mpl)
junk bonds
boom (m) boom (n)
bordo: a bordo on
board
borrador (m)
(rough) draft
bosquejo (m) rough
draft *or* outline
brazo (m) derecho
right-hand man
británico (-ca)
British

bruto (-ta) gross (adj)

buen precio good value (for money)

buena calidad good quality

buena compra good buy

buena gestión good management

bueno (-na) good

bulto (m) packet (n)

buque (m) ship (n)

buque cisterna tanker

buque de carga freighter

buque de contenedores container ship

buque de salvamento salvage vessel

buque gemelo (de la misma flota) sister ship

buque mercante merchant ship or merchant vessel

burocracia (f) bureaucracy or red tape

búsqueda (f) de clientes canvassing

Cc

caber hold (v) or contain (v)

cada tres meses quarterly (adv)

cadena (f) chain

campaña de ventas sales campaign or sales drive

campaña publicitaria advertising campaign or publicity campaign

campo (m) area or field

campo (m) [rural] country

campo de aplicación [mandato] terms of reference

canal (m) channel (n)

canales (mpl) de distribución channels of distribution or distribution channels

cancelación (f) cancellation

cancelación de una cita cancellation of an appointment
cancelado (-da) off *or* cancelled
cancelar cancel *or* write off [debt]
candidato (-ta) candidate
candidato (-ta) a un puesto de trabajo applicant for a job
candidato (-ta) propuesto (-ta) nominee (n)
canje (m) parcial part exchange *or* trade-in
canjear exchange (v)
canon (m) royalty
cantidad (f) quantity (qty) *or* amount (n)
cantidad total total amount
capacidad (f) capacity
capacidad de almacenamiento o de almacenaje storage capacity

capacidad de endeudamiento borrowing power
capacidad de fabricación manufacturing capacity
capacidad hotelera hotel accommodation
capacidad industrial industrial capacity
capacitación (f) training
capacitado (-da) qualified
capacitar train (v) *or* qualify
capaz able *or* capable
capaz de capable of
capital (m) capital
capital circulante working capital
capital disponible available capital
capital en acciones equity capital *or* share capital
capital inicial initial capital
capital nominal nominal capital

capital-riesgo (m)
risk capital *or*
venture capital
capitalista (mf)
capitalist
capitalización (f)
capitalization
capitalización
bursátil market
capitalization
capitalización de las
reservas capitaliza-
tion of reserves
capitalizar capitalize
carga (f) cargo *or*
shipment
carga aérea air
freight
carga de un camión
lorry-load
carga en cubierta
deck cargo
carga por peso
muerto deadweight
cargo
carga útil payload
cargamento (m)
load (n)
cargar load (v)
cargar en cuenta
debit an account

cargar en exceso
overcharge (v)
cargar un camión o
un barco load a
lorry *or* a ship
cargar una compra
en cuenta charge a
purchase
cargo (m) charge (n)
cargo: a cargo de
chargeable (to)
cargo (m) [puesto]
job title *or* position
cargos (mpl)
adicionales
additional charges
cargos en concepto
de interés interest
charges
carnet (m) [socio]
membership card
carnet (m) [docu-
mento] carnet
caro (-ra) dear *or*
expensive
caro: muy caro
highly-priced
carpeta (f) folder (n)
carpeta: dar car-
petazo a shelve (v)
carretera (f) road

carretilla (f) elevadora de horquilla fork-lift truck
carta (f) letter
carta adjunta o explicatoria covering letter or covering note
carta certificada registered letter
carta comercial business letter
carta de crédito letter of credit (L/C)
carta de general circular letter of credit
carta de crédito irrevocable irrevocable letter of credit
carta de intención letter of intent
carta de nombramiento letter of appointment
carta de porte waybill
carta de presentación introduction [letter]
carta de reclamación letter of complaint

carta de recomendación letter of reference
carta de reiteración follow-up letter
carta de solicitud letter of application
carta tipo o carta estándar standard letter
carta urgente express letter
cartel (m) cartel
cartelera (f) hoarding [for posters]
cartera (f) [maletín] briefcase
cartera (de valores) portfolio
cartera con las iniciales personalized briefcase
cartón (m) cardboard or carton
cartulina (f) card [material]
casa (f) house [for family]
casa comercial business or house

casa: de la casa
in-house
casa matriz parent
company
cash flow (m)
cash flow
**cash flow actual-
izado** discounted
cash flow (DCF)
catalogar index (v)
catálogo (m) cata-
logue *or* list (n)
**catálogo de ventas
por correo** mail-
order catalogue
categoría (f)
category
**categoría (f)
[clase]** class
or tax bracket
**categoría: de
segunda categoría**
second-class
causa (f) [proceso]
court case
causa: a causa de
owing to
cedente (mf)
assignor
ceder en arriendo
lease (v)

**celebrar una
reunión** hold a
meeting
**censor (m) jurado
de cuentas** certi-
fied accountant
censor (-ra) auditor
central central
**central (f) tele-
fónica** telephone
exchange
centralita (f)
switchboard
**centralita tele-
fónica** telephone
switchboard
centralización (f)
centralization
**centralización de
las compras** central
purchasing
centralizar
centralize
centro (m) centre
centro comercial
business centre *or*
shopping centre
**centro de benefi-
cios** profit centre
centro de costes
cost centre

centro de la ciudad
city centre *or* down-
town (n) (US)
centro de trans-
porte depot
centro industrial
industrial centre
centro de repara-
ciones service centre
cercano (-na) close to
cero (m) zero *or* nil
cerrado (-da)
closed *or* shut (adj)
cerradura (f) lock (n)
cerrar close (v)
or shut (v) *or*
close down
cerrar [sobre]
seal (v)
cerrar con llave
lock (v)
cerrar un trato
clinch a deal
cerrar una cuenta
close an account
cerrar una cuenta
bancaria close
a bank account
cerrar una tienda o
una oficina lock up
a shop *or* an office

certificado (m)
certificate
certificado de adu-
ana clearance cer-
tificate
certificado de
aprobación certifi-
cate of approval
certificado de
depósito certificate
of deposit
certificado de
garantía certificate
of guarantee
certificado de
origen certificate
of origin
certificado de
registro certificate
of registration
certificado (-da)
registered (adj)
certificar certify
(v) *or* register (v)
cesión (f) cession
cesión-arren-
damiento (f)
lease-back
cesionario (-ria)
assignee
cheque (m) cheque

cheque abierto
open cheque
cheque al portador
cheque to bearer
cheque conformado
certified cheque
cheque cruzado
crossed cheque
**cheque de adminis-
tración** cashier's
check (US)
cheque de sueldo
salary cheque *or* pay
cheque
cheque en blanco
blank cheque
**cheque en pago de
dividendos** divi-
dend warrant
cheque sin cruzar
open cheque
cheque sin fondos
rubber check (US)
**chequeo (m) al
azar** random check
**cheques (mpl) con
el nombre impreso**
personalized
cheques
chocar crash (v)
chófer (m) driver

choque (m) crash
(n) *or* accident
cíclico (-a) cyclical
ciclo (m) cycle
ciclo de trabajo run
(n) *or* work routine
ciclo del producto
product cycle
ciclo económico
economic cycle *or*
trade cyle
ciento: por ciento
per cent
cierre (m) closing
(n) *or* closure
cierre: al cierre
closing (adj)
cierre del ejercicio
year end
**cif (coste, seguro y
flete)** c.i.f. (= cost,
insurance and freight)
cifra (f) figure
cifra de negocios
turnover *or* sales
**cifras (fpl) ajus-
tadas estacional-
mente** seasonally
adjusted figures
cifras de ventas
sales figures

cifras estimadas
estimated figures
cifras históricas
historical figures
cifras reales actuals
cifras sin comprobar
unchecked figures
cima (f) top (n) *or*
peak *or* highest point
cinta (f) magnética
magnetic tape *or*
mag tape
circuito cerrado
closed circuit TV
circulación (f) circulation [of money]
circular (f) circular
(n) *or* circular letter
circular (v) run (v)
cita (f) appointment *or* meeting
citación (f) judicial
summons
citar quote (v)
clarificar clear (v)
* clarify (v)
claro (-ra) clear
(adj) *or* easy to
understand
clase (f) [categoría]
class *or* tax bracket

**clase: de primera
clase** first-class
**clase económica o
turista** economy
class
**clase preferente
(en aviones)**
business class
clasificación (f)
classification *or* rating
clasificación crediticia credit rating
clasificar classify
or index (v)
cláusula (f) clause
or article
cláusula adicional
rider
cláusula de excepción escape clause
**cláusula de
exclusión** exclusion
clause
**cláusula de
reembolso** payback
clause
cláusula de renuncia waiver clause
**cláusula de
rescisión**
cancellation clause

cláusula penal
penalty clause
**cláusula que pro-
hibe la huelga**
no-strike agreement
or no-strike clause
cláusula resolutoria
termination clause
clausura (f) closure
**clausurar una
sesión** close a
meeting
clave (f) key
cliente (mf) client
or customer
cliente habitual
regular customer
clientela (f)
clientele *or* custom
**clientes (mpl)
eventuales**
potential customers
clip (m) paperclip
club (m) club *or*
society
co-propiedad (f)
joint ownership
**co-propietario
(-ria)** joint owner
coacreedor (-ra)
co-creditor

coaseguro (m)
co-insurance
cobertura (f) cover
or hedge (n) *or*
hedging
**cobertura del divi-
dendo** dividend cover
**cobertura del
seguro** insurance
cover
**cobertura periodís-
tica** media coverage
cobrable cashable
cobrador (-ra)
collector
**cobrador (m) de
alquileres** rent
collector
cobrar charge (v)
or collect (v) *or*
encash
cobrar: por cobrar
receivable
cobrar a la entrega
charges forward
cobrar de más
overcharge (v)
cobrar de menos
undercharge (v)
cobrar un cheque
cash a cheque

cobrar una deuda
collect a debt
cobro (m) collection
cobro a la entrega
cash on delivery
(c.o.d.)
cobro de morosos
debt collection
cobro en metálico
encashment
cobro por recogida
collection charges *or*
collection rates
cobro: a cobro rever-
tido reversed charge
or toll free (US)
coche (m) de
alquiler hire car
coche en
gran demanda
best-selling car
codificación (f)
coding
código (m) code
código de almace-
namiento stock code
código de barras
bar code
código fiscal o
código impositivo
tax code

código postal post-
code *or* zip code
(US) *or* area code
códigos (mpl) legi-
bles por ordenador
computer-readable
codes
codirección (f)
joint management
codirector (-ra)
co-director
codirector (-ra)
gerente joint
managing director
coeficiente (m)
rate (n)
coeficiente de
amortización
depreciation rate
coeficiente de
ajuste de precios
price differential
coeficiente de
errores error rate
coeficiente de ocu-
pación load factor
coeficiente de
rentabilidad
profitability
coincidir (con)
agree with

colaboración (f) collaboration *or* contribution

colaborar collaborate

colateral collateral (adj)

colectivo (-va) collective

colgar: no cuelgue hold the line please

colocar place (v)

columna (f) del debe debit column

columna del haber credit column

comenzar begin *or* start (v)

comerciable marketable

comercial commercial (adj)

comercialización (f) commercialization *or* merchandizing

comercialización a gran escala mass marketing

comercializar commercialize (v) *or* merchandize (v)

comercializar un producto merchandize a product

comerciante (mf) dealer *or* merchant *or* trader *or* merchandizer

comerciante al por mayor wholesaler *or* wholesale dealer

comerciante al por menor retail dealer

comerciante exclusivo sole trader

comerciar handle (v) *or* sell

comerciar (en) deal in *or* trade in

comerciar con alguien deal with someone *or* do business with someone

comercio (m) commerce *or* trade (n) *or* trading

comercio al por menor retailing

comercio de exportación export trade

comercio de visibles visible trade

comercio electrónico
e-commerce (n)
comercio exterior
external trade *or*
export trade *or*
foreign trade
comercio floreciente
flourishing trade
comercio interior
domestic trade
**comercio interna-
cional** international
trade
comercio invisible
invisible trade
comercio legal
lawful trade
comercio marítimo
maritime trade
**comercio multilat-
eral** multilateral
trade
comercio recíproco
reciprocal trade
comercio unilateral
one-way trade
cometer commit (v)
comienzo (m)
beginning *or* start (n)
comisión (f)
commission

**comisión (f) [corre-
taje]** brokerage *or*
broker's commission
comisión de arbitraje
arbitration board *or*
arbitration tribunal
comisionista (mf)
commission agent
**comisionista al por
mayor** factor (n)
comité (m) commis-
sion *or* committee
cómodo (-da)
convenient
compañía (f)
company
**compañía asociada
o afiliada** associate
company *or* sister
company
compañía de seguros
insurance company
compañía fiduciaria
trust company
**compañía filial
o compañía sub-
sidiaria** subsidiary
company
**compañía indepen-
diente** independent
company

compañía naviera o compañía marítima shipping company *or* shipping line

compañía que financia la compra a plazos hire-purchase company

comparable comparable

comparación (f) comparison

comparar compare

comparar con compare with

comparar precios shop around

compartir share (v)

compartir una oficina share an office

compensación (f) compensation

compensar [deducir] set against

compensar [indemnizar] compensate *or* make up for

competencia (f) competition

competencia (f) [pericia] expertise

competencia desleal unfair competition

competencia dura stiff competition

competencia encarnizada cut-throat competition

competente competent *or* capable

competidor (-ra) competitor

competir (con) compete (with)

competitividad (f) competitiveness

competitivo (-va) competitive *or* competing (adj)

con precio competitivo competitively priced

complementario (-ria) complementary

completamente nuevo (-va) brand new

completar complete (v)

completo (-ta) complete (adj) *or* comprehensive *or* full-scale

componer repair (v)
compra (f) pur-
chase *or* purchasing
or buying
compra a granel
bulk buying
compra a plazos
hire purchase (HP)
compra al contado
cash purchase *or*
spot purchase
compra apalancada
leveraged buyout
(LBO)
compra de futuros
forward buying
compra de una
empresa por sus
ejecutivos manage-
ment buyout (MBO)
compra febril panic
buying
compra impulsiva
impulse purchase
comprador (-ra)
buyer *or* purchaser
or shopper
comprador impul-
sivo impulse buyer
comprador genuino
genuine purchaser

comprar buy *or*
purchase (v)
comprar a futuros
buy forward
comprar en
efectivo buy
for cash
compras (fpl)
shopping
comprender
understand
comprobación (f)
check (n) *or*
examination
comprobación
de los recursos
económicos
means test
comprobante (m)
voucher
comprobante de
caja sales receipt
comprobar check
(v) *or* monitor
comprometerse
undertake (v)
compromiso (m)
compromise (n)
compromiso (m)
[promesa] under-
taking *or* promise

compromiso (m)
[cita] appointment
or meeting
compromiso (m)
[obligación] obli-
gation *or* duty
compromisos (mpl)
commitments
compulsa (f) certi-
fied copy *or* true copy
común common
común: en común
jointly
comunicación (f)
communication
comunicación hori-
zontal horizontal
communication
comunicación verti-
cal vertical
communication
comunicaciones (fpl)
communications
comunicado (m)
communication *or*
message
comunicado de
prensa press
release
comunicar commu-
nicate *or* announce

comunidad (f)
community
con cum
conceder grant (v)
or extend (v)
conceder [adju-
dicar] award (v)
conceder [dar]
allow *or* give
conceder una licen-
cia license
concertación (f)
harmonization *or*
reconciliation
concesión (f) con-
cession *or* right *or*
franchise (n)
concesión de un
préstamo lending
concesionario (-ria)
concessionaire *or*
dealer *or* franchisee
or licensee
conciliación (f)
conciliation
conciliación de
cuentas reconcilia-
tion of accounts
concluir conclude
or wind up *or*
complete

conclusión (f)
conclusion (n) *or*
close (n)
condición (f)
condition
condición: a
condición de que
on condition that *or*
provided that
condición: sin
condiciones
unconditional
condición: en las
condiciones
acordadas on
agreed terms
condición (f)
[salvedad] proviso
condición jurídica
legal status
condicionado (-da)
qualified *or* with
reservations
condicional
conditional
condiciones (fpl)
terms *or* conditions
condiciones: en
condiciones favor-
ables on favourable
terms

condiciones de
empleo conditions
of employment
condiciones de
pago terms of
payment
condiciones de
servicio terms of
employment
condiciones de
trabajo working
conditions
condiciones de
venta conditions
of sale *or* terms
of sale
condominio (m)
joint ownership
conducir drive (v)
conductor (m)
driver
conectar connect
or interface (v)
conexión (f)
connection *or* tie-up
or link
conexión (f)
[informática]
computer port
confeccionar
make out

conferencia (f) de prensa press conference
confesar confess *or* declare
confianza (f) confidence
confianza: de confianza reliable
confiar entrust
confidencia (f) tip (n)
confidencial confidential
confidencialidad (f) confidentiality
confirmación (f) confirmation
confirmar confirm
confirmar: sin confirmar unconfirmed
confirmar a alguien en su puesto de trabajo confirm someone in a job
confirmar una reserva confirm a booking
confiscación (f) forfeiture
confiscar confiscate *or* seize

conflicto (m) de intereses conflict of interest
conflictos (mpl) colectivos industrial disputes
conflictos laborales labour disputes
conforme a [según] according to *or* under
conformidad (f) [acuerdo] compliance
congelación (f) freeze (n)
congelación de créditos credit freeze
congelación de salarios wage freeze
congelado (-da) frozen
congelar freeze (v)
congelar salarios y precios freeze wages and prices
conglomerado (m) conglomerate
congreso (m) congress *or* conference
conjuntamente jointly

**conjunto (m) de
medidas económi-
cas** package of eco-
nomic measures
conjunto (-ta) joint
**conjunto: en con-
junto** overall
conmutar commute
or exchange
**conocimiento (m)
de embarque** bill
of lading
conseguir get *or*
manage to
**conseguir hacer
algo** succeed in
conseguir fondos
secure funds *or*
raise money
**conseguir un con-
trato** win a contract
consejero (-ra)
consultant *or*
adviser
**consejero (-ra)
[director]** director
**consejo (m) (de
administración)**
board (n) of
directors
conservación (f)
maintenance

conservar maintain
considerar consider
consigna (f) left
luggage office
consignación (f)
consignment
consignador (-ra)
consignor
consignar consign
or dispatch (v)
consignar [asignar]
appropriate (v)
consignatario (-ria)
consignee
**consolidación (f)
de fondos** funding
(of debt)
**consolidación de un
préstamo** restruc-
turing of a loan
consolidado (-da)
consolidated
consolidar consoli-
date *or* establish
consorcio (m)
consortium
**consorcio emisor o
asegurador** under-
writing syndicate
constante constant
or recurrent **constar
de** consist of

constitución (f) de una sociedad incorporation

constituir en sociedad incorporate (a company)

constituirse parte civil bring a civil action

construcción: en construcción under construction

construir build *or* develop

consultar consult

consultar a un abogado take legal advice

consultoría (f) consultancy firm

consumidor (-ra) consumer

consumo (m) consumption

consumo doméstico o consumo interior home consumption

contabilidad (f) accounting *or* bookkeeping

contabilidad de costes cost accounting

contabilidad de costes actuales current cost accounting

contabilidad de ingresos revenue accounts

contable (mf) accountant *or* bookkeeper

contable de costes cost accountant

contable jefe chief accountant *or* controller (US)

contactar contact (v)

contacto (m) contact (n)

contado: al contado cash (adv)

contar count (v)

contenedor (m) container

contener contain *or* hold (v)

contener [parar] check (v) *or* stop

contenerización (f)
containerization
contenido (m)
contents
contestación (f)
answer (n) *or*
reply (n)
contestador (m)
automático
answering machine
contestar answer (v)
or reply (v)
contestar el telé-
fono answer the
telephone
contestar una carta
answer a letter
contingencia (f)
contingency
continuación (f)
continuation
continuamente
continually
continuar continue
or proceed (v)
continuo (-nua) con-
tinual *or* continuous
contra OPA (f)
reverse takeover
contraasiento (m)
contra entry

contracción (f)
shrinkage
contractual
contractual
contraer deudas
incur debts
contraoferta (f)
counterbid *or*
counter-offer
contrapartida (f)
contra entry
contrario (-ria)
contrary
contraste (m)
contrast (n)
contratar
contract (v)
contratar personal
hire staff
contratista (mf)
contractor
contratista de
transporte por
carretera haulage
contractor
contratista del
Estado government
contractor
contrato (m)
contract (n) *or*
agreement (n)

contrato: según contrato contractually or according to the contract

contrato a plazo fijo fixed-term contract

contrato de Bolsa contract note

contrato de corta duración short-term contract

contrato de empleo contract of employment

contrato de seguros insurance contract

contrato de venta bill of sale

contrato en exclusiva exclusive agreement

contrato permanente permanent contract

contribución (f) contribution

contribución de capital contribution of capital

contribuir contribute

contribuyente (mf) contributor or taxpayer

control (m) control (n) or check or inspection

control: de control supervisory

control de alquileres o de rentas rent control

control de calidad quality control

control de crédito credit control

control de divisas exchange control

control de existencias stock control or inventory control (US)

control de materiales materials control

control de precios price control

control presupuestario budgetary control

controlado (-da) por el Estado government-controlled

controlar control (v) *or* monitor (v)

controlar un negocio control a business

convenido (-da) agreed

conveniente convenient

convenio (m) agreement *or* covenant (n)

convenio salarial colectivo collective wage agreement

conversaciones fructíferas productive discussions

conversión (f) conversion

conversión de divisas currency conversion

conversión de un préstamo refunding of a loan

convertibilidad (f) convertibility

convertir convert

convocar call *or* convene

cooperación (f) co-operation

cooperar co-operate

cooperativa (f) co-operative (n)

cooperativo (-va) co-operative (adj)

coparticipación (f) copartnership

copia (f) copy (n) *or* duplicate (n)

copia auténtica o certificada certified copy

copia carbón carbon copy

copia de reserva o de seguridad backup copy

copia exacta true copy

copia falsa forgery

copia impresa hard copy

copia impresa [de ordenador] computer printout

copiar copy (v) *or* duplicate (v)

copiar [escribir] write out

copiar una factura duplicate an invoice

copropiedad (f)
co-ownership *or*
part-ownership
copropietario (-ria)
co-owner *or*
part-owner
corona (f) krone
or krona
corporación (f)
corporation *or* guild
corrección (f)
correction
correcto (-ta)
correct (adj) *or* right
or accurate
corredor (m) de
seguros insurance
broker
corredor (-ra) de
bolsa stockbroker
correduría (f) de
bolsa stockbroking
corregir correct (v)
or rectify *or* revise
correo (m) mail
(n) *or* post (n)
correo aéreo
airmail (n)
correo electrónico
electronic mail
(email)

correo entrante
incoming mail
correo por via ter-
restre o marítima
surface mail
correos (mpl)
post (n)
correr un riesgo
run a risk
correspondencia (f)
correspondence *or*
mail
correspondencia
de salida
outgoing mail
correspondencia
recibida
incoming mail
corresponder
agree with
corresponder a
algo correspond
with something
correspondiente
(mf) correspondent
corresponsal (mf)
correspondent *or*
journalist
corretaje (m)
brokerage *or*
broker's commission

corriente common *or* frequent

corriente [actual] current

corriente [ordinario] ordinary *or* regular

corriente: precio corriente average price

corrientes: de los corrientes instant (adj)

corto: a corto plazo short-term (adj) *or* on a short-term basis

costar cost (v)

costas (fpl) costs

costas judiciales legal costs *or* legal charges *or* legal expenses

coste (m) o charge (n) cost (n)

coste de almacenaje storage (n)

coste de la gestión de deudas factoring charges

coste de producción production cost

coste del transporte haulage costs *or* haulage rates

coste de ventas cost of sales

coste de vida cost of living

coste descargado landed costs

coste directo direct cost

coste incremental incremental cost *or* marginal cost

coste inicial historic(al) cost

coste marginal marginal cost

coste total total cost

coste unitario o coste por unidad unit cost

coste, seguro y flete (cif) cost, insurance and freight (c.i.f.)

costear los gastos de alguien defray someone's expenses

costes (mpl) de distribución
distribution costs

costes de envío
shipping charges *or* shipping costs

costes de fabri-cación manu-facturing costs

costes de lanzamiento
launching costs

costes de puesta en marcha
start-up costs

costes excesivos
excessive costs

costes fijos
fixed costs

costes laborales
labour costs

costes laborales indirectos indirect labour costs

costes sociales
social costs

costes variables
variable costs

costo (m) cost (n)

costo más honorar-ios cost plus

costoso (-sa)
costly *or* expensive

costumbre (f)
routine (n)

cotejar check (v) *or* compare (v)

cotidiano (-na)
day-to-day

cotización (f)
quote (n) *or* quotation

cotización de aper-tura opening price

cotizar [calcular]
quote (v)

cotizar [contribuir]
contribute (v)

crack (m) financial crash (n)

crear una compañía
set up a company

creciente increas-ing *or* mounting

crecimiento (m)
growth

crecimiento económico
economic growth

crédito (m) credit (n)

crédito: a crédito
on credit

crédito a corto plazo
short-term credit
crédito a largo plazo long credit *or*
extended credit
crédito abierto
open credit
crédito al consumidor
consumer credit
crédito bancario
bank credit
crédito barato
cheap money
crédito blando
soft loan
crédito congelado
frozen credits
crédito de apoyo
standby credit
crédito instantáneo
instant credit
crédito por impuestos pagados
tax credit
crédito renovable
revolving credit
crédito sin interés
interest-free credit
crédito 'stand by'
standby credit

crisis (f) de liquidez
liquidity crisis
crisis del dólar
dollar crisis
crisis económica [depresión] slump
(n) *or* depression
crisis financiera
financial crisis
crónico (-ca)
chronic
cruzar un cheque
cross a cheque
cuadrar [ajustar]
reconcile
cuadrar [saldar]
balance (v)
cuadrícula (f) grid
cualificado (-da)
skilled *or* qualified
cualificado: no cualificado
unskilled
cualificado: muy cualificado highly
qualified
cuanto: en cuanto a
regarding
cuarta parte (f) o cuarto (m)
quarter [25%]

cuarto trimestre
fourth quarter
cúbico (-ca) cubic
cubierta (f) deck
cubierto: precio
del cubierto
cover charge
cubierta (f)
[funda] cover (n)
cubrir cover (v)
cubrir gastos break
even *or* cover costs
or meet expenses
cubrir un riesgo
cover a risk
cuenta (f) account
cuenta (f) [restau-
rante] bill (n)
cuenta: a cuenta
on account
cuenta: anticipo a
cuenta advance on
account
cuenta: anticipo de
caja a cuenta cash
advance
cuenta: por cuenta y
riesgo del comprador
caveat emptor
cuenta a plazo
deposit account

cuenta abierta
open account *or*
charge account
cuenta acreedora
account in credit
cuenta administrada
por un apoderado
nominee account
cuenta bancaria
bank account
cuenta bloqueada
frozen account *or*
account on stop
cuenta compensada
contra account
cuenta con saldo pos-
itivo account in credit
cuenta conjunta
joint account
cuenta corriente
current account *or*
drawing account *or*
cheque account
cuenta de ahorro
savings account
cuenta de caja
cash account
cuenta de capital
capital account
cuenta de crédito
credit account

cuenta de depósito
deposit account
**cuenta de garantía
bloqueada** escrow
account
**cuenta de gastos
de representación**
expense account
**cuenta de no
residente** external
account
**cuenta de pérdidas
y ganancias** profit
and loss account
cuenta detallada
itemized account
**cuenta en descu-
bierto** overdrawn
account
**cuenta en
participación**
joint account
cuenta inactiva
dead account
cuenta numerada
numbered account
**cuenta presupues-
taria** budget account
**cuentas a cobrar *o*
por cobrar** accounts
receivable

**cuentas a pagar *o*
por pagar** accounts
payable
cuentas anuales
annual accounts
**cuentas de fin de
mes** month-end
accounts
cuentas de gestión
management accounts
**cuentas de media-
dos de mes**
midmonth accounts
**cuentas semes-
trales** half-yearly
accounts
cuentas sin verificar
unaudited accounts
cuestión (f) matter
(n) *or* question (n)
cuestionar
question (v)
cuestionario (m)
questionnaire
culpa (f) blame (n)
culpa (f) [falta]
fault *or* blame
culpar blame (v)
cumbre (f) peak
(n) *or* top (n) *or*
highest point

cumplidor (-ra)
reliable
cumplimiento (m)
[realización]
fulfilment
cumplimiento (m)
[ejecución]
execution
cumplir carry out
or fulfil (v)
cumplir
[satisfacer] meet
cumplir [ejecutar]
execute
cumplir un plazo
establecido meet a
deadline
cumplir una promesa
keep a promise
cuota (f) quota
or fee
cuota de depre-
ciación allowance
for depreciation
cuota de
importación
import quota
cuota de inscripción
registration fee
cuota de mercado
market share
cupo (m) quota

cupo de importación
import quota
cupón (m) coupon
cupón: con cupón de
interés cum coupon
cupón: sin cupón de
interés ex coupon
cupón de anuncio
coupon ad
cupón de regalo
gift coupon
curriculum (vitae)
(m) curriculum
vitae (CV)
cursar un pedido
place an order
curso (m) comercial
commercial course
curso de actual-
ización o curso de
reciclaje refresher
course
curso de gestión
empresarial man-
agement course
cursos (mpl) de
iniciación induction
courses *or* induction
training
curva (f) curve
curva de ventas
sales curve

Dd

dañado (-da)
damaged
dañar damage (v)
daño (m)
damage (n)
daños (mpl) causados por incendio
fire damage
daños materiales
damage to property
daños por tormenta
storm damage
daños y perjuicios
damages
dar give
dar [conceder]
allow
dar [producir]
produce (v)
dar carpetazo
shelve (v)
dar empleo
employ (v)
dar instrucciones
brief (v) or issue
instructions
dar por resultado
result in

dar publicidad
publicize or plug (v)
dar una entrada
pay or put money
down
dar una propina
tip (v)
darse cuenta real-
ize or understand
darse prisa
hurry up
datos (mpl) data
datos de salida
computer output
debajo: por
debajo de under or
less than
debate (m) debate
or discussion
debe (m) debit or
debtor side
debe y haber
debits and credits
deber owe
debidamente duly
or legally
debido a due to or
owing to
debido (-da) owing
débil slack or weak
débito (m) debit
(n) or charge (n)

decidir decide *or* resolve

decidirse por la opción más fácil take the soft option

decimal (m) decimal (n)

decisión (f) decision

decisión (f) [fallo] ruling (n)

decisivo (-va) deciding

declaración (f) declaration *or* statement *or* announcement

declaración (f) [renta] return (n)

declaración de aduana customs declaration

declaración de ingresos nulos nil return

declaración de quiebra declaration of bankruptcy

declaración de renta tax return *or* tax declaration

declaración de siniestro insurance claim

declaración del IVA VAT declaration

declaración oficial official return

declarado (-da) declared

declarar declare *or* state (v)

declarar [renta] return (v)

declarar a alguien en quiebra declare someone bankrupt

declarar mercancías en la aduana declare goods to customs

decomisar forfeit (v)

decomiso (m) forfeiture *or* forefeit (n)

decreciente decreasing (adj) *or* falling

decretar rule (v) *or* give decision

deducción (f) deduction

deducción (f) de impuestos tax deductions

deducciones (fpl) personales personal allowances

deducible deductible

deducir deduct (v)

deducir [compensar] set against

deducir [inferir] deduce *or* infer (v)

deducir del sueldo dock (v)

defectivo (-va) defective

defecto (m) defect *or* (mechanical) fault *or* imperfection

defecto: en su defecto failing that

defectuoso (-sa) defective *or* faulty

defender defend

defenderse en juicio defend a lawsuit

defensa (f) defence

defensor (m) del pueblo ombudsman

déficit (m) deficit *or* shortfall

déficit comercial trade deficit trade gap

deflación (f) deflation

deflacionista deflationary

defraudación (f) fraud

DEG (derechos especiales de giro) special drawing rights (SDRs)

dejar [abandonar] leave (v)

dejar de hacer algo fail to do something

dejar un margen allow for

dejar un margen del 10% para el porte allow 10% for carriage

delegación (f) delegation

delegado (-da) delegate (n) *or* deputy (n)

delegado (-da) del personal worker director

delegar delegate (v)

delito (m) por omisión nonfeasance

demanda (f) demand (n)

demanda (f) [reclamación] claim (n)

demanda de pago call (n) for money

demanda de pago de acciones call (n)

demanda efectiva effective demand

demanda estacional seasonal demand

demanda excesiva run (n)

demanda por daños y perjuicios action for damages

demanda: oferta y demanda supply and demand

demandado (-da) defendant

demandante (mf) claimant or plaintiff

demandar sue

demora (f) delay (n)

demorar delay (v)

demostración (f) demonstration

demostrar demonstrate

departamental departmental

departamento (m) department or division or section

departamento de 'marketing' marketing department

departamento de atención al cliente customer service department

departamento de compras buying department or purchasing department

departamento de contabilidad accounts department

departamento de diseño design department

Departamento de Estado government department

departamento de exportación export department

departamento de facturación invoicing department

departamento de informática computer department

departamento de personal personnel department

departamento de producción production department

departamento de publicidad publicity department

departamento de reclamaciones claims department

departamento de relaciones públicas public relations department

departamento de reservas room reservations

depender de depend on

dependienta (f) saleswoman *or* shop assistant

dependiente (m) salesman *or* shop assistant

depositante (mf) depositor

depositar [ingresar] deposit (v) *or* bank (v)

depósito (m) bank deposit *or* down payment

depósito (m) [almacén] store (n) *or* storeroom *or* stockroom

depósito (m) [almacenamiento] storage (n)

depósito (m) [almacén de mercancías] goods depot

depósito a la vista demand deposit

depósito a plazo time deposit

depósito a plazo fijo fixed deposit

depósito aduanero
bonded warehouse
depósito no
reembolsable non-
refundable deposit
depósito
reembolsable
refundable deposit
depósitos (mpl)
bancarios bank
deposits
depósitos con
interés interest-
bearing deposits
depreciación (f)
depreciation
depreciación de un
activo writedown (n)
depreciar(se) depre-
ciate *or* amortize
depreciar el valor
de un activo write
down [an asset]
depresión (f) depres-
sion *or* slump (n)
derecho (m)
law *or* right (n) *or*
entitlement
derecho (-cha)
right (adj)
derecho civil civil law

derecho de aduana
customs duty
derecho de con-
tratos contract law
derecho de ocu-
pación security of
tenure
derecho de paso
right of way
derecho de
retención lien
derecho de veto
right of veto
derecho
internacional
international law
derecho marítimo
maritime law
derecho mercantil
commercial law
derechohabiente
(m) rightful claimant
derechos (mpl)
admission fee
derechos de autor
royalty
derechos de
dársena port
charges *or* port dues
derechos de expo-
rtación export duty

derechos de impo-rtación import duty
derechos espe-ciales de giro (DEG) special draw-ing rights (SDRs)
derechos portuar-ios harbour dues
derivar de derive from *or* result from
derrumbamiento (m) collapse (n)
derrumbarse collapse (v)
desaceleración (f) slowdown
desacelerar slow down
desaconsejar advise against
desacreditar discredit (v)
desacuerdo (m) disagreement
desaparecido (-da) missing *or* unaccounted for
desarrollar develop
desarrollo (m) development *or* growth

desarrollo de pro-ductos product development
desarrollo económico eco-nomic development
desbordar flood (v)
descanso (m) break (n) *or* rest (n)
descarga (f) y carga de un avión turnround
descargar unload
descargar mer-cancías en un puerto land goods at a port
descargo (m) [deuda] discharge (n)
descargo (m) final final discharge
descender fall (v) *or* drop (v)
descenso (m) decline (n) *or* down-turn *or* decrease
descentralización (f) decentralization
descentralizar decentralize *or* hive off

descontable
discountable
descontar discount
(v) *or* knock off *or*
deduct (v)
**descontar del
sueldo** dock (v)
describir describe
descripción (f)
description
**descripción
comercial** trade
description
**descripción del
puesto de trabajo**
job description *or*
job specification
**descubierto (m)
[sobregiro]**
overdraft
descuento (m)
discount (n) *or*
rebate
**descuento: con
descuento** off *or*
reduced by
**descuento al por
mayor** wholesale
discount
descuento básico
basic discount

**descuento para
comerciantes del
sector** trade dis-
count *or* trade terms
**descuento por
cantidad** quantity
discount
**descuento por pago
al contado** cash
discount
**descuento por
volumen** volume
discount
descuidado (-da)
negligent
desechable
disposable
desecho (m)
waste (n)
desembarcar
land (v)
desembolsar
disburse *or* pay out
desembolso (m)
disbursement *or*
expenditure *or* outlay
desembolsos (mpl)
outgoings *or*
expenditure
desempleado (-da)
unemployed

desempleo (m)
unemployment
desfalcador (-ra)
embezzler
desfalcar embezzle
desfalco (m)
embezzlement
desfavorable
unfavourable
desgastar erode
desgaste (m)
natural (fair) wear
and tear
desglosar break
down (v) *or* itemize
desglose (m)
breakdown (n)
desgravable
taxdeductible
desgravación (f)
concession
desgravación fiscal
tax allowance *or*
tax relief *or*
tax concession
deshacerse de
unload *or* offload *or*
get rid of
deshacerse de las
existencias sobrantes
dispose of excess stock

deshacerse de algo
get rid of something
deshonorar
dishonour
desistir de una
acción abandon an
action
desocupar vacate (v)
despachar
dispatch (v)
despachar pedidos
atrasados
release dues
despachar un pedido
fulfil an order
despacho (m)
[envío] dispatch
(n) *or* sending (out)
despacho (m)
[oficina] office
despacho aduanero
o de aduanas
customs clearance
despacho de bil-
letes booking office
despacho de pedi-
dos order fulfilment
desparejado
(-da) odd
despedir discharge
or pay off

despedir a alguien
sack someone
despedir a un
empleado dismiss
an employee
despedir por falta
de trabajo lay off
workers
despegar take off
desperdiciar waste
(v) *or* use too much
desperdicio (m)
waste (n) *or* wastage
desperfectos (mpl)
breakages
despido (m)
dismissal *or* sacking
despido (m) [exce-
dente de plantilla]
redundancy
despido injusto
unfair dismissal *or*
wrongful dismissal
desregulación (f)
deregulation
destacado (-da)
outstanding *or*
exceptional
destinatario (-ria)
addressee *or*
receiver

destino (m)
destination
destitución (f)
removal *or* sacking
destreza (f) skill
desvalorización (f)
devaluation
desvalorizar devalue
detallado (-da)
detailed
detallar detail (v)
or itemize *or*
break down
detalle (m) detail (n)
detalles (mpl)
particulars
detallista (mf)
retailer
detener [frenar]
plug (v) *or* block (v)
or stop (v)
detener el pago de
un cheque stop a
cheque
deteriorado (-da)
damaged *or*
shop-soiled
determinar
determine
deuda (f) debt *or*
indebtedness

deuda incobrable
irrecoverable debt
or write-off
deuda morosa
bad debt
deudas (fpl)
liabilities
deudas a corto plazo
short-term debts
**deudas a largo
plazo** long-term
debts
deudas a pagar
debts due
**deudas garanti-
zadas** secured debts
deudas pendientes
outstanding debts
deudor (-ra)
debtor *or* defaulter
**deudor (-ra)
hipotecario (-ria)**
mortgager *or*
mortgagor
**deudor (-ra)
judicial** judgment
debtor
devaluación (f)
devaluation
devaluar
devalue (v)

devengar earn (v) *or*
bear (v) *or* yield (v) *or*
accrue (v) (interest)
devolución (f)
return (n)
**devolución (f)
[reembolso]**
refund (n)
devolver return (v)
or send back
**devolver una carta
al remitente** return
a letter to sender
devolver una letra
dishonour a bill
día (m) day
día: al día per day
or up-to-date
día de ajuste
quarter day
día festivo bank
holiday
diagrama (m)
diagram
diagrama de flujo
flow chart *or* flow
diagram
**diario (m) de bol-
sillo** pocket diary
diario (-ria) daily
or day-to-day

dictado (m)
dictation
dictáfono (m)
dictating machine
dictar dictate
diferencia (f)
difference *or*
discrepancy
diferencial
differential (adj)
diferencias (fpl) de
precio differences
in price
diferente
different
diferido (-da)
deferred
diferir differ
diferir [aplazar]
defer *or* adjourn
diferir el pago
defer payment
difícil difficult
dificultad (f)
difficulty (n)
difundir a través de
la red de emisoras
network (v)
difusión (f)
circulation
dígito (m) digit

dilución (f) del
capital dilution of
equity
dimensiones
(fpl) dimensions
or size *or*
measurements
dimisión (f)
resignation
dimitir resign
dinero (m) money
dinero: sin dinero
broke (adj)
dinero barato
cheap money
dinero efectivo
cash (n)
dinero en mano
spot cash
dinero escaso tight
money
dinero para gastos
menores petty cash
dinero para gastos
personales
spending money
dinero suelto
change (n)
diplomado (-da)
certificated
dique (m) dock (n)

dirección (f)
direction
dirección (f)
[gerencia]
management
dirección (f)
[señas] address (n)
dirección comercial
business address
dirección conjunta
joint management
dirección de
personal personnel
management
dirección de
reenvío forwarding
address
dirección postal
accommodation
address
dirección
telegráfica cable
address
directamente
direct (adv)
directiva (f)
directive
directivo (-va)
managerial
directo (-ta) direct
(adj)

director (-ra)
director *or* manager
director (-ra)
adjunto (-ta)
deputy manager
director (-ra) com-
ercial sales manager
director (-ra) de
banco bank
manager
director (-ra) de
una empresa
company director
director (-ra) de
exportación export
manager
director (-ra) de
finanzas finance
director
director (-ra) de
hotel hotel
manager
director (-ra) de
'marketing'
marketing manager
director (-ra) de
planta floor
manager
director (-ra) de
producción
production manager

director (-ra) de proyecto project manager

director (-ra) de publicidad publicity manager

director (-ra) de reclamaciones claims manager

director (-ra) de sucursal branch manager

director (-ra) ejecutivo (-va) executive director

director (-ra) externo (-na) outside director

director (-ra) en funciones acting manager

director (-ra) general general manager

director (-ra) general adjunto (-ta) deputy managing director

director (-ra) gerente managing director (MD)

director (-ra) no ejecutivo (-va) non-executive director

director (-ra) principal senior manager *or* senior executive

director (-ra) regional area manager

directorio (m) directory

directorio comercial classified directory

directriz (f) guideline *or* directive

dirigido (-da) a un mercado popular down-market

dirigir direct (v) *or* channel (v)

dirigir [gestionar] manage

dirigir [llevar] run (v)

dirigir [obrar] operate

dirigir un negocio control a business

disco (m) disk

disco duro
hard disk
discrepancia (f)
discrepancy *or*
variance
disculpa (f)
apology
disculparse
apologize
discurrir flow (v)
discusión (f)
discussion *or*
argument
discusión (f)
[debate] debate
discutir discuss
diseñar design (v)
diseño (m)
design (n)
diseño de produc-
tos product design
diseño industrial
industrial design
diseño registrado
registered design
disminución (f)
decrease *or*
lowering
disminución (f)
[impuestos]
abatement

disminución de
valor decrease in
value
disminuir decline
(v) *or* decrease (v)
or fall off
disolver dissolve
disolver una
sociedad dissolve a
partnership
dispararse soar
disponer arrange *or*
set out
disponibilidad (f)
availability
disponible
available *or*
vacant
disposición (f)
provision
dispositivo (m)
device
disquete (m) *o*
diskette (m)
diskette
disquetera (f)
disk drive
distinto (-ta)
different
distribución (f)
distribution

distribución exclu-siva distributorship
distribuidor (-ra) distributor *or* stockist
distribuir distribute
distribuir un dividendo pay a dividend
distrito (m) district *or* area
distrito comercial commercial district
disuadir advise against
diversificación (f) diversification
diversificar diversify
dividendo (m) dividend
dividendo: con dividendo cum dividend
dividendo: sin divi-dendo ex dividend
dividendo final final dividend
dividendo mínimo minimum dividend

dividendo por acción earnings per share *or* earnings yield
dividendo por superávit surplus dividend
dividendo provisional interim dividend
dividir divide *or* share (v)
dividir [separar] separate (v)
divisas (fpl) foreign exchange
divisas de reserva reserve currency
división (f) division
divulgación (f) disclosure
divulgar disclose *or* release (v)
doble double (adj)
doble imposición (f) double taxation
doble reserva (f) double-booking
docena (f) dozen

documentación (f)
documentation
documental
documentary
documento (m)
document
documento adjunto
enclosure
documento
escrito instrument
documento falso
forgery
documento no
negociable
non-negotiable
instrument
documentos (mpl)
documents *or*
papers
documentos falsos
faked documents
dólar (m) dollar
domiciliación (f)
bancaria direct
debit *or* standing
order
domicilio (m)
domicile
domicilio: a domi-
cilio house to house
or door to door

domicilio particular
home address
domicilio social
registered office *or*
headquarters (HQ)
dorso (m) back (n)
dotación (f) de
personal manning
dpto. (= departa-
mento) dept
(=department)
dracma (m)
[moneda] drachma
dueña (f)
proprietress
or landlady
or owner
dueño (m)
proprietor *or*
landlord *or* owner
dumping (m)
dumping
duplicación (f)
duplication
duplicado (m)
duplicate (n)
duplicar duplicate
(v) *or* double (v)
duro (-ra) hard

Ee

echar al correo
post *or* mail (v)
ecológico (-ca)
environmentally
friendly
economía (f) econ-
omy *or* economics
economía de libre
mercado free
market economy
economía de
oferta supply side
economics
economía dirigida
controlled economy
economía estable
stable economy
economía madura
mature economy
economía mixta
mixed economy
economía
sumergida black
economy
economías de
escala economies
of scale

económico (-ca)
economic *or*
economical
economista (mf)
economist
economista de
mercado market
economist
economizar
economize (v) *or*
save (on)
ecu *o* ECU (m) ecu
or ECU (European
currency unit)
edad (f) de
jubilación
retirement age
edificio (m)
building *or* facility
or premises
edificio principal
main building
efectivo (m)
ready cash
efectivo: en
efectivo cash
efectivo en caja
cash in hand
efectivo (-va)
effective *or*
actual

efecto (m) effect (n) *or* instrument (n)
efecto de favor accommodation bill
efecto indirecto spinoff
efecto negociable bankable paper
efecto secundario knock-on effect
efectos a cobrar receivables
efectos embargados (vendidos a bajo precio) distress merchandise
efectuar effect (v)
eficacia (f) effectiveness *or* efficiency
eficaz efficient
eficiencia (f) efficiency *or* effectiveness
eficiente efficient
ejecución (f) execution *or* implementation *or* enforcement

ejecutar exectute (v) *or* implement (v) *or* enforce (v)
ejecutivo (m) de cuentas account executive
ejecutivo de ventas sales executive
ejecutivo (-va) executive
ejecutivo (-va) auxiliar junior executive *or* junior manager
ejecutivo (-va) en formación management trainee
ejemplar (m) copy (n)
ejercer exercise (v) *or* perform (v)
ejercer derecho de opción exercise an option
ejercicio (m) exercise (n)
ejercicio del derecho de opción exercise of an option

ejercicio económico
financial year
ejercicio fiscal
tax year
**elaboración (f) de
datos** data processing
elaborar process (v)
**elaborar
[producto]**
manufacture (v)
elaborar cifras
process figures
elasticidad (f)
elasticity
elección (f)
election *or* choice
elegir elect *or* choose
elemento (m)
factor (n)
**elevador (m) de gra-
nos** grain elevator
eludir evade
elusión (f) evasion
elusión de impuestos
tax avoidance
embalador (-ra)
packer
embalaje (m)
packaging *or*
packing *or*
package

**embalaje de exposi-
ción** display pack
**embalaje de
plástico tipo
burbuja** blister
pack *or* bubble pack
**embalaje
hermético**
airtight packaging
**embalaje vacío o
ficticio** dummy pack
embalar pack (v)
embalar [caja]
case (v) *or* crate (v)
**embalar mer-
cancías en cajas
de cartón** pack
goods into cartons
embarcadero (m)
wharf
embarcar embark
embarcarse
board (v)
embarcarse en
embark on
embargador (-ra)
sequestrator
embargar seize
embargo (m)
embargo *or* seizure
or sequestration

embarque (m)
embarkation
embaucar fiddle (v)
embolsar pocket (v)
embotellamiento
(m) bottleneck
emergencia (f)
emergency
emisión (f) issue (n)
emisión de
acciones share issue
emisión de acciones
gratuitas scrip
issue
emisión de dere-
chos rights issue
emisión gratuita
bonus issue
emisión
publicitaria TV
commercial
emitir issue (v)
emolumentos
(mpl) fee
empaletar palletize
empaquetador (-ra)
packer
empaquetar parcel
(v) or pack (v)
empezar start (v)
or begin (v)

empezar un
negocio a cero
cold start
emplazamiento (m)
summons
empleado (-da)
employee or
employed
empleado (-da) de
oficina office
worker or clerk
empleado (-da) del
servicio de
información
information officer
empleado (-da)
para mantener
llenos los estantes
shelf filler
emplear employ or
use (v)
emplear de nuevo
re-employ
emplear más
personal take on
more staff
empleo (m)
employment or
appointment or job
empleo: sin empleo
unemployed

empleo a tiempo parcial part-time work *or* part-time employment

empleo de la capacidad capacity utilization

empleo eventual temporary employment

empleo fijo staff appointment

empleo seguro secure job

emprendedor (-ra) go-ahead (adj)

emprender undertake

emprender un negocio go into business

empresa (f) enterprise *or* business *or* company *or* undertaking

empresa a pequeña escala small-scale enterprise

empresa comercial commercial undertaking

empresa competidora rival company

empresa con fines de lucro profit-oriented company

empresa conjunta joint venture

empresa de alquiler de maquinaria plant-hire firm

empresa de transporte público common carrier

empresa de transportes haulage contractor *or* carrier

empresa de ventas por correo mailorder business *or* mail-order firm

empresa en ruinas wreck (n)

empresa familiar family company

empresa mediana middle-sized company

empresa privada private enterprise

empresa que comercia con otra trading partner

empresarial entrepreneurial

empresario (-ria) employer *or* entrepreneur *or* businessman *or* businesswoman

empresas (fpl) rivales rival firms *or* competing firms

empréstito (m) loan capital

empuje (m) drive (n) *or* energy

encargado (-da) [almacén, tienda] manager

encargado (-da) de compras buyer

encargado (-da) del libro de compras bought ledger clerk

encargado (-da) del libro de ventas sales ledger clerk

encargar [confiar] entrust

encargar [hacer un pedido] order (v)

encargarse de undertake

encarte publicitario [de una revista] magazine insert

encauzar channel (v)

enchufe (m) electric plug *or* connection

enchufe (m) [influencia] useful contact

encogimiento (m) shrinkage

encontrar find (v) *or* meet (v)

encontrar: no encontrar miss (v)

encontrarse (con) meet

encubrimiento (m) de activos conceal- ment of assets

encuesta (f) opinion poll *or* questionnaire

endémico (-ca) chronic

endeudado (-da) indebted

endeudarse get into debt *or* run into debt

endosante (mf) endorser

endosar un cheque endorse a cheque

endosatario (-ria) endorsee

endoso (m) endorsement

energía (f) energy

enjuiciar prosecute

enlace (m) tie-up *or* link

enmendar amend

enmienda (f) amendment

ensayo (m) test (n) *or* trial

enseñar show (v) *or* teach (v)

entablar enter into

entablar negociaciones open negotiations

entablar un pleito take legal action

entender understand

entrada (f) entrance *or* admission *or* entering

entrada (f) [billete] ticket

entrada (f) [depósito] down payment

entrada de favor complimentary ticket

entradas (fpl) receipts

entrar en enter *or* go in

entrar en dársena dock (v)

entrar en vigor operate (v)

entrega (f) delivery

entrega con acuse de recibo recorded delivery

entrega futura future delivery

entrega gratuita free delivery

entrega urgente express delivery

**entregado: no
entregado**
undelivered
entregar deliver *or*
hand in *or* hand over
**entregar: para
entregar a** care of
or c/o
entrevista (f)
interview (n)
entrevistado (-da)
interviewee
entrevistador (-ra)
interviewer
entrevistar
interview (v)
enumerar list (v)
**envasado (-da) al
vacío** shrink-wrapped
envasar pack (v)
**envase (m)
[embalaje]** packing
or packaging *or*
pack (n)
**envase (m) [recipi-
ente]** container
envase al vacío
shrink-wrapping
**envase no retorn-
able** non-returnable
packing

**envases (mpl)
devueltos** returned
empties
enviar send *or*
dispatch
**enviar por carga
aérea** airfreight (v)
enviar por correo
post (v) *or* mail (v)
**enviar por
correo aéreo**
airmail (v)
**enviar por correo
urgente** express (v)
enviar por fax
fax (v)
enviar por télex
telex (v)
**enviar un paquete
por correo aéreo**
send a package by
airmail
**enviar un paquete
por vía terrestre o
marítima** send a
package by
surface mail
**enviar una carga
por vía marítima**
send a shipment
by sea

enviar una factura por correo send an invoice by post

envío (m) dispatch (n)

envío (m) [carga] shipment

envío (m) [expedición] shipping or forwarding

envío (m) [giro] remittance

envío (m) [remesa] consignment

envío agrupado de mercancías consolidated shipment

envío de publicidad por correo direct mailing or mailing shot

envío de revistas por correo magazine mailing

envío por correo mailing

envíos (mpl) a granel bulk shipments

envoltorio (m) wrapping or wrapper

envolver wrap up or parcel (v)

epígafres (mpl) de un acuerdo heads of agreement

equilibrar balance (v)

equilibrio (m) balance (n)

equipaje (m) luggage or baggage

equipaje de mano hand luggage

equipaje no reclamado unclaimed baggage

equipar equip

equiparación (f) equalization

equipo (m) equipment

equipo de consumidores consumer panel

equipo de oficina office equipment

equipo de ventas sales team

equipo defectuoso faulty equipment

equipo directivo management team

equipo pesado
heavy equipment
**equipos (mpl) de
oficina** business
equipment
equitativo (-va)
fair (adj)
equivocación (f)
mistake *or* error
equivocado (-da)
wrong
erosionar erode
errar miss (v)
erróneo (-nea)
erroneous *or* wrong
error (m) error (n)
or slip (n) *or*
mistake (n)
error aleatorio
random error
error de cálculo
miscalculation
**error de copia o de
oficina** clerical
error
error de ordenador
computer error
escala (f) scale *or*
range (n)
escala: sin escalas
non-stop

**escala de
rendimiento**
earning capacity
**escala móvil
de salarios**
incremental scale
**escala salarial o
escala de salarios**
wage scale
escalar escalate
escalonar stagger
escaparate (m)
shop window *or*
window display
escasez (f)
shortage
**escasez de mano
de obra** manpower
shortage
escaso (-sa) short of
escogido (-da)
choice (adj)
escribir write
escribir a alguien
correspond with
someone
**escribir sin
abreviar** write out
(in full)
escrito (m)
writing

escrito (-ta) a mano handwritten
escritorio (m) desk
escritura (f) writing *or* handwriting
escritura (f) [título] deed
escritura de cesión deed of assignment
escritura de constitución articles of association
escritura de convenio deed of covenant
escritura de sociedad deed of partnership
escritura de transferencia deed of transfer
escudo (m) [moneda] escudo
escuela (f) de secretariado secretarial college
escuela empresarial business school
escuela superior de comercio commercial college
esencial essential

esfuerzo (m) effort
espacio (m) space *or* room
espacio en blanco blank (n)
espacio para oficinas office space
espacio publicitario advertising space
especial special
especialista (mf) specialist
especialización (f) specialization
especializado (-da) [trabajador] skilled
especializar specialize
especificación (f) specification
especificar specify
esperar instrucciones await instructions
espionaje (m) industrial industrial espionage
esquina (f) corner (n)
estabilidad (f) stability *or* steadiness

**estabilidad de los
precios** price
stability
estabilización (f)
stabilization
**estabilizar los
precios** peg prices
estabilizar (se)
stabilize *or* level out
estable stable
establecer
establish *or* set (v)
establecerse settle
**establecimiento
(m)** establishment
[business]
estación (f) season
estación (f) [tren]
train station
**estación de
ferrocarril** railway
station
**estación de mer-
cancías** freight depot
**estación de trabajo
[de ordenador]**
computer
workstation
estacional seasonal
estadísticas (fpl)
statistics

**estadístico (-ca)
(adj)** statistical
estadístico (-ca)
statistician
estado (m) [país]
state (n) *or* country
**estado (m)
[condición]**
condition *or* state
estado de cuenta
bank balance
**estado de cuenta
mensual** monthly
statement
estado de cuentas
statement of account
**estado de
cuentas semestral**
half-yearly statement
**estado de flujo de
caja** cash flow
statement
**estadounidense
(mf)** American
estafa (f) fraud (n)
estafador (-ra)
racketeer
estampilla (f)
stamp (n)
estancado (-da)
stagnant

estancamiento (m)
stagnation

estancia (f) stay

estándar standard
(adj)

estandarización (f)
standardization

**estandarizar (nor-
malizar)** standardize

estantería (f)
shelves *or* shelving

**estantería (f) [vit-
rina]** display unit
or display stand

estar de acuerdo
agree with

**estar en punto
muerto** be
deadlocked

estatal government
(adj)

estatutos (mpl)
articles of
association

estibador (m)
stevedore

estimación (f)
estimate (n) *or*
estimation

estimado (-da)
estimated

estimar estimate (v)

estimular boost (v)

**estimular la
economía** stimulate
the economy

estímulo (m)
stimulus *or* boost
(n) *or* incentive

estipulación (f)
stipulation *or*
provision

estipular stipulate

estrategia (f)
strategy

**estrategia
comercial** business
strategy

**estrategia de
'marketing'**
marketing strategy

estratégico (-ca)
strategic

estropear spoil

estropearse break
down (v)

estructura (f)
structure (n)

**estructura cuadric-
ular** grid structure
estructural
structural
estucturar
structure (v)
estudiar study (v)
estudio (m)
study (n) *or*
survey (n)
**estudio de
desplazamientos y
tiempos** time and
motion study
estudio de mercado
market research
**estudios (mpl)
sobre el terreno**
field work
etapa (f) stage (n)
etiqueta (f) label (n)
etiqueta (de señas)
address label
**etiqueta de correo
aéreo** airmail sticker
etiqueta de precio
price tag *or* price
ticket *or* price label
etiquetado (m)
labelling

etiquetar label (v)
eurocheque (m)
Eurocheque
eurodivisa (f)
Eurocurrency
eurodólar (m)
Eurodollar
euromercado (m)
Euromarket
europeo (-a)
European
evadir evade
evadir impuestos
evade tax
evaluación (f)
valuation
or evaluation
**evaluación de la
rentabilidad**
measurement of
profitability
evaluar evaluate
evaluar los costes
evaluate costs
evasión (f) evasion
**evasión de capital(
es)** flight of capital
**evasión de
impuestos** tax avoid-
ance *or* tax evasion

eventual prospective

eventualidad (f) contingency

evitar avoid *or* prevent

exactamente exactly

exacto (-ta) exact *or* accurate

examen (m) examination *or* test

examinar examine

excedencia (f) leave of absence

excedente (m) surplus *or* excess

excedente de plantilla [despido] redundancy (n)

excedente laboral overmanning

exceder exceed

excelente excellent *or* first-class

excepcional exceptional

excepto excluding

excepto except

excesivo (-va) excessive

exceso (m) excess *or* surplus

exceso de capacidad excess capacity

exceso de equipaje excess baggage

exceso de existencias overstocks

excluir exclude

exclusión (f) exclusion

exclusiva sole right

exclusividad (f) exclusivity

exclusivo (-va) sole

excusa (f) apology

exención (f) exemption

exención fiscal tax exemption *or* exemption from tax

exento (-ta) exempt (adj)

exento de alquiler rent-free

exento de impuestos exempt from tax *or* tax-exempt

exhibición (f) exhibition *or* display

exhibidor (-ra)
demonstrator
exhibir o exponer
display (v)
exigir require
or demand (v)
or claim (v)
exigir el reembolso
ask for a refund
eximir exempt (v)
existencias (fpl)
stock or inventory (n)
existencias finales
closing stock
existencias iniciales
opening stock
éxito (m) success
éxito: con éxito
successful
éxito: sin éxito
unsuccessful
expandir expand
expansión (f)
expansion
expansión
industrial
industrial expansion
expedición (f)
forwarding or
shipping or
consignment (n)

expedidor (-ra)
shipper
expedidor (-ra)
forwarding agent
expediente (m)
dossier or file or
record
expedir ship (v) or
dispatch (v)
experimentado
(-da) experienced
experimentar una
recuperación stage
a recovery
experto (-ta)
experienced
expiración (f)
expiration or
expiry
expirar expire
explicación (f)
explanation
explicar explain
explorar explore
explotar exploit
exponer exhibit (v)
or display (v)
exponer [describir]
describe
exportación (f)
export (n)

exportación: de exportación exporting (adj)

exportaciones (fpl) exports

exportador (-ra) exporter *or* exporting (adj)

exportar export (v)

exposición (f) display (n) *or* exhibition *or* show

exposición (f) [riesgo] exposure

expositor (-ra) exhibitor

expresar express (v)

expreso (-sa) express (adj)

expropiación (f) forzosa compulsory purchase

extender make out

extender un cheque write out a cheque

extensión (f) telephone extension

exterior external

exterior [externo] outside

externo (-na) external *or* outside

extirpar excise (v)

extra extra

extracto (m) de cuentas bank statement

extranjero (m) overseas (n)

extranjero: en el extranjero abroad *or* overseas (adj)

extranjero (-ra) foreign

extraoficial unofficial

extraoficialmente off the record

extraordinario (-ria) extraordinary

extras (mpl) extras

extras (mpl) opcionales optional extras

Ff

fábrica (f) factory
fábrica (f) [planta]
plant (n) *or* factory
fabricación (f)
manufacturing *or*
manufacture (n)
fabricante (m)
manufacturer *or*
producer
fabricar
manufacture
(v) *or* produce
fabricar en serie
mass-produce
**fabricar coches
en serie**
massproduce cars
fácil easy
facilidad (f)
facility
facilidad de venta
saleability
**facilidades (fpl)
de crédito** credit
facilities

**facilidades de
pago** easy terms
factibilidad (f)
feasibility
factor (m)
factor (n)
**factor de riesgo
(en una inversión)**
downside factor
factor del coste
cost factor
factor decisivo
deciding factor
factor negativo
minus factor
factor positivo
plus factor
**factores (mpl)
cíclicos** cyclical
factors
**factores de
producción** factors
of production
factura (f) bill (n)
or invoice (n)
factura con el IVA
VAT invoice
factura de hotel
hotel bill

factura detallada itemized invoice *or* detailed account

factura por duplicado duplicate receipt *or* duplicate of a receipt or invoice

factura pro forma pro forma (invoice)

facturación (f) billing *or* invoicing

facturación (f) [ingresos] sales revenue

facturar bill (v) *or* invoice (v)

facturar [el equipaje] check in [at airport]

facturas (fpl) impagadas unpaid invoices

fallar fail *or* not to succeed *or* miss

fallecido (-da) dead (adj)

fallo (m) [decisión] ruling (n)

fallo (m) [defecto] mechanical fault

falseado (-da) false

falsear fiddle (v)

falsificación (f) falsification *or* forgery *or* fake (n)

falsificado (-da) counterfeit (adj)

falsificar falsify *or* forge *or* fake (v)

falsificar [embaucar] fiddle (v)

falsificar dinero counterfeit (v) (money)

falso (-sa) false

falso (-sa) [falsificado] counterfeit (adj)

falta (f) fault *or* blame

falta (f) [escasez] shortage

falta de entrega non-delivery

falta de fondos lack of funds

fama (f) fame

fase (m) phase *or* stage (n)

favor: de favor
complimentary
favorable
favourable
fax (m) fax (n)
fe: de buena fe
bona fide
fecha (f) date (n)
fecha: con fecha de
dated
fecha: en fecha
futura forward
fecha: sin fecha
undated
fecha de amorti-
zación o de rescate
redemption date
fecha de caducidad
sell by date or
expiry date
fecha de cumplim-
iento completion date
fecha de entrada en
vigor effective date
fecha de entrega
delivery date
fecha de lanzamiento
launching date
fecha de recepción
date of receipt

fecha de venci-
miento maturity
date
fecha inicial
starting date
fecha tope o fecha
límite closing date
or deadline
fechador (m) date
stamp
fechar date (v)
feria (f) show (n)
or fair
feria comercial
trade fair
ferrocarril (m) rail
or railway (GB) or
railroad (US)
ferry (m) ferry
ferry roll-on roll-
off roll on/roll off
ferry
fiabilidad (f)
reliability
fiable reliable
fiador (-ra) guar-
antor or surety
fianza (f)
guarantee or
security or surety

ficha (f) filing card *or* index card
ficha de ordenador computer file
fichero (m) file (n) *or* card index (n)
fichero (m) [de ordenador] computer file
fichero de tarjetas card-index file
fidelidad (f) a la marca brand loyalty
fidelidad a un establecimiento customer loyalty
fiesta (f) civil bank holiday
fiesta oficial statutory holiday
fiesta nacional public holiday
fijación (f) fixing
fijación colectiva de precios common pricing
fijación de los precios pricing

fijación de precios competitivos competitive pricing
fijación de precios marginal marginal pricing
fijar fix *or* arrange *or* set
fijar los daños assess damages
fijar objetivos set targets
fijar una reunión para las 3 de la tarde fix a meeting for 3 p.m.
fijo (-ja) fixed *or* set (adj)
fijo (-ja) [uniforme] flat (adj)
filial (adj) affiliated
filial (f) subsidiary (n)
fin (m) end (n)
fin: con fines lucrativos profit-making
fin: sin fines lucrativos non profit-making

fin de mes
month end
final (adj) final *or*
closing (adj)
final (m) end (n)
finalización (f)
completion
finalizar finalize
finalizar [terminar]
end (v)
financiación (f)
funding *or* financing
**financiación del
déficit presupues-
tario** deficit
financing
financiamiento (m)
financing
financiar finance
(v) *or* fund (v)
**financiar una
operación** finance
an operation
financieramente
financially
financiero (-ra)
financial
finanzas (fpl)
finance (n) *or*
finances

finanzas públicas
public finance
fingir fake (v)
finiquito (m)
settlement
firma (f) signature
firma (f) [empresa]
firm (n)
**firma de un
contrato** comple-
tion of a contract
firmante (mf)
signatory
firmar sign (v)
**firmar como tes-
tigo** witness (v)
firmar un cheque
sign a cheque
firmar un contrato
sign a contract
firme firm (adj) *or*
strong
fiscal (adj) fiscal
(adj)
fiscal (m)
prosecution counsel
fletador (-ra)
charterer
fletamento (m)
chartering

fletamento (m)
[flete] freightage
fletar charter (v)
fletar [cargar]
take on freight
fletar un
avión charter an
aircraft
flete (m) freight *or*
freightage
flete aéreo air
freight
flete de vuelta
homeward freight
flexibilidad (f)
flexibility
flexible flexible
flojo (-ja) slack *or*
loose
flojo (-ja) [débil]
weak
florecer flourish
floreciente boom-
ing *or* flourishing
florín (m)
[moneda] guilder
flotación (f) float (n)
flotante floating
flotar una divisa
float (v) a currency

fluctuación (f)
fluctuation
fluctuante
fluctuating
fluctuar fluctuate
fluir flow (v)
flujo (m) flow (n)
flujo de caja
cash flow
flujo de caja
negativo negative
cash flow
flujo de caja positivo
positive cash flow
flujo de caja
descontado
discounted
cash flow (DCF)
FMI (Fondo
Monetario
Internacional) IMF
(=International
Monetary Fund)
folleto (m) leaflet
or prospectus
folleto publicitario
brochure
folleto publicitario
enviado por correo
mailing piece

fondo (m) bottom
fondo (m) [finan-zas] fund (n)
fondo de caja cash float
fondo de comercio goodwill
fondo de pensiones pension fund
fondo para gastos menores petty cash
fondo para imprevis-tos contingency fund
Fondo Monetario Internacional (FMI) International Monetary Fund (IMF)
fondos (mpl) mutuos o fondos de inversión unit trust
fondos públicos public funds
formación (f) training (n)
formación (f) de mandos management training
formación en el puesto de trabajo in-house training

formación profe-sional en el trabajo on-the-job training
formación profe-sional fuera del trabajo off-the-job training
formal formal
formalidad (f) formality
formalidades adu-aneras customs formalities
formar form (v)
formarse train (v) *or* learn
formulario (m) form (n)
formulario de declaración de la renta tax declaration form
formulario de solicitud application form
fórmulas (fpl) judiciales form of words
fotocopia (f) photocopy (n) *or* photocopying

fotocopiadora (f) copier *or* photocopier

fotocopiaje (m) photocopying

fotocopiar photocopy (v)

fracasado (-da) unsuccessful

fracasar fail *or* flop (v)

fracaso (m) failure *or* flop (n)

frágil fragile

franco (m) [moneda] franc

franco [libre] franco

franco a bordo free on board (f.o.b.)

franco a domicilio carriage paid

franco de porte carriage free

franco en almacén price ex warehouse

franco en fábrica price ex works

franco en muelle price ex quay

franco sobre vagón o franco vagón FF.CC. free on rail

franquear frank (v) *or* stamp (v)

franqueo (m) postage

franqueo (m) concertado postage paid *or* postpaid

franqueo y embalaje postage and packing (p. & p.)

franquicia (f) franchise *or* franchising

franquiciador (-ra) franchiser

franquiciar franchise (v)

fraude (m) fraud

fraude fiscal tax evasion

fraudulentamente fraudulently

fraudulento (-ta) fraudulent

frecuencia (f) de visitas de un representante call rate

frecuente frequent

frenar plug (v) *or* block (v) *or* stop (v)

freno (m) brake *or* check (n)

frontera (f) border

fuego (m) fire (n)

fuente (f) de ingre-sos source of income

fuera de control out of control

fuera de horas de oficina outside office hours

fuera de horas punta off-peak

fuerte strong

fuerte competencia keen competition

fuerza (f) strength

fuerza: a la fuerza forced

fuerza mayor act of God *or* force majeure

fuerzas (fpl) del mercado market forces

fuga (f) flight

fuga de capital(es) flight of capital

funcionamiento (m) [maquinaria] operating *or* running (n)

funcionamiento (m) [rendimiento] performance

funcionario (-ria) official (n) *or* civil servant

funcionario (-ria) de aduanas customs officer *or* customs official

función: en funciones acting

funda (f) cover (n) *or* top (n)

fundamental basic (adj) *or* fundamental

fundar una com-pañía set up a company *or* float a company

furgoneta (f) de reparto delivery van

fusión (f) merger

fusionar merge

futura: en fecha futura forward

futuros (mpl) futures

Gg

galería (f) comercial shopping mall

gama (f) range (n)

gama de precios price range

gama de productos product line

gama de productos de una compañía product mix

ganancia (f) gain (n) *or* profit (n) *or* return (n)

ganancia neta clear profit

ganancias (fpl) earnings

ganancias netas net earnings *or* net income

ganancias: cuenta de pérdidas y ganancias profit and loss account

ganar gain (v)

ganar [sueldo] earn (v)

ganar dinero make money

ganga (f) bargain (n)

garante (m) backer *or* guarantor *or* surety (n)

garantía (f) guarantee *or* warranty *or* collateral (n)

garantía (f) [fianza] surety (n) *or* security

garantizar guarantee (v) *or* warrant (v)

garantizar el pago underwrite

gasolina a precio reducido cut-price petrol

gastar spend

gastar excesivamente overspend

gastar más de lo presupuestado overspend one's budget

gastar menos
underspend
gasto (m) expense
or expenditure *or*
outlay
gasto de
tramitación
handling charge
gastos (mpl)
expenses
gastos: sin gastos
de franqueo
post free
gastos a cobrar a la
entrega charges
forward
gastos
adicionales y com-
plementarios extra
charges
gastos
administrativos
administrative
expenses
gastos aparte
extras
gastos
bancarios bank
charges

gastos corrientes
running costs *or*
running expenses
gastos de
capital capital
expenditure
gastos de demora
demurrage
gastos de descarga
landing charges
gastos de embalaje
packing charges
gastos de
explotación
operating costs *or*
operating
expenses
gastos de franqueo
postal charges *or*
postal rates
gastos de
mantenimiento
running costs *or*
running expenses
gastos de
producción
overheads *or*
overhead costs *or*
expenses

gastos de publicidad publicity expenditure

gastos de transporte freight costs

gastos del consumidor *o* de consumo consumer spending

gastos generales *o* gastos de producción overheads *or* overhead costs *or* expenses

gastos generales de fabricación manufacturing overheads

gastos iniciales start-up costs

gastos menores petty expenses *or* incidental expenses

gastos no autorizados unauthorized expenditure

gastos reemborsables out-of-pocket expenses

gastos totales total expenditure

general general *or* across-the-board

general [completo] full-scale (adj)

género (m) merchandise (n)

genuino (-na) genuine

gerencia (f) management

gerente (mf) manager

gestión (f) management

gestión de cartera portfolio management

gestión de deudas con descuento factoring

gestión lineal line management

gestionar negotiate (v)

**gestionar deudas
con descuento**
factor (v)
girar draw (v)
**girar (volumen de
ventas)** turn
over (v)
**girar en descu-
bierto** overdraw
giro (m) [envío]
remittance
giro (m) [letra]
draft (n)
giro a la vista
sight draft
giro bancario bank
draft *or* banker's
draft *or* giro system
**giro bancario [letra
bancaria]** bank
bill (GB)
giro postal postal
order *or* money
order
**giro postal interna-
cional** foreign
money order
global overall *or*
comprehensive

global [mundial]
worldwide (adj)
gobierno (m)
government (n)
**gobierno: del
gobierno**
government (adj)
**grado: de grado
inferior** low-level
graduado (-da)
graduated
gradual gradual
**gráfico (n) *o* grá-
fica (f)** graph (n)
or chart (n)
**gráfico circular o
gráfico sectorial**
pie chart
gráfico de barras
bar chart
gráfico de ventas
sales chart
gramo (m) gram *or*
gramme
gran demanda (f)
keen demand
gran gasto (m)
heavy expenditure
grande large *or* big

grande [impor-tante] heavy *or* important

grandes almacenes (mpl) store (n) *or* large shop *or* department store

grandes costes (mpl) heavy costs *or* heavy expenditure

granel: a granel loose

grapa (f) staple (n)

grapadora (f) stapler

grapar staple (v)

grapar papeles staple papers together

gratificación (f) por méritos merit award *or* merit bonus

gratis gratis *or* free *or* free of charge

gratuitamente gratis *or* free (adv)

gratuito (-ta) free (adj)

gravamen (m) lien

gravamen sobre las importaciones import levy

gravar impose

gravar con un impuesto tax (v)

gremio (m) guild

grúa (f) crane

gruesa (f) gross (n) (= 144)

grupo (m) group

grupo de trabajo working party

grupos (mpl) socioe-conómicos socio-economic groups

guardar save (v) *or* store (v)

guardar [orde-nador] back up (v) *or* save (v)

guardar [tener] hold (v) *or* keep (v)

guardia (m) de seguridad security guard

guerra (f) de pre-cios price war *or* price-cutting war

guía (f) comercial commercial directory *or* trade directory

guía telefónica telephone book *or* telephone directory

guía urbana street directory
guía (mf) de turismo courier *or* guide (n)

Hh

haber (m) credit balance *or* credit side
habilidad (f) skill
habitación (f) room
habitaciones (fpl) de hotel hotel accommodation
habitante (mf) inhabitant *or* occupier
habitante (mf) [residente] resident (n)
habitual usual *or* routine (adj)
hacer do (v) *or* make (v)
hacer bajar los precios force prices down
hacer cumplir enforce

hacer efectivo encash
hacer falta take (v) *or* need (v)
hacer frente (a) cope (v) (with)
hacer funcionar run (v) *or* work (a machine)
hacer negocios transact business
hacer publicidad con mucho bombo hype (v)
hacer subir los precios force prices up
hacer trabajo eventual temp (v)
hacer un asiento post an entry
hacer un borrador draft (v)
hacer un depósito pay money down
hacer un inventario take stock
hacer un muestreo sample (v)
hacer un pedido order (v)

hacer una lista
make a list *or* list (v)
hacerse cargo
take over
hacerse un seguro
take out a policy
hacia abajo down
or downward
hacia el centro
downtown (adv)
Hacienda (f) Publica
the Treasury
hasta up to
hecho a medida oa
la orden custom-
built *or* custom-made
hectárea (f)
hectare
herramienta (f) imp-
lement (n) *or* tool (n)
hipermercado (m)
hypermarket *or*
superstore
hipoteca (f) mort-
gage (n)
hipotecar mort-
gage (v)
historial (m) per-
sonal record
hoja (f) de cálculo
spreadsheet

hoja de papel
sheet of paper
hoja de sueldo ode
salario pay slip
holding (m)
holding company
hombre (m) man (n)
hombre de
confianza right-
hand man
hombre de nego-
cios businessman
honorarios (mpl)
fee *or* honorarium
hora (f) hour
hora: por hora
hourly *or* per hour
hora de apertura
opening time
hora de cierre
closing time
hora-hombre (f)
man-hour
horario (m)
timetable (n)
horario bancario
banking hours
horario comercial
opening hours
horario de oficina
office hours

**horario de presen-
tación (en el aerop-
uerto)** check-in time
**horas (fpl) de ofic-
ina** business hours
**horas extraordinar-
ias** overtime
horas punta peak
period or rush hour
hotel (m) hotel
hotel homologado
graded hotel
hueco (m) gap
**hueco de un
mercado** niche
**hueco en el
mercado** gap in
the market
huelga (f) strike (n)
**huelga de brazos
caídos** sit-down
strike
huelga de celo go-
slow or work-to-rule
huelga de protesta
protest strike
**huelga de
solidaridad**
sympathy strike
huelga general
general strike

huelga salvaje
wildcat strike
huelguista (mf)
striker
hundimiento (m)
collapse (n)
hundirse collapse
(v) or sink (v)
**hundirse [caer en
picado]** slump (v)
hurto (m) pilferage
or pilfering (n)
**hurto en las tien-
das** shoplifting

Ii

**I+D (investigación
y desa rrollo)**
research and devel-
opment (R & D)
igual equal (adj)
igualar equal (v)
igualdad (f)
equality or parity
ilegal illegal

ilegalidad (f)
illegality
ilegalmente
illegally
ilícito (-ta) illicit
imagen (f) de
marca brand image
magen pública
public image
imagen pública de
una empresa
corporate image
imitación (f)
imitation *or* fake (n)
impagado (-da)
unpaid
impago (m) de una
deuda non-
payment
impar odd
impedir prevent
imperfección (f)
imperfection
imperfecto (-ta)
imperfect
imponer impose (v)
importación (f) imp-
ort *or* importing (n)
importación-
exportación
import-export

importaciones (fpl)
imports
importaciones (fpl)
visibles visible
imports
importador (-ra)
importer (n) *or*
importing (adj)
importancia (f)
importance
importante
important *or* major
importante
[grande] heavy
importar import (v)
importar [valer]
matter (v)
importe (m)
amount
importe debido
amount owing
importe pagado
amount paid
imposible de con-
seguir unobtainable
imposición (f)
[depósito] deposit
imposición (f)
[impuesto] taxation
imposición alta
high taxation

imposición directa
direct taxation
imposición en efec-
tivo cash deposit
imposición indirecta
indirect taxation
impositor (-ra)
depositor
imprenta (f)
printer
imprescindible
essential
impresión (f)
printout
impreso (m) form (n)
impreso de solici-
tud applicationform
impreso de
declaración de
aduana customs
declaration form
impresora (f)
printer *or* computer
printer
impresora de líneas
line printer
impresora de rueda
de margarita daisy-
wheel printer
impresora láser
laser printer

impresora matricial
dot-matrix printer
imprimir print out
impuesto (m) tax
(n) *or* taxation (n)
impuesto ad valo-
rem ad valorem tax
impuesto atrasado
back tax
impuesto básico
basic tax
impuesto de circu-
lación road tax
impuesto de socie-
dades corporation tax
impuesto de venta
purchase tax
impuesto del tim-
bre stamp duty
impuesto directo
direct tax
impuesto indirecto
indirect tax
impuesto no inclu-
ido exclusive of tax
impuesto pagado
tax paid
impuesto para
financiar la forma-
ción profesional
training levy

impuesto progresivo graded tax

impuesto progresivo sobre la renta graduated income tax

impuesto sobre el consumo excise duty

impuesto sobre el valor añadido (IVA) value added tax (VAT)

impuesto sobre el volumen de ventas turnover tax

impuesto sobre la renta income tax

impuesto sobre la venta sales tax

impuesto sobre las plusvalías capital gains tax

impuesto sobre las ventas de bienes o servicios output tax

impuestos (mpl) duty

impuestos incluidos inclusive of tax

impuestos retenidos en el origen tax deducted at source

impulsar boost (v)

impulso (m) impulse *or* boost (n)

inalcanzable unobtainable

inalterado (-da) unchanged

inasequible unavailable

inauguración (f) opening (n)

inaugural opening (adj)

incapaz incapable

incautación (f) seizure

incautar seize (v)

incendio (m) fire (n)

incentivo (m) incentive

incluido (-da) inclusive

incluido: no incluido exclusive of

incluir include (v)

incluir incorporate

inclusive o inclusivo (-va) inclusive

incompetencia (f) [incapacia] incompetence (n)

**incompetencia (f)
[ineficacia]**
inefficiency
**incompetente
[incapaz]**
incompetent
**incompetente [ine-
ficaz]** inefficient
incondicional
unconditional
incorporado (-da)
built-in
incorporar
incorporate (v)
incorrectamente
incorrectly
incorrecto (-ta)
incorrect
incremental
incremental
incremento (m)
increment (n) *or*
increase (n)
**incumplimiento
(m)** default (n)
incumplir default
(v) *or* break (v)
**incumplir los
pagos** default on
payments
incurrir en incur

**indemnidad (f) oin-
demnización (f)**
indemnity *or*
indemnification
**indemnización por
daños y perjuicios**
compensation for
damage
indemnizar
indemnify
**indemnizar [resar-
cir]** make good
**indemnizar [com-
pensar]** compensate
**indemnizar a
alguien por una
pérdida** indemnify
someone for a loss
independiente
independent
indexación (f)
indexation
indicador (m) indica-
tor *or* index number
**indicadores (mpl)
económicos** eco-
nomic indicators
indicar show (v) *or*
specify (v)
**indicar [citar refe-
rencia]** quote (v)

índice (m) index number

índice de crec-imiento growth index

índice de ocupación occupancy rate

índice de precios al comsumo retail price index

índice de precios al consumo (IPC) consumer price index

índice de precios al por mayor wholesale price index

índice del coste de vida cost-of-living index

índice ponderado weighted index

indiciación (f) indexation

indirecto (-ta) indirect

indisponibilidad (f) unavailability

industria (f) industry

industria clave key industry

industria con alto coeficiente de capital capital-intensive industry

industria de servicios service industry or tertiary industry

industria nacionalizada nationalized industry

industria pesada heavy industry

industria principal staple industry

industria próspera o en pleno auge boom industry

industria secundaria secondaryindustry

industria terciaria tertiary industry

industrial industrial

industrial (mf) industrialist (n)

industrialización (f) industrialization

industrializar industrialize

ineficacia (f) inefficiency

ineficaz inefficient
inexplicado (-da)
unexplained *or*
unaccounted for
inferior lower (adj)
inflación (f) inflation
inflación de costes
cost-push inflation
inflacionario (-ria)
o inflacionista
inflationary
influencia (f)
influence (n)
influir influence (v)
información (f)
information
información de
vuelos flight
information
información privile-
giada insider dealing
información pub-
licitaria sales
literature
informar inform
(v) *or* report (v)
informar [advertir]
advise
informar [dar
instrucciones]
brief (v)

informar sobre la
marcha report on
progress
informático (-ca)
computerized
informatizado (-da)
computerized
informatizar
computerize
informe (m) report
(n) *or* survey (n)
informe (m) [reg-
istro] record (n)
informe anual
annual report
informe confiden-
cial confidential
report
informe de
viabilidad (de un
proyecto)
feasibility report
informe provisional
interim report
informe sobre la
marcha de un tra-
bajo progress report
infracción (f) adu-
anera infringement
of customs
regulations

infracción fiscal
tax offence
infraestructura (f)
infrastructure
infringir break (v)
or infringe (v)
infringir la ley
break the law
ingeniero (-ra) de
producto product
engineer
ingeniero (-ra) de
obra site engineer
inglés (-esa)
English or British
ingresar bank (v)
or deposit (v)
ingresar en caja
take (v)
ingreso (m) revenue
ingreso (m) [depó-
sito] deposit (n)
ingreso (m)
[entrada] entry or
admission
ingreso fijo regular
income
ingreso real real
income or real wages
ingreso total total
revenue

ingresos (mpl)
income or earnings
or salary
ingresos (mpl)
[entradas] receipts
ingresos (mpl)
[recaudación] take
(n) or money taken
ingresos brutos
gross earnings
ingresos de un
negocio takings
ingresos de ventas
sales revenue
ingresos invisibles
invisible earnings
ingresos libres de
impuestos non-
taxable income
ingresos netos net
receipts or net earn-
ings or net income
ingresos por publi-
cidad revenue from
advertising
ingresos por alquiler
rental income
iniciación (f)
induction
iniciado (m)
insider

inicial initial (adj) *or* starting (adj)

iniciar initiate *or* pioneer (v)

iniciar conversaciones initiate discussions

iniciativa (f) initiative

inicio (m) start (n)

injusto (-ta) unfair

inmediatamente immediately

inmediato (-ta) immediate *or* instant (adj) *or* prompt

inmovilizar capital lock up capital

innovación (f) innovation

innovador (-ra) innovator (n) *or* innovative (adj)

innovar innovate

inquietud (f) concern (n) *or* worry (n)

inquilino (-na) tenant *or* lessee *or* occupant

inquilino (-na) en posesión sitting tenant

inscribir [registrar] enter

inscribir (en un registro) register (v)

inscribir una compañía en un registro register a company

inscribirse [registrarse] register (v)

inscripción (f) registration

inscripción (f) [entrada] entering

insignificante petty *or* negligible

insistir en hold out for

insolvencia (f) insolvency *or* bankruptcy

insolvente insolvent *or* bankrupt

inspección (f) inspection *or* survey (n)

inspección aduanera customs examination

inspección de daños damage survey

inspeccionar inspect *or* survey (v)

inspector (-ra) inspector *or* controller
inspector (-ra) de calidad quality controller
inspector (-ra) de fábrica factory inspector
inspector (-ra) de Hacienda tax inspector
inspector (-ra) de obra surveyor
inspector (-ra) del IVA VAT inspector
instalaciones (fpl) facilities
instalaciones de almacenaje storage facilities
instalaciones portuarias harbour facilities
instalar la maquinaria en una fábrica tool up (v)
instantáneo (-nea) instant (adj) *or* immediate
institución (f) institution

institución financiera financial institution
institucional institutional
instituir institute (v)
instituto (m) institute (n)
instrucción (f) instruction *or* directive
instrucciones (fpl) directions for use
instrucciones de envoi forwarding instructions or shipping instructions
instrumento (m) instrument *or* implement (n)
instrumento (m) [medio] medium (n)
instrumento negociable negotiable instrument
insuficiencia (f) insufficiency *or* shortfall
intangible intangible
integración (f) horizontal horizontal integration

integración vertical
vertical integration
**intensificar (el con-
trol)** tighten up on
intercambiable
exchangeable
intercambiar exch-
ange (v) or swap (v)
intercambio (m)
exchange (n)swap (n)
interés (m)
interest (n)
**interés (m) [atrac-
ción]** appeal (n) or
attraction
interés acumulado
accrued interest
interés acumulativo
cumulative interest
interés compuesto
compound interest
interés elevado
high interest
interés fijo fixed
interest
interés personal
vested interest
interés simple
simple interest
interesar
interest (v)

interesar [atraer]
appeal to (v) or
attract
**intereses (mpl)
creados** vested
interest
interfaz (m)
interface (n)
interino (-na)
temp (n)
**interino (-na) [en
funciones]**
acting (adj)
interior internal
interior [nacional]
domestic or
inland (GB)
intermediario (-ria)
intermediary or
middleman
**intermediario (-ria)
[agente]** broker
internacional
international
Internet (m)
Internet (n)
interno (-na) internal
**interno (-na) [de la
casa]** in-house
interpretar
interpret

intérprete (mf)
interpreter
interrumpir
discontinue
interrupción (f)
interruption *or*
breakdown (n)
intervención (f)
audit (n)
intervenir las
cuentas audit (v)
interventor (-ra)
auditor
introducción (f)
introduction
introducir introduce
introducir datos
input information
introducir gradual-
mente phase in
inundación (f)
flood (n)
inundar flood (v)
inundar el mercado
glut (v) *or* flood (v)
the market
invalidación (f)
invalidation
invalidar void (v)
or invalidate
invalidez (f)
invalidity

inválido (-da)
invalid *or* void (adj)
invariable uncha-
nged *or* constant
inventariar
inventory (v) *or*
take stock
inventario (m)
inventory *or* stock-
taking *or* stock list
inventario de posi-
ción (en almacén)
picking list
inversión (f)
investment
inversión (f) [revo-
cación] reversal
inversión: gastos
de inversion
capital expenditure
inversión segura
safe investment *or*
secure investment
inversión sin rlesgo
risk-free investment
inversiones de
interés fijo
fixed-interest
investments
inversiones en val-
ores seguros blue-
chip investments

**inversiones
exterlores** foreign
investments
inversionista (mf)
investor
inversor (-ra)
investor
**inversores (mpl)
institucionales**
institutional
investors
invertir invest
investigación (f)
investigation *or*
research (n)
**investigación (f)
[petición de
informes]** inquiry
**investigación de
conflictos** problem
solving or trou-
bleshooting
**investigación sobre
el consumo** con-
sumer research
**investigación y
desarrollo (I+D)**
research and devel-
opment (R & D)
investigador (-ra)
researcher *or*
research worker

investigar investi-
gate or research (v)
**investigar [perse-
guir]** follow up
invitación (f)
invitation
invitar invite
**IPC (índice de pre-
cios al consumo)**
consumer price
index
ir go
ir a la huelga
strike (v) *or* go on
strike
**ir de compras o de
tiendas** shopping
ir haciendo get
along
irregular irregular
**irregularidades
(fpl)** irregularities
irrevocable
irrevocable
irse leave (v)
itinerario (m)
itinerary
**IVA (impuesto
sobre el valor aña-
dido)** VAT (= value
added tax)
izquierdo (-da) left

Jj

jefe (adj) chief (adj)
jefe (-fa) manager
or head *or* boss
jefe ejecutivo chief
executive
**jefe (-fa) de
almacén** stock
controller
**jefe (-fa) de com-
pras** purchasing
manager
**jefe (-fa) de depar-
tamento *o* de sec-
ción** departmental
manager *or* head of
department
**jefe (-fa) de dis-
tribución** distribu-
tion manager
**jefe (-fa) de equipo
de ventas** field
sales manager
jefe (-fa) de oficina
chief clerk
**jefe (-fa) de publi-
cidad** advertising
manager

**jefe (-fa) de per-
sonal** personnel
manager
jornada (f) day *or*
working day
joven young
joven: más joven
junior *or* younger
jubilación (f)
retirement
jubilarse retire
(from one's job)
judicial legal
juego (m) game *or*
set (n)
**juego completo en
caja de presen-
tación** boxed set
juez (mf) judge (n)
juicio (m) lawsuit
or court case *or* trial
**juicio (m) [senten-
cia]** judgement *or*
judgment
**junta (f) de direc-
tores** management
or managers
junta directiva
board of directors
junta general
general meeting

junta general anual annual general meeting (AGM)
juntar join (v)
jurídico (-ca) legal
jurisdicción (f) jurisdiction
justificar justify *or* warrant (v)
justificar [respon-der] account for
justo (-ta) fair (adj)
juzgar judge (v)

Kk

kilo (m) o kilo-gramo (m) kilo *or* kilogram
kilometraje (m) distance *or* mileage (allowance)

Ll

laboral occupa-tional *or* labour
lado (m) side
laguna (f) fiscal tax loophole
lanzamiento (m) launch (n) *or* launching
lanzamiento float (n) *or* flotation (of company)
lanzamiento de una socledad floating of a company
lanzar launch (v)
lanzar al mercado bring out
largo (-ga) long
largo plazo long-term
largo plazo: a largo plazo long-range
leasing (m) leasing
legal legal *or* lawful *or* statutory
legalizar authenticate

legible por orde-nador computer-readable

legislación (f) legislation

legítimo (-ma) rightful

lenguaje (m) buro-crático officialese

lenguaje de progra-mación programming language

lenguaje infor-mático _o_ de orde-nador computer language

lento (-ta) slow

letra (f) handwriting

letra (f) [bancaria] bill (n) _or_ draft

letra a largo plazo long-dated bill

letra al propio cargo note of hand _or_ promissory note

letra bancaria bank bill (GB)

letra de cambio bill of exchange

letras (fpl) a cobrar bills receivable

letras a corto vencimiento short-dated bills

letras a pagar bills payable

letras por cobrar bills for collection

letrero (m) notice _or_ sign (n)

levantar lift (v) _or_ remove

levantar acta minute (v)

levantar un embargo lift an embargo

levantar una sesión close a meeting

ley (f) law

ley de la oferta y la demanda law of supply and demand

ley de prescripción statute of limitations

ley de rendimien-tos decrecientes law of diminishing returns

ley de sociedades anómimas company law

liberación (f)
release (n)
liberalización (f)
liberalization *or*
deregulation
liberalizar libera-
lize *or* decontrol
liberar free (v) *or*
release (v)
libra (f) pound
libra esterlina
pound sterling
librado (-da)
drawee
librador (-ra)
drawer
libramiento (m)
order (n)
libre free (adj) *or*
vacant
libre [franco]
franco
libre cambio o**libre
comercio** free trade
**libre de derechos de
aduana** free of duty
libre de impuestos
duty-free *or* free of
tax *or* tax-free
**libre: de libre dedica-
ción** freelance (adj)

**libreta (f) de ahor-
ros** bank book
libro (m) book (n)
libro de caja
cash book
libro de pedidos
order book
libro de registro
register (n)
libro de ventas
sales book
**libro diario [con-
tabilidad]** journal
or accounts book
libro mayor ledger
**libro mayor de
compras** purchase
ledger *or* bought
ledger
**libro mayor de
resultados** nominal
ledger
**libro mayor de ven-
tas** sales ledger
**libro registro de
accionistas** register
of shareholders
licencia (f) licence
or permit
**licencia (f) [autor-
ización]** licensing

**licencia de export-
ación** export licence
or export permit
**licencia de
importación** import
licence *or* import
permit
**licencia por materni-
dad** maternity leave
**licenciado (-da) en
practices** graduate
trainee
licitación (f)
bidding (n)
licitador (m)
tenderer *or* bidder
**licitar para un con-
trato** tender for a
contract
lícito (-ta) lawful
or legal
**líder (m) del mer-
cado** market leader
limitación (f) limi-
tation *or* restriction
limitado (-da)
limited
limitar limit (v) *or*
restrict
limitar el crédito
restrict credit

límite (m) limit (n)
límite de crédito
credit limit *or*
lending limit
**límite de descu-
bierto bancario**
overdraft facility
límite de precios
price ceiling
línea (f) line (n)
línea aérea airline
línea de carga
load line
línea de productos
product line
línea exterior
outside line
**línea ocupada
[teléfono]** engaged
línea telefónica
telephone line
línea de flotación
load line
liquidación (f)
liquidation *or*
winding up
**liquidación (f)
[rebajas]** sale (n)
**liquidación de una
deuda** clearing (of
a debt)

liquidación de activo realization of assets
liquidación de inventario stocktaking sale
liquidación forzosa compulsory liquidation
liquidación total por cierre closing-down sale
liquidación voluntaria voluntary liquidation
liquidar sell off
liquidar existencias clear (v) or liquidate stock
liquidar propiedades realize property
liquidar una compañía liquidate a company
liquidar una cuenta settle an account
liquidar una deuda clear a debt
liquidar una sociedad wind up a company

liquidez (f) liquidity
lira (f) lira
lista (f) list (n)
lista de bultos packing list or packing slip
lista de contenidos packing list or packing slip
lista de correos poste restante
lista de destinatarios mailing list
lista de direcciones address list
lista de existencias stocklist
lista de precios price list or scale of charges
lista de precios fija fixed scale of charges
lista del contenido de un paquete docket
lista negra black list (n)
listado (m) de ordenador computer listing
listo (-ta) ready
litro (m) litre

llamada (f)
(phone) call
**llamada a cobro
revertido** reverse
charge call *or* collect
call (US)
llamada de fuera
incoming call
**llamada interna-
cional** interna-
tional call
llamada local
local call
llamada rutinaria
routine call
llamada telefónica
phone call *or*
telephone call
**llamadas interna-
cionales directas**
international direct
dialling
**llamar (por
teléfono)** call (v)
or phone (v) *or*
telephone (v)
**llamar a cobro
revertido** reverse
the charges
llave (f) key
llegada (f) arrival

llegadas (fpl)
arrivals
llegar arrive *or*
reach
**llegar: que está por
llegar** due
llegar a un acuerdo
reach an agreement
llegar al máximo
peak (v)
llenar fill (a gap)
lleno (-na) full
llevar take (v) *or*
carry *or* transport (v)
llevar [dirigir] run
(v) *or* manage
llevar [producir]
bear (v)
**llevar a alguien
ante los tribunales**
take someone to
court
**llevar negocia-
ciones** conduct
negotiations
**llevar un
negocio** carry on a
business
local local (adj)
local (m) [edificio]
premises

local comercial
business premises
local de exposición
(exhibition) stand
local sin vivienda
incorporada
lock-up premises
logotipo (m) logo
lonja (f)
commodity market
or commodity
exchange
lote (m) batch (n)
or lot
lucrativo (-va)
money-making *or*
profit-making *or*
profitable
lugar (m) place (n)
or site *or* venue *or*
spot
lugar de trabajo
place of work
lugar de reunión
meeting place

Mm

macroeconomía (f)
macro-economics
magistratura (f)
del trabajo
industrial tribunal
mal equipado (-da)
underequipped
mal pagado (-da)
underpaid
mala adminis-
tración (f)
maladministration
or mismanagement
mala calidad (f)
poor quality
mala compra (f)
bad buy
malentendido (m)
misunderstanding
maleta (f) case (n)
or suitcase
maletas (fpl)
baggage *or*
luggage
maletín (m)
briefcase
malgastar waste (v)

malversación (f)
misappropriation *or*
embezzlement
malversador (-ra)
embezzler
malversar
misappropriate
or embezzle
mandante (m)
principal (n)
mandar por correo
post (v) *or* mail (v)
mandar trabajo
fuera farm
out work
mandato (m)
mandate *or* writ
mandato (m)
[campo de apli-
cación] terms of
reference
mandato (m)
[periodo] tenure
mando (m)
control (n)
mando a distancia
remote control
mandos (mpl)
intermedios middle
management
manejable
manageable

manejar handle (v)
or manage *or* operate
manejo (m) handling
manejo: de fácil
manejo user-friendly
manejo de materi-
ales materials
handling
manera (f) means
or ways
manifiesto (m)
manifest
manipulación (f)
handling
mano: de segunda
mano secondhand
mano: en manos de
los tribunales sub
judice
mano: escrito a
mano handwritten
mano (f) de obra
manpower *or* work-
force *or* labour force
mano de obra
barata cheap labour
mano de obra cuali-
ficada skilled labour
mano de obra local
local labour
mantener maintain
or keep up

mantenimiento (m)
maintenance
mantenimiento de
relaciones mainte-
nance of contacts
mantenimiento de
suministros main-
tenance of supplies
manual (adj)
manual (adj)
manual (m)
manual (n)
manual de
funcionamiento
operating manual
manual de
mantenimiento
service manual
manufacturar
manufacture (v)
manzana (f)
[edificios] block (n)
maqueta (f) mock-
up *or* model (n)
máquina (f) machine
máquina de cambio
change machine
máquina
franqueadora
franking machine
maquinaria (f) plant
(n) *or* machinery

maquinaria pesada
heavy machinery
maquinista (mf)
machinist *or*
operator
marca (f) brand
marca (f) [señal]
mark (n)
marca comercial
trademark *or* trade
name *or* brand name
marca registrada
registered trademark
marcador (m)
marker pen
marcar mark (v)
marcar [teléfono]
dial (v)
marcar directa-
mente dial direct
marcar un número
dial a number
marcha (f)
progress (n)
marcha: en marcha
going
marcharse leave
(v) *or* go away
marco (m) frame (n)
marco alemán
mark (n) *or*
Deutschmark

margen (m) margin
**margen de bene-
ficio** profit margin
or mark-up
**margen de
beneficio bruto**
gross margin
**margen de cober-
tura** backwardation
margen de error
margin of error
margen neto net
margin
marginal marginal
marina (f) mercante
merchant navy
marino (-na)
marine
marítimo (-ma)
maritime
más more *or* plus
masa (f) mass
**master (m) en
administración de
empresas** Master's
degree in Business
Administration
(MBA)
**material (m) de
embalaje** packag-
ing material

**material de exposi-
ción** display material
medio (-dia)
[mitad]
**materias (fpl) pri-
mas** raw materials
matrícula (f)
registration (fee)
**matriz (f) [de un
talonario]** counter-
foil *or* cheque stub
maximización (f)
maximization
maximizar maximize
máximo (m)
maximum (n)
máximo (-ma)
maximum (adj)
**mayor [impor-
tante]** major
**mayor
[principal]** main
mayor [superior]
senior
mayoría (f)
majority
mayorista (mf)
wholesale dealer *or*
wholesaler
mechera (f)
shoplifter

media (f) mean (n)
media ponderada
weighted average
media docena (f)
half a dozen *or* a
half-dozen
mediación (f)
mediation
mediador (-ra)
mediator
mediador de con-
flictos problem
solver *or* trouble-
shooter
mediana (f) median
mediano (-na)
medium *or* medium-
sized *or* average (adj)
mediar mediate
medición (f) de la
rentabilidad
measurement of
profitability
medida (f) de
tiempo timing
medida de volumen
o de capacidad
cubic measure
medida: hecho a la
medida custom-
built or custom-made

medidas (fpl)
measures *or*
measurements
medidas de
precaución safety
precautions
medidas de
seguridad safety
measures
medidas de
seguridad (en una
oficina) office
security
medidas fiscales
fiscal measures
medio (m)
medium (n)
medio (m)
[manera] means
medio (-dia)
[mitad] half (adj)
medio (-dia) mean
(adj) *or* average (adj)
or medium (adj)
mediocre mediocre
or low-quality
medios (mpl)
[instalaciones]
facilities
medios (mpl)
[recursos] means

**medios de comuni-
cación** mass media
**medios de trans-
porte** transport
facilities
**medios fraudulen-
tos** false pretences
mejor (el, la) best
mejor postor
highest bidder
mejora (f) upturn
or improvement
mejorar recover *or*
get better
memorandum (m)
memo *or* memo-
randum
memoria (f)
(computer) memory
**memoria (f) [info-
rme]** report (n)
mencionar mention
or refer to
menor junior (adj)
or younger
menos minus *or* less
menos de under *or*
less than
**menos de lo necesa-
rio [escaso]** short of

mensaje (m)
message
mensajero (-ra)
messenger *or* courier
mensual
monthly (adj)
mensualmente
monthly (adv)
mercadeo (m)
merchandizing
mercado (m)
market (n) *or*
marketplace
**mercado (m)
[salida]** outlet
mercado a futuros
forward market
mercado alcista
bull market
mercado bajista
bear market
mercado cautivo
captive market
mercado cerrado
closed market
**Mercado Común
Europeo** Common
Market
**mercado de compra-
dores** buyer's market

mercado de divisas foreign exchange market

mercado de valores stock market

mercado de vende-dores seller's market

mercado débil weak market

mercado interior home market *or* domestic market

mercado libre open market

mercado limitado limited market

mercado mundial world market

mercado nacional home market *or* domestic market

mercado negro black market

mercado potencial potential market

mercado previsto target market

Mercado Unico Europeo Single European Market

mercados (mpl) extranjeros over-seas markets

mercados monetar-ios money markets

mercadotecnia (f) marketing

mercancía (f) commodity

mercancías (fpl) goods *or* merchandise (n)

mercancías a precio reducido cut-price goods

mercancías con impuestos adu-aneros pagados duty-paid goods

mercancías dañadas por un incendio fire-damaged goods

mercancías en tránsito goods in transit

mérito (m) merit

mermas (fpl) leakage

mes (m) month

mes: del presente mes instant (adj)

mes civil calendar month

mesa (f) de despacho desk

meta (f) target (n)

mezclado (-da) mixed

microeconomía (f) micro-economics

microordenador (m) microcomputer

miembro (m) member

miembros: los miembros membership

mil millones (mpl) billion

millón (m) million

millonario (-ria) millionaire

mínimo (m) low (n) or minimum (n)

mínimo (-ma) minimum (adj)

ministerio (m) (government) department

ministerio (m) de Hacienda Exchequer

ministro (m) del gobierno secretary or government minister

minoría (f) minority

minorista (mf) retail dealer or retailer

minusvalías (fpl) capital loss

minuto (m) minute (n)

misceláneo (-nea) miscellaneous

misión (f) comercial trade mission

mitad (f) half (n)

mitad de precio half-price sale

mixto (-ta) mixed

modelo (m) model (n) or standard (n)

modelo a escala model (n) or mock-up

modelo de prueba demonstration model

modelo económico economic model

modem (m) modem

moderado (-da)
moderate (adj)
moderar
moderate (v)
moderno (-na)
modern *or* up to date
moderno: muy
moderno state-of-
the-art
modificación (f)
alteration
modificar alter
modo (m) mode
modo de empleo
directions for use
modo de pago
mode of payment
moneda (f) coin *or*
currency
moneda bloqueada
blocked currency
moneda convertible
convertible currency
or hard currency
moneda de curso
legal legal currency
or legal tender
moneda débil soft
currency
moneda estable
stable currency

moneda extranjera
foreign currency
moneda fuerte
strong currency
moneda infla-
cionista inflated
currency
moneda suelta
change (n) *or* small
change
monetario (-ria)
monetary
monopolio (m) mon-
opoly *or* corner (n)
monopolio absoluto
absolute monopoly
monopolización (f)
monopolization
monopolizar
monopolize
montacargas (m)
goods elevator
montaje (m)
assembly
moratoria (f)
moratorium
moroso ([extra
charge] slow
payer
mostrador (m)
counter

mostrador de facturación check-in counter

mostrar (el funcionamiento de algo) demonstrate

mostrar show (v)

mostrar un beneficio show a profit

motivación (f) motivation

motivado (-da) motivated

motor (m) drive (n)

movilidad (f) mobility

movilizar mobilize

movilizar capital mobilize capital

movimiento (m) movement

movimientos (mpl) de capital movements of capital

movimientos de existencias stock movements

mudanza (f) move or removal

mudar(se) move (house, office)

muebles (mpl) accesorios fittings

muebles de oficina office furniture

muelle (m) quay or dock (n) or wharf

muerto (-ta) dead (adj)

muestra (f) (trial) sample

muestra aleatoria random sample

muestra de inspección check sample

muestra gratuita free sample

muestra pequeña swatch

muestreo (m) sample or sampling

muestreo aleatorio random sampling

muestreo de aceptación acceptance sampling

muestreo por áreas sampling

mujer (f) de negocios businesswoman

multa (f) fine (n)

multar fine (v)
multicopista (f)
copying machine
multilateral
multilateral
multinacional (f)
multinational (n)
múltiple
multiple (adj)
multiplicación (f)
multiplication
multiplicar multiply
multitud (f) crowd
or multitude *or*
mass of people
mundial
worldwide (adj)
mundialmente
worldwide (adv)
mundo (m) world
mutua (f) de
seguros mutual
(insurance) company
mutuo (-tua)
mutual (adj)
muy cualificado
(-da) o muy
capacitado (-da)
highly qualified

Nn

nación (f) más
favorecida most-
favoured nation
nacional national
or domestic
nacional: de ámbito
nacional
nationwide
nacionalización (f)
nationalization
nada (f) nothing
naufragar wreck (v)
naufragio (m)
wreck (n)
nave (f) de carga
loading bay
necesario (-ria)
necessary
necesidad (f) need
necesitar need (v)
negar(se) refuse (v)
negarse a cumplir
un acuerdo repudi-
ate an agreement
negarse a pagar
dishonour
negativa (f) refusal

negligencia (f)
negligence
negociable negotiable
negociación (f)
bargaining *or*
negotiation
negociaciones (fpl)
conjuntas joint
discussions
negociaciones
salariales wage
negotiations
negociador (-ra)
negotiator
negociar negotiate
(v) *or* bargain (v)
negociar en
deal in (v)
negocio (m)
bargain (n) *or* deal (n)
negocio (m)
[empresa] busi-
ness *or* concern (n)
negocio descuidado
neglected business
negocio deshonesto
(pero no ilegal)
sharp practice
negocio duro hard
bargain *or* hard
bargaining

negocio ilícito
racketeering
negocio suplemen-
tario sideline
negocios (mpl)
business
negocios: por asun-
tos de negocios on
business
neto (-ta) net (adj)
nivel (m) level
nivel: de bajo nivel
low-level
nivel de existen-
cias stock level
nivelarse level off
or level out
niveles (mpl) de
dotación de
personal manning
levels
niveles de salarios
wage levels
noche (f) night
nombramiento (m)
appointment
nombramiento de
administrador
judicial letters of
administration
nombrar appoint

**nombrar por coop-
ción** co-opt someone
nombre (m) name
**nombre: en nombre
de** on behalf of
**nombre (m) com-
ercial** brand name
or trademark or
trade name
norma (f) norm or
standard (n)
norma (f) [regla]
rule (n)
normal [estándar]
normal or standard
(adj)
normal [corriente]
regular or usual
normalización (f)
standardization
normalizar
standardize
normas (fpl)
regulations
normas de conducta
code of practice
**normas de produc-
ción** production
standards
normas de seguridad
safety regulations

nota (f) note (n)
nota de abono
credit note
nota de adeudo
debit note
nota de aviso
advice note
nota de cobertura
cover note
nota de crédito
credit note
**nota de envío o de
expedición**
shipping note or
consignment note
or dispatch note
notable outstand-
ing or exceptional
notario (m) notary
public
noticia (f) news
or item
notificación (f)
notice (n) or
notification
**notificación de
despido o de
dimisión** notice
**notificación de
renovación**
renewal notice

notificar notify
novedad (f) novelty
or (new)departure
**nuevo nom-
bramiento (m)**
reappointment
nuevo pedido (m)
reorder (n)
nulo (-la) null
or void
numerar number (v)
numérico (-ca)
numeric *or* numerical
número (m)
number (n)
**número (m)
[ejemplar]** copy
(n) *or* issue (n)
**número de
apartado de
correos** box number
número de cheque
cheque number
**número de cuenta
del Girobank** giro
account number
número de factura
invoice number

**número de llamada
gratuita** toll free
number (US)
número de lote
batch number
número de pedido
order number
**número de
referencia**
reference number
**número de registro
o número de
matrícula**
registration
number
número de serie
serial number
número de teléfono
phone number *or*
telephone number
**números (mpl)
impares** odd
numbers

Oo

obedecer obey *or* comply with

objetivo (m) objective (n) *or* target (n) *or* aim (n)

objetivo: cumplir un objetivo meet a target

objetivo: no cumplir un objetivo miss a target

objetivo de producción production targets

objetivo de ventas sales target

objetivos (mpl) a largo plazo long-term objectives

objeto (m) de una OPA takeover target

objetos (mpl) salvados salvage (n)

obligación (f) obligation *or* duty

obligación perpetua irredeemable bond

obligación redimible callable bond

obligaciones (fpl) loan stock

obligaciones (fpl) [responsabilidades] responsibilities

obligaciones a corto plazo current liabilities

obligacionista (mf) debenture holder

obligatorio (-ria) compulsory *or* binding

obrero (m) workman *or* (manual)worker

obreros (mpl) cualificados skilled workers

obreros semicualificados semi-skilled workers

obsequiar give *or* present (v)

obsequio (m) (free) gift *or* present (n)

obsequio publicitario premium offer

obsolescencia (f)
obsolescence
obsolescente
obsolescent
obsoleto (-ta)
obsolete
obtener obtain *or* get
**obtener beneficios
brutos** gross (v)
**obtener beneficios
netos** net (v)
obtener el título de
qualify as
**obtener la libertad
de alguien bajo fia-
nza** bail someone out
**ocupación (f)
[empleo]** occupa-
tion *or* employment
**ocupación (f)
[posesión]** tenure
or occupancy
**ocupación tempo-
ral** temporary
employment
ocupado (-da) busy
or engaged
ocupante (mf)
occupant *or* occupier
ocupar un vacío
fill a gap

ocuparse de
attend to
oferta (f) offer (n)
oferta (f) [puja]
bid (n)
**oferta (f) [sumin-
istro]** supply (n)
**oferta (f) [tra-
bajo]** tendering *or*
tender
**oferta de adquisi-
ción disputada o
rebatida** contested
takeover
**oferta de
lanzamiento**
introductory offer
oferta de ocasión
bargain offer
oferta de venta
offer for sale
oferta en metálico
cash offer
oferta especial
special offer
oferta final
closing bid
oferta inicial
opening bid
oferta monetaria
money supply

oferta pública de adquisición (OPA) takeover bid
oferta y demanda supply and demand
ofertas (fpl) bidding
ofertas de trabajo appointments vacant *or* situations vacant
ofertas lacradas sealed tenders
oficial official (adj)
oficial: no oficial unofficial
oficina (f) office
oficina: de oficina clerical
oficina central head office
oficina central de correos general post offfice
oficina de colocación employment agency *or* employment bureau
oficina de distribución modificable open-plan office

oficina de expedición dispatch department
oficina de información information bureau
oficina de informática computerbureau
oficina de reclamaciones complaints department
oficina del registro civil registry office
oficina general general office
oficina principal main office
oficinas (fpl) de alquiler offices to let
oficinista (mf) clerk
oficioso (-sa) unofficial
ofrecer offer (v)
OIT (Organización Internacional del Trabajo) ILO (=International Labour Organization)

omisión (f) omission
omitir omit
**opción (f) de
compra** option to
purchase
opcional optional
**OPEP (Organización
de los Países
Exportadores de
Petróleo)** OPEC
(= Organization of
Petroleum Exporting
Countries)
operación (f) oper-
ation *or* transaction
operación al contado
cash transaction
**operación en multi-
ples divisas** multi-
currency operation
**operación fraudu-
lenta** fraudulent
transaction
**operación llaves
en mano** turnkey
operation
operacional
operational
**operaciones (fpl) en
bolsa** dealing (on
the Stock Exchange)

**operador (-ra) de
cambios** foreign
exchange broker *or*
foreign exchange
dealer
**operador (-ra) de
teclado** keyboarder
operario (-ria)
operator *or* worker
operativo (-va)
operative (adj)
opinión (f) pública
public opinion
oportunamente duly
oportunidad (f)
opportunity
**oportunidades de
mercado** market
opportunities
optar [decidir]
decide
**optar por una línea
de conducta** decide
on a course of action
optativo (-va)
optional
orden (mf) order (n)
orden (f) [mandato]
writ *or* warrant (n)
**orden (f) de com-
pra** purchase order

orden (f) de domiciliación (bancaria) banker's order
orden (f) de expedición delivery order
orden (f) de pago bank mandate *or* money order
orden (m) alfabético alphabetical order
orden (m) cronológico chronological order
orden (m) del día agenda
ordenador (m) computer
ordenador (m) personal personal computer (PC)
ordenar order (v) *or* arrange *or* put in order
ordinario (-ria) ordinary *or* regular
organigrama (m) organization chart *or* flow chart
organismo (m) organization
organismo paraestatal quango
organización (f) organization
organización lineal line organization
Organización de los Países Exportadores de Petróleo (OPEP) Organization of Petroleum Exporting Countries (OPEC)
Organización Internacional del Trabajo (OIT) International Labour Organization (ILO)
organización y métodos organization and methods
organizar organize *or* arrange
organizativo (-va) organizational
órgano (m) administrativo administrative body or authority
órgano decisorio decision-making body

órganos (mpl) de gestión managerial posts

origen (m) origin

original

original (adj)

oro (m) en lingotes bullion

oscilación (f) fluctuation

oscilar [fluctuar] fluctuate

oscilar [variar] range (v)

otorgar grant (v) *or* award (v)

Pp

pactar [convenir] covenant (v)

pacto (m) covenant (n) *or* agreement (n)

padrino (m) sponsor (n)

paga (f) pay (n)

paga de vacaciones holiday pay

paga extraordinaria de Navidad Christmas bonus

pagadero (-ra) payable

pagadero a la entrega payable on delivery

pagadero a la vista payable on demand

pagadero a sesenta días payable at sixty days

pagadero por adelantado payable in advance

pagado (-da) paid

pagado: muy bien pagado highly-paid

pagado (-da) por adelantado prepaid

pagador (-ra) payer

pagar pay (v) or pay out

pagar: sin pagar unpaid

pagar (costes) bear (v) (costs)

pagar [devolver]
repay
pagar a plazos pay
in instalments
**pagar al contado o
en efectivo**
pay cash
pagar con cheque
pay by cheque
**pagar con tarjeta
de crédito** pay by
credit card
pagar intereses
pay interest
**pagar la cuenta y
marcharse**
check out
**pagar los intereses
de una deuda**
service a debt
**pagar por adelan-
tado** prepay or pay
in advance
pagar una cuenta
pay a bill
pagar una deuda
discharge a debt or
redeem a debt
pagar una factura
pay an invoice or
settle an invoice

**pagar una recla-
mación** settle a
claim
pagaré (m) accom-
modation bill or
promissory note or
note of hand
pagaré (m) [vale]
IOU (= I owe you)
**pagaré (m) de inte-
rés fijo** debenture
**páginas (fpl) amar-
illas** yellow pages
pago (m) payment
or repayment
**pago (m) [de una
deuda]** discharge (n)
**pago (m) [finiq-
uito]** settlement
pago a cuenta
interim payment or
payment on account
pago a destajo
payment by results
pago al contado
cash terms or
spot cash
pago anticipado
advance payment
pago anual yearly
payment

pago aplazado
deferred payment
pago atrasado back
payment
pago en efectivo
cash payment *or*
payment in cash
pago en especie
payment in kind
pago en exceso
overpayment
pago en metálico
payment in cash
pago íntegro full
payment
**pago mediante
cheque** payment by
cheque
pago mínimo
minimum payment
pago parcial partial
payment
**pago por adelan-
tado** prepayment *or*
money up front
pago simbólico
token payment
**pago total de una
deuda** full
discharge of a debt

pago único lump sum
**pagos (mpl) a
cuenta** progress
payments
pagos de la hipoteca
mortgage payments
pagos mensuales
monthly payments
pagos por etapas
staged payments
pagos semestrales
half-yearly payment
país (m) country *or*
state
país de origen
country of origin
**país en vías de
desarrollo**
developing country
**países (mpl) expor-
tadores de petróleo**
oil-exporting
countries
**países productores
de petróleo**
oil-producing
countries
**países subdesar-
rollados** underde-
veloped countries

palabras (fpl) de agradecimiento speech of thanks
paleta (f) pallet
panel (m) panel
pantalla (f) monitor (n) or screen
papel (m) carbón carbon paper
papel carbón: sin papel carbón carbonless
papel continuo continuous stationery
papel de envolver wrapping paper
papel de estraza brown paper
papel reciclado recycled paper
papeleo (m) paperwork
papeleo (m) [burocracia] red tape
papeles (mpl) [documentos] papers
paquete (m) parcel (n) or pack (n) or packet

paquete (m) [acciones] block (n) (of shares)
paquete de cigarrillos packet of cigarettes
paquete de sobres pack of envelopes
par par
parada (f) stop (n)
parado (-da) unemployed
paraíso (m) fiscal tax haven
parar stop (v) or check (v)
parar: sin parar non-stop
parecer appear or seem
paridad (f) parity
paro (m) stoppage or stopping
paro (m) [desempleo] unemployment
paro estructural structural unemployment
paro técnico work-to-rule

parte (f) part or party

parte (f) [proporción] proportion

parte acusadora prosecution

parte contratante contracting party

parte superior top (n)

parte (m) de baja doctor's certificate

participación (f) share (n)

participación de beneficios equity

participación en los beneficios profit-sharing

particular private

partida (f) batch (n)

partida (f) [de un balance] item (n)

partidas (fpl) excepcionales exceptional items *or* extraordinary items

pasado (-da) de moda old-fashioned

pasaje (m) fare

pasaje sencillo one-way fare

pasante (mf) junior clerk

pasar [tiempo] spend

pasar a cuenta nueva carry over a balance or carry forward

pasar información a un fichero card-index (v)

pasar modelos model (v)

pasar por la criba screen (v)

pasarse a switch over to

pasivo (m) liabilities

pasivo a largo plazo long-term liabilities

pasivo circulante current liabilities

paso (m) de información a un fichero card-indexing

patentado (-da) patented

patentar un invento patent an invention
patente (f) patent
patente de invención letters patent
patente solicitada o **patente en tramitación** patent applied for *or* patent pending
patrimonio (m) capital *or* net worth *or* heritage
patrocinado (-da) por el Estado government-sponsored
patrocinador (-ra) sponsor (n)
patrocinar sponsor (v)
patrocinio (m) sponsorship
patrón (m) standard (n)
peaje (m) toll
pedido (m) order (n)
pedido (-da) on order
pedido cursado al representante comercial journey order

pedido no servido o **por servir** unfulfilled order
pedido por correo mail-orde
pedido suplementario repeat order
pedido urgente rush order
pedidos (mpl) pendientes back orders *or* outstanding orders
pedidos (mpl) por servir dues *or* back orders
pedir ask *or* ask for
pedir [solicitar] request (v)
pedir información inquire (v)
pedir más detalles ask for further details *or* particulars
pedir perdón apologize (v)
pedir prestado borrow (v)
peligro (m) de incendio fire risk

pena (f) penalty
penalizar penalize (v)
pendiente out-
standing *or* pending
**penetración (f) en
el mercado** market
penetration
**penetrar un mer-
cado** penetrate a
market
pensión (f) pension
pequeño (-ña) small
**pequeñas empresas
(fpl)** small busi-
nesses
**pequeño empre-
sario (m)** small
businessman
pequeño hurto (m)
pilferage *or* pilfering
**pequeños
accionistas (mpl)**
minor shareholders
per [a, por] per
per cápita per capita
perder lose
(something)
**perder [tren,
avión]** miss (v)
perder dinero lose
money

perder un depósito
forfeit a deposit
perder un pedido
lose an order
perder valor depre-
ciate *or* lose value
pérdida (f) loss *or*
wastage
**pérdida de
clientela** loss of
customers
pérdida de ejercicio
trading loss
**pérdida de
trabajadores por
jubilación** natural
wastage
**pérdida de un
pedido** loss of an
order
pérdida de valor
depreciation *or* loss
of value
pérdida neta net loss
pérdida parcial
partial loss
**pérdida sobre el
papel** paper loss
pérdida total
write-off *or*
dead loss

pérdidas (fpl)
leakage
pérdidas de capital
capital loss
perecedero (-ra)
perishable
pericia (f) expertise
periféricos (mpl)
peripherals
periódico (m)
newspaper
periódico (-ca)
periodic *or*
periodical (adj)
periodo (m) period
**periodo de conser-
vación de un pro-
ducto** shelf life of a
product
periodo de preaviso
period of notice
periodo de prueba
probation *or* trial
period
**periodo de reembo-
lso** payback period
periodo de reflexión
cooling off period
periodo de validez
period of validity
permanecer stay (v)

permanencia (f)
stay (n)
permiso (m) per-
mit (n) *or* permis-
sion *or* leave (n)
**permiso de
exportación** export
licence *or* export
permit
**permiso de resi-
dencia** residence
permit
permiso de trabajo
work permit
permitir permit *or*
allow
permitirse un gasto
afford
perseguir chase *or*
follow up
**persona: por per-
sona** per head
**persona (f) autor-
izada** licensee
**persona dedicada a
las relaciones
públicas** public
relations man
personal personal
personal (m) per-
sonnel *or* staff (n)

personal adminis-trativo office staff *or* managerial staff

personal clave key personnel *or* key staff

personal de aten-ción al público counter staff

personal de oficina clerical staff

personal de ventas sales force *or* sales people

personal de ventas muy motivado highly motivated sales staff

personal del hotel hotel staff

personal eventual temporary staff

personal fijo regular staff

personal reducido al mínimo skeleton staff

personalidad (f) jurídica legal status

perspectivas (fpl) prospects

pertenecer belong to

pertinente relevant

pesado (-da) heavy

pesar weigh

pesar en exceso be overweight

peso (m) weight

peso (m) [mon-eda] peso

peso bruto gross weight

peso escaso false weight

peso máximo weight limit

peso muerto deadweight

peso neto net weight

petición (f) request (n)

petición: a petición on request

petición de informes inquiry

petición de informes sobre crédito status inquiry

petición de pago (de acciones) call (n)

petróleo (m) oil

petrolero (m)
oil tanker
PIB (Producto Interior
Bruto) GDP (= gross
domestic product)
pieza (f) piece
pieza de recambio *o*
pieza de repuesto
spare part
piloto (mf) pilot (n)
pionero (-ra)
pioneer (n)
piso (m) floor
piso (m) [aparta-
mento] flat (n) or
appartment (US)
plan (m) plan (n) or
project (n)
plan (m) [sistema]
arrangement
plan de emergencia
contingency plan
plan de pensiones
pension scheme
plan de trabajo de
una empresa
corporate plan
plan general
overall plan
plan periódica-
mente actualizado
rolling plan

plan remunerativo
money-making plan
planear plan (v)
planes de contin-
gencia standby
arrangements
planificación (f)
planning
planificación a
largo plazo
long-term planning
planificación de la
mano de obra
manpower planning
planificación
económica
economic planning
planificación
empresarial
corporate planning
planificación
estratégica
strategic planning
planificador (-ra)
planner
planificar plan (v)
planificar las inver-
siones plan investments
plano (m) plan (n)
or drawing (n)
planta (f)
floor plan

planta (f) [fábrica]
plant (n) or
factory
plantear raise (v)
plantilla (f) staff or
establishment
**plata (f) en lin-
gotes** bullion
plaza (f) (job)
vacancy *or*
position (n)
**plaza (f) [mer-
cado]** market (n)
plaza del mercado
marketplace *or* square
plazo (m) term *or*
notice *or* instalment
plazo (m) [límite]
time limit
plazo (m)
[periodo] period
plazo: a plazo
forward
plazo de entrega
delivery time
plazo de espera
lead time
**plazo de tiempo lím-
ite** time limitation
plazo límite
deadline

plazo medio
medium-term
pleito (m) lawsuit
**plena: en plena
dedicación** full-time
**pluriempleado (-
da)** moonlighter
pluriempleo (m)
moonlighting
**plus (m) de
carestía de vida**
cost-of-living bonus
plusvalía (f)
capital gains
**PNB (Producto Naci-
onal Bruto)** GNP (=
gross national product)
poder (m) power
**poder (m) [procu-
ración]** proxy
poder adquisitivo
purchasing power *or*
spending power
**poder de
negociación**
bargaining power
**poder notarial *o*
poderes (mpl)**
power of attorney
poderhabiente (mf)
proxy

política (f) policy
política comercial de reciprocidad arancelaria fair trade
política crediticia credit policy
política de precios pricing policy
política de precios flexibles flexible pricing policy
política presupuestaria budgetary policy
póliza (f) de seguros insurance policy *or* assurance policy
póliza (f) a todo riesgo all-risks policy
póliza provisional cover note
ponderación (f) weighting
poner put (v) *or* place (v)
poner a la venta release (v)
poner al día update (v)
poner el sello stamp (v)

poner en contenedores containerize (v)
poner en la lista negra blacklist (v)
poner en libertad free (v)
poner en práctica un acuerdo implement an agreement
poner en una caja case (v) or put in a box
poner la dirección *o* las señas address (v) (a letter, a parcel)
poner las iniciales a initial (v)
poner por escrito put in writing
poner precio a price (v)
poner término a un acuerdo terminate an agreement
poner un negocio set up in business
popular popular
por via
porcentaje (m) percentage

porcentaje de aumento percentage increase

porcentaje de comisión cost plus

porcentaje de descuento percentage discount

porcentaje fijo flat rate

pormenores (mpl) particulars

portacontenedores container ship

portador (-ra) bearer or payee

portátil portable

porte (m) carriage or freight

porte debido carriage forward or freight forward

porte pagado carriage paid or postpaid or postage paid

poseedor (-ra) holder

poseer possess (v) or own (v)

posesión (f) possession or ownership or tenure

posfechar postdate

posibilidad (f) possibility

posibilidad de comparación comparability

posible possible

posible comprador (-ra) prospective buyer

posición (f) position or place (n)

posición (f) [status] status

positivo (-va) positive

posponer postpone or hold over

postal postal

postal (f) card or postcard

postor (m) bidder or tenderer

postura (f) position

postura (f) negociadora bargaining position

potencial potential (adj)

potencial (m) potential (n)

practicar el 'dumping' dump goods on a market
prácticas (fpl) comerciales justas fair dealing
prácticas restrictivas restrictive practices
práctico (-ca) handy
precauciones (fpl) safety precautions
precintar seal (v)
precinto (m) seal (n)
precinto de aduana customs seal
precio (m) price (n) or charge (n)
precio (m) [tarifa] rate (n) or tariff
precio: a precio reducido cut-price
precio a destajo piece rate
precio acordado o precio convenido agreed price
precio actual current price
precio al cierre closing price

precio al contado cash price
precio al detallista trade price
precio al por mayor wholesale price
precio al por menor retail price
precio competitivo competitive price
precio con entrega de artículo usado trade-in price
precio de apertura opening price
precio de catálogo list price or catalogue price
precio de compra purchase price
precio de conversión conversion price or conversion rate
precio de coste cost price
precio de descuento discount price
precio de entrada admission charge
precio de entrega delivered price

precio de entrega inmediata spot price

precio de fábrica factory price

precio de intervención intervention price

precio de mercado market price *or* market rate

precio de ocasión bargain price

precio de oferta offer price *or* supply price

precio de reventa resale price

precio de subvención supportprice

precio de transporte freight rates

precio de venta selling price

precio de venta recomendado manufacturer's recommended price (MRP)

precio del crudo odel petróleo oil price

precio en fábrica price ex works

precio en firme firm price

precio excesivo overcharge (n)

precio facturado invoice price

precio fijo set price

precio inicial starting price *or* upset price

precio irrisorio bargain price

precio justo fair price

precio máximo maximum price

precio máximo autorizado ceiling price

precio medio average price

precio mínimo aceptable reserve price

precio módico moderate price

precio neto net price

precio por unidad unit price

precio reducido cut price *or* reduced rate

precio simbólico token charge

precio sin des- cuento full price

precio todo incluido inclusive charge *or* all-in price

precio tope ceiling price

precio umbral threshold price

precio vigente going rate

precios (mpl) com- petitivos keen prices

precios estables stable prices

precios exagerados inflated prices

precios flexibles flexible prices

precios mínimos o precios de saldo knockdown prices

precios populares popular prices

precios reventados rock-bottom prices

precipitarse rush (v)

precisar specify

predecir forecast (v)

preempaquetar prepack *or* prepackage

preferencia (f) pref- erence or choice (n)

preferencial o pref- erente preferential

preferir prefer

prefijo (m) dialling code

prefinanciación (f) pre-financing

pregunta (f) question (n)

preguntar ask (v) *or* inquire (v) *or* question (v)

premio (m) award (n)

prensa (f) press (n)

preocupación (f) concern (n) *or* worry

preparación (f) de pedidos order processing

preparación de presupuestos budgeting

preparado (-da) ready

preparar train (v)

preparar [elaborar]
process (v)
preparar [redactar]
draw up
preparar un contrato draw up a contract
preparar un horario
timetable (v)
preparar una factura raise an invoice
prepararse train (v)
prescribir
prescribe (v)
preselección (f)
shortlist (n)
preseleccionar
shortlist (v)
presentación (f)
presentation *or* production
presentación (f) [introducción]
introduction
presentar present (v) *or* produce (v)
presentar [entregar] hand in
presentar [introducir] introduce

presentar [organizar] stage (v) *or* organize
presentar [petición, demanda] file (v) (a petition)
presentar excusas apologize
presentar una cuenta o una factura render an account
presentar una letra a la aceptación
present a bill for acceptance
presentar una letra al pago present a bill for payment
presentar una reconvención
counter-claim (v)
presentarse report (v) (to a place)
presentarse a una entrevista report for an interview
presente
present (adj)
presente: del presente mes instant

presidente (-ta) chairman

presidente y direc- tor gerente chairman and managing director

prestamista (mf) (money)lender

préstamo (m) borrowing *or* loan

préstamo a corto plazo short-term loan

préstamo a largo plazo long-term loan

préstamo a plazo fijo term loan

préstamo bancario bank loan

préstamo garanti- zado secured loan

préstamo sin interés soft loan

préstamos (mpl) bancarios bank borrowings

prestar lend (v) *or* loan (v)

prestatario (-ria) borrower *or* debtor

prestigio (m) prestige

presupuestar budget (v)

presupuestario (- ria) budgetary

presupuesto (m) budget (n)

presupuesto (m) [cotización] quote (n) *or* quotation *or* estimate

presupuesto de explotación opera- tional budget *or* operating budget

presupuesto de gastos generales overhead budget

presupuesto de promoción promotion budget

presupuesto de publicidad advertising budget

presupuesto de ventas sales budget

presupuesto del Estado (govern- ment) budget

presupuesto provi- sional provisional budget

presupuesto publicitario publicity budget

pretender [alegar] claim (v)

prevención (f) prevention

prevenir prevent or pre-empt

preventivo (-va) preventive

prever forecast (v) or foresee or anticipate

prever [estipular] provide for

previo (-via) previous or prior

previsión (f) forecast or forecasting

previsión a largo plazo long-term forecast

previsión de mano de obra manpower forecasting

previsión de mercado market forecast

previsión de ventas sales forecast

previsión provisional de ventas provisional forecast of sales

previsto (-ta) projected

prima (f) bonus (n)

prima al comisionista del credere

prima de incentivo incentive bonus or incentive payments

prima de productividad productivity bonus

prima de renovación renewal premium

prima de riesgo risk premium

prima de seguros (insurance) premium

prima por ausencia de siniestralidad no-claims bonus

primario (-ria) primary

primer trimestre first quarter

primera opción first option

primeras entradas, primeras salidas first in first out (FIFO)

primero (-ra) first

primero (-ra) [inicial] initial (adj)

primero (-ra) [principal] prime

principal principal (adj) *or* chief *or* main

principal (m) [capital] principal (n)

principio (m) principle

principio (m) [inicio] start (n)

prisa (f) rush (n)

privado (-da) private

privatización (f) privatization

privatizar privatize

privilegio (m) fiscal tax concession

probar sample (v) *or* test (v)

probatorio (-ria) probationary

problema (m) problem

proceder proceed

procedimiento (m) process (n) *or* procedure

procedimiento de selección selection procedure

procedimientos (mpl) judiciales judicial processes

procesamiento (m) prosecution *or* legal action

procesamiento por lotes batch processing

procesar prosecute

proceso (m) [juicio] trial *or* court case *or* lawsuit

proceso de datos data processing

proceso judicial legal proceedings

procesos (mpl) decisorios decision-making processes

procesos industriales industrial processes

procuración (f)
proxy
procurador (-ra)
attorney
producción (f) pro-
duction *or* output
producción en serie
mass production
**producción interior
o producción
nacional** domestic
production
producción total
total output
producir produce (v)
or make *or* bring in
**producir [deven-
gar]** carry (v)
**producir [orde-
nador]** output (v)
**producir a gran
escala** mass-produce
producir en exceso
overproduce
productividad (f)
productivity
productivo (-va) pro-
ductive *or* profitable
producto (m) product
**producto defectu-
oso** reject (n)

**producto destinado
a un mercado de
masas** mass-
market product
producto derivado
by-product
producto ficticio
dummy
producto final end
product
**Producto Interior
Bruto (PIB)** gross
domestic product
(GDP)
**Producto Nacional
Bruto (PNB)** gross
national product
(GNP)
**producto presti-
gioso** prestige
product
producto principal
staple product
**producto sensible a
los cambios de
precio** price-
sensitive product
productor (-ra)
producer
productos (mpl)
produce (n)

productos acabados
finished goods
productos competi-
tivos competitive
products
productos de marca
propia own label
goods *or* own brand
goods
productos de
primera calidad
high-quality goods
productos
devueltos sin
vender returns *or*
unsold goods
productos en
competencia
competing products
productos manu-
facturados
manufactured goods
productos pere-
cederos perishables
productos semia-
cabados semi-
finished products
profesional (adj)
professional (adj)
profesional (mf)
professional (n)

programa (m) pro-
gramme *or* program
programa de inves-
tigación research
programme
programa de
ordenador
computer program
programa infor-
mático software
programa piloto
pilot scheme
programación (f)
scheduling
programación de
ordenador com-
puter programming
programador (-ra) de
ordenadores com-
puter programmer
programar un
ordenador program
a computer
progresar
progress (v)
progresivo (-va)
progressive *or* gradual
progreso (m)
progress (n)
prohibición (f) ban
(n) *or* embargo(n)

prohibición de hacer horas extras overtime ban

prohibición de importar import ban

prohibir ban (v) *or* forbid *or* embargo (v)

prohibitivo (-va) prohibitive

prolongación (f) extension

prolongar extend

promedio (m) average (n) *or* mean (n)

promedio ponderado weighted average

promesa (f) promise (n) *or* undertaking

prometer promise (v)

promoción (f) promotion *or* publicity

promoción: en o de promoción promotional

promoción de un producto promotion of a product

promoción de ventas sales promotion *or* sales drive

promocionar promote *or* advertise

promocionar la imagen pública de una empresa promote a corporate image

promocionar un nuevo producto promote a new product

pronosticar forecast (v) *or* tip (v)

pronóstico (m) forecast (n)

pronto (-ta) prompt

pronto early *or* soon

pronto pago (m) prompt payment

propicio (-cia) favourable

propiedad (f) ownership (n) *or* property (n)

propiedad colectiva collective ownership or common ownership

propiedad conjunta multiple ownership

propiedad inmobiliaria real estate

propiedad privada
private property *or*
private ownership
propietaria (f) pro-
prietress *or* landlady
propietario (m) pro-
prietor *or* landlord
propietario (-ria)
owner
propietario (-ria)
legítimo (-ma)
rightful owner
propietario (-ria)
único (-ca) sole
owner
propina (f) tip (n)
proponer propose
proponer una
enmienda move an
amendment
proponer(se)
propose to
proponerse
[aspirar a] aim (v)
proporción (f)
proportion
proporcional
proportional
proposición (f)
proposition *or* pro-
posal *or* suggestion

propósito (m) aim (n)
propuesta (f) pro-
posal *or* proposition
prorrata pro rata
prórroga (f)
renewal *or* extension
prorrogar extend
or renew
prorrogar un
arrendamiento
renew a lease
proseguir continue
prospecto (m)
prospectus *or* leaflet
prosperar flourish
or boom (v)
próspero (-ra)
prosperous *or* flour-
ishing *or* booming
protección (f)
protection *or* defence
protección (f)
[cobertura]
hedging *or* hedge
protección al
consumidor
consumer protection
proteccionista pro-
tective *or* protectionist
protector (-ra)
protective

proteger protect *or* safeguard or defend

protesta (f) protest (n)

protestar (contra algo) protest (v)(against somthing)

protestar una letra protest a bill

protesto (m) protest (n)

prototipo (m) de contrato model agreement

proveedor (-ra) supplier

proveer provide (v) *or* supply (v)

provisión (f) de fondos provision *or* allocation of funds

provisional provisional

próximo (-ma) close to

proyectado (-da) projected

proyectar project (v) *or* plan (v) *or* design (v)

proyecto (m) project *or* plan

proyecto (m) [borrador] draft (n) *or* rough plan

proyecto de ley bill (n)

prueba (f) proof

prueba (f) [ensayo] trial *or* test

prueba: a prueba on approval

prueba: de prueba probationary

prueba documentada documentary proof

prueba gratuita free trial

pruebas (fpl) documentales documentary evidence

publicación (f) asistida por ordenador desk-top publishing(DTP)

publicación (f) periódica periodical (n)

publicar [anunciar] advertise

publicar [divulgar] release (v) *or* make public

publicidad (f) publicity *or* advertising
publicidad a escala nacional national advertising
publicidad en el punto de venta point of sale material (POS material)
publicidad exagerada hype (n)
publicidad por correo direct-mail advertising *or* mail shot
publicidad sin interés (por correo) junk mail
público (-ca) public (adj)
público (-ca) [común] common
puente-báscula (m) weighbridge
puerta (f) door
puerta: de puerta en puerta door-to-door
puerto (m) port *or* harbour
puerto de contenedores container port

puerto de embarque port of embarkation
puerto de escala port of call
puerto de registro port of registry
puerto distribuidor entrepot port
puerto franco free port
puesta (f) en marcha (de un negocio) start-up
puesta al día updating
puesta en práctica implementation
puesto (m) post (n) *or* position *or* job *or* place (n)
puesto aduanero customs entry point
puesto clave key post
puesto de trabajo [empleo] job
puesto de trabajo [informática] workstation
puja (f) bid (n)
pujar más alto outbid

punto (m) point
punto (m)
[discusión] item
(on agenda)
punto de partida
starting point
punto de referencia
benchmark
punto de reunión
venue
punto de venta
point of sale (p.o.s.
or POS)
punto decimal
decimal point
punto máximo
peak (n)
punto muerto
breakeven point *or*
deadlock (n)
punto porcentual
percentage point
puntos (mpl) de
venta electrónicos
electronic point of
sale (EPOS)
PYME (pequeña y
mediana empresa)
small and middle-
sized businesses

Qq

quebrado (m)
bankrupt (n)
quebrado no reha-
bilitado undis-
charged bankrupt
quebrado rehabili-
tado certificated
bankrupt
quebrar crash (v)
or fail
quedar remain *or*
be left
quedarse stay (v)
or remain
quedarse atrás fall
behind
queja (f) complaint
quejarse complain
(about)
querellante (mf)
plaintiff
quiebra (f)
bankruptcy
quiebra: en quiebra
bankrupt (adj)
quiebra comercial
commercial failure

quitar remove
quitar [rebajar]
take off *or* deduct
quórum (m) quorum

Rr

racionalización (f)
rationalization
racionalizar
rationalize
radicar base (v)
rama (f) branch (n)
rampa (f) de carga
loading ramp
rápidamente rapi-
dly *or* fast (adv)
rápido (-da) rapid *or*
prompt *or* fast (adj)
rápido (-da) [urge-
nte] express (adj)
ratero (-ra) de
tiendas shoplifter
ratificación (f)
ratification
ratificar ratify

raya (f) line (n)
razón (f) [motivo]
reason
razón (f) [relación]
ratio
razón social
corporate name
reacción (f)
feedback *or* response
reactivación (f)
recovery *or*
turnround *or* upturn
reajustar adjust *or*
readjust
reajuste (m)
adjustment *or*
readjustment
real real *or* actual
realización (f)
fulfilment
realizar realize
realizar activos
realize assets
realizar un
proyecto *o* un plan
realize a project *or*
a plan
realizar una opera-
ción de cesión-
arrendamiento
lease back

reanudar resume
reanudar las nego-ciaciones resume negotiations
reasegurador (-ra) reinsurer
reasegurar reinsure
reaseguro (m) reinsurance
rebaja (f) rebate *or* discount *or* reduction
rebaja (f) **[recorte]** cut (n)
rebajar mark down *or* deduct *or* reduce
rebajar un precio reduce a price
rebajas (fpl) de fin de temporada end of season sale
rebajas a mitad de precio half-price sale
rebajas de precios price reductions
recadero (m) deliveryman
recado (m) message
recargar mark up
recargo (m) surcharge (n) *or* overcharge (n)

recargo de importación import surcharge
recaudación (f) takings *or* take (n)
recaudación de impuestos levy (n) *or* tax collection
recaudador (-ra) collector
recaudador (-ra) de impuestos tax collector
recaudar levy (v)
recepción (f) reception (desk)
recepcionista (mf) receptionist *or* reception clerk
recesión (f) recession
rechazar reject (v) *or* turn down
rechazo (m) rejection *or* refusal
recibir receive *or* take (v) *or* get
recibir una llamada take a call
recibo (m) receipt
recibo de aduana customs receipt

recibo de depósito
deposit slip *or*
paying-in slip
reciclaje (m) pro-
fessional retraining
reciclar recycle *or*
retrain
recipiente (m)
container
reciprocidad (f)
reciprocity
recíproco (-ca)
reciprocal
reclamación (f)
claim (n)
reclamación de
pago demand (n)
(for payment)
reclamar claim (v)
or demand (v)
recobrar recover
(v) *or* repossess (v)
recoger collect (v)
recogida (f)
collection
recomendación (f)
recommendation
recomendar
recommend
reconciliación (f)
reconciliation

reconocer a un
sindicato recognize
a union
reconocer una
firma honour a
signature
reconocimiento (m)
recognition
reconocimiento de
un sindicato union
recognition
reconvención (f)
counter-claim (n)
récord (adj) record
or record-breaking
récord (m) record (n)
récord de ventas
record sales
recordar remind *or*
remember
recordatorio (m)
reminder
recortar cut (v)
recorte (m) cut (n)
rectificación (f)
rectification *or*
correction
rectificar rectify *or*
correct (v)
recuperable
recoverable

recuperación (f)
recovery *or* retrieval
recuperación (f)
[precios] rally (n)
recuperación de
datos data retrieval
recuperar [reco-
brar] recover *or*
repossess
recuperar
[rescatar] retrieve
or get back
recuperarse
[mejorar] recover
recuperarse
[precios] rally (v)
recursos (mpl)
resources *or* means
recursos
financieros
financial resources
recursos naturales
natural resources
red (f) network (n)
Red (f) Web (n)
red de distribución
distribution network
redactar draft (v)
or draw up
redactar un contrato
draft a contract *or*
draw up a contract

redactar una carta
draft a letter
redimir pay off *or*
redeem (v)
redistribuir
redistribute
rédito (m) interest
(n) *or* rate of interest
redondear por
defecto round down
redondear por
exceso round up
reducción (f) reduc-
tion *or* decrease (n) *or*
lowering *or* shrinkage
reducción (f)
[desaceleración]
slowdown
reducción de costes
cost-cutting
reducción de
empleos job cuts
reducción de gas-
tos retrenchment
reducción de los
impuestos tax
reductions
reducir reduce
reducir [desacel-
erar] slow down
reducir a escala
scale down

**reducir gradual-
mente** phase out
**reducir drástica-
mente [los precios]**
slash prices
reducir gastos
reduce expenditure *or*
cut down on expenses
reducir los precios
lower prices
reducir un precio
reduce a price
redundante
redundant
reelección (f)
re-election
reelegir re-elect
reembolsable refund-
able *or* repayable
reembolsar refund
(v) *or* repay *or*
pay back
**reembolsar
[redimir]** pay off
reembolso (m)
repayment
**reembolso (m) [rein-
tegro]** reimbursement
or rebate *or* refund (n)
**reembolso de gas-
tos** reimbursement
of expenses

reembolso total
full refund
reemplazar replace
reemplazo (m)
replacement
reempleo (m) re-
employment
**reestructuración
(f)** restructuring
**reestructuración de
la compañía**
restructuring of the
company
reestructurar
restructure
reexportación (f)
re-export (n)
reexportar
re-export (v)
referencia (f)
reference
referente a
relating to
referirse refer
referirse a apply to
**refinanciación (f)
de un préstamo**
refinancing of a loan
**refinanciar un
crédito o una deuda**
roll over credit *or*
a debt

refrendar countersign

refugio (m) shelter

regalar give (away)

regalar [obsequiar] present (v)

regalo (m) present (n) *or* gift

regatear haggle (v) *or* bargain (v)

región (f) region *or* area

regional regional

regir rule (v) *or* run *or* be in force

registrado (-da) registered

registrador (-ra) registrar

registrar record (v) *or* register (v)

registrar una marca comercial register a trademark

registrar una propiedad register a property

registrarse [inscribirse] register (v) *or* check in

registro (m) register (n) *or* registry

registro (m) [informe] record

registro (m) [inscripción] registration

registro (m) [inspección] examination *or* inspection

registro de compañias companies' register

Registro Marítimo de Lloyd Lloyd's register

Registro Mercantil Registrar of Companies

regla (f) law *or* rule (n)

reglamentación (f) regulation

reglamentar regulate

reglamentario (-ria) statutory

reglamento (m) regulations

reglamento sobre incendios fire regulations

regreso (m) return (n)

regulación (f)
regulation
**regulado (-da) por el
Estado** government-
regulated
regular (adj)
regular (adj)
regular regulate (v)
rehusar refuse (v)
reimportación (f)
reimport (n)
reimportar
reimport (v)
reintegro (m)
reimbursement *or*
withdrawal
reinversión (f)
reinvestment
reinvertir reinvest (v)
reivindicación (f)
claim (n)
**reivindicación
salarial** wage claim
relación (f) rela-
tion *or* connection
relación (f) [lista]
list (n)
relación (f) [razón]
ratio
**relación: con
relación a** further to

**relación de direc-
tivos de una
empresa** register of
directors
relación de gastos
statement of
expenses
**relación precio-
ganancias**
price/earnings ratio
(P/E ratio)
relacionar connect
relaciones (fpl)
relations
**relaciones labo-
rales** industrial
relations
relaciones públicas
public relations (PR)
relativo a regard-
ing *or* relating to
rematar knock
down (v) *or* reduce
remate (m) dis-
tress sale
remesa (f) [envío]
consignment
**remesa (f) [par-
tida]** batch (n)
remite (m) return
address

remitente (mf)
sender *or* consignor
remitir remit (v) *or*
refer
remitir adjunto
enclose
remitir por cheque
remit by cheque
remontarse soar
remuneración (f)
remuneration *or*
payment
remunerar
remunerate
remunerativo (-va)
money-making
rendimiento (m)
[actuación]
performance
rendimiento (m)
[capacidad] (pro-
duction) capacity
rendimiento (m)
[producción]
output (n) *or*
throughput
rendimiento (m)
[rentabilidad]
yield (n) *or* return
rendimiento bruto
gross yield

rendimiento corri-
ente current yield
rendimiento de la
inversión return on
investment (ROI)
rendimiento efec-
tivo effective yield
rendimiento máx-
imo peak output
rendimiento neto
net yield
rendir yield (v) *or*
bear (v)
rendir cuentas a
alguien report to
someone
renovación (f)
renewal
renovación de
existencias
restocking
renovación urbana
redevelopment *or*
urban renewal
renovar redevelop
or renew
renovar existencias
restock
renovar un abono *o*
una suscripción
renew a subscription

renovar un pedido reorder (v) *or* repeat an order

renta (f) [alquiler] rent (n)

renta (f) [ingresos] income (n)

renta (f) [rendimiento] yield (n)

renta bruta gross income

renta de inversiones investment income

renta fija fixed income

renta imponible taxable income

renta nominal nominal rent

renta personal personal income

renta por alquiler rental income

renta que no llega a cubrir los costes uneconomic rent

renta real real income *or* real wages

renta total total income

renta vitalicia life interest

rentabilidad (f) profitability *or* cost-effectiveness

rentabilidad del dividendo dividend yield

rentable paying (adj) *or* cost-effective

rentable [lucrativo] profit-making *or* profitable

renuncia (f) renunciation *or* resignation

renuncia (f) [abandono de responsabilidad] disclaimer

renuncia (f) [desistimiento] waiver

renunciar a abandon

renunciar a un pago waive a payment

reorganización (f) reorganization

reorganizar reorganize

reparación (f) repair (n)

reparar repair (v)
repartir distribute
(v) *or* share out
repartir [entregar]
deliver (v)
repartir un riesgo
spread a risk
reparto (m)
distribution (n) *or*
delivery (n)
**reparto de mer-
cancías** delivery of
goods
repercusión (f)
knock-on effect
repertorio (m)
index (n) *or* list (n)
repetir repeat
**repetirse: que se
repite** recurrent
reponer replace (v)
repostar restock
**representación (f)
exclusiva** sole
agency
representante (mf)
representative
**representante (mf)
[vendedor]**
salesman *or* sales
representative

**representante a
comission**
commission rep
**representante
exclusivo** sole agent
representar represent
representativo (-va)
representative (adj)
repudiar repudiate
repuesto (m)
replacement
reputación (f) rep-
utation *or* standing
**requerimiento (m)
de pago** demand
(n) for payment
requerir require
or need
requisitos (mpl)
requirements
resarcir repay (v)
or indemnify (v) *or*
compensate (v)
**resarcirse de las
pérdidas** recoup
one's losses
rescatable
redeemable
**rescatador (-ra) de
empresas** white
knight

rescatar retrieve (v)
rescatar una póliza
surrender a policy
rescatar una prenda
redeem a pledge
rescate (m)
retrieval *or* recovery
or salvage (n)
rescate (m) [pól-iza] surrender (n)
(of insurance policy)
rescate (m) [prés-tamo] redemption
(of a loan)
rescindir rescind
rescindir un contrato
cancel a contract
reserva (f) booking
or reservation
reserva (f)
[almacén] reserve
or store (n)
reserva (f) [pro-visión] supply (n)
or provision
reserva anticipada
advance booking
reserva en bloque
block booking
reserva en dólares
dollar balance

reservar reserve
(v) *or* book (v)
reservar con
exceso overbook
reservar la misma
plaza a dos per-sonas double-book
reservas (fpl)
reserve (n) *or*
reserves *or* supplies
or stockpile
reservas: con
reservas qualified
reservas de divisas
currency reserves
reservas de caja
cash reserves
reservas de mate-rias primas stock
of raw materials
reservas ocultas
hidden reserves
reservas para
imprevistos
emergency reserves
resguardo (m) slip
(n) *or* receipt (n)
residencia (f)
residence
residente
resident (adj)

residente (mf)
resident (n)
residuos (mpl)
waste (n)
resignar resign
resolución (f)
resolution
resolver resolve (v)
resolver un
problema solve a
problem
respaldar back up
(v) *or* support
respaldo (m)
financiero financial
backing
respetar respect (v)
responder answer
(v) *or* reply (v) *or*
respond (v)
responder de
account for
responsabilidad (f)
responsibility *or*
liability
responsabilidad
contractual con-
tractual liability
responsabilidad
ilimitada unlimited
liability

responsabilidad
limitada limited
liability
responsabilidades
(fpl) responsibilities
responsable
responsible (for)
responsable de
liable for
responsable (mf)
de la capacitación
training officer
responsable (mf) del
progreso de un tra-
bajo progress chaser
responsable (mf)
de relaciones
públicas public
relations officer
respuesta (f) reply
(n) *or* answer (n) *or*
response (n)
respuesta (f) [reac-
ción] feedback
resto (m) rest *or*
remainder
restricción (f) res-
traint *or* restriction
restricción a las
importaciones
import restrictions

restricción comercial restraint of trade
restrictivo (-va) restrictive
restringir restrict (v)
resultado (m) result (n)
resultados (mpl) (company) results
resultar result in
resultar de result from
retención (f) de impuestos en origen withholding tax
retención fiscal tax deductions
retener keep back *or* withhold
retirada (f) withdrawal
retirar withdraw
retirar gradualmente phase out
retirar una oferta withdraw an offer
retirar una oferta de adquisición withdraw a takeover bid
retirarse [jubilarse] retire (v)

retirarse (de una elección) stand down
retiro (m) withdrawal
retiro (m) [jubilación] retirement *or* pension
retornable returnable
retrasar hold up (v) *or* delay
retrasarse fall behind
retraso (m) hold-up (n) *or* delay
retraso: con retraso late (adv)
retroactivo (-va) retroactive
reunión (f) meeting *or* assembly
reunión de ventas sales conference
reunión del consejo de administración board meeting
reunión de personal staff meeting
reunir recursos pool resources
reunirse meet (v)
revaluación (f) revaluation *or* reassessment

revaluar revalue *or* reassess

revelación (f) disclosure

revelación de información confidencial disclosure of confidential information

revelar disclose

revelar una información disclose a piece of information

reventa (f) resale

reverso (m) back (n)

revertido (-da) reverse (adj)

revés (m) setback

revisar revise (v) *or* inspect (v)

revisar [máquina] service (v)

revisar las cuentas audit the accounts

revisión (f) [máquina] service (n)

revisión de sueldos salary review

revista (f) magazine *or* journal *or* periodical (n)

revista profesional especializada trade magazine *or* trade journal

revocar revoke *or* reverse (v) *or* countermand

riesgo (m) risk (n) *or* exposure

riesgo financiero financial risk

rincón (m) corner (n)

ritmo (m) de producción rate of production

robo (m) theft

rollo (m) publicitario sales pitch

romper las negociaciones break off negotiations

romper un acuerdo break an agreement

romperse break down (v)

rotación (f) turnover

rotación de existencias stock turnover

rotulador (m) marker pen

rótulo (m) sign (n)
roturas (fpl)
breakages
rubricar initial (v)
ruego (m)
request (n)
ruptura (f)
breakdown (n)
ruta (f) habitual
run (n) *or* regular
route
rutina (f) routine (n)
rutinario (-ria)
routine (adj)

Ss

sacar [dinero]
draw *or* withdraw
[money]
sacar el título de
qualify as
saco (m) bag
sala (f) room
sala de conferencias
conference room

sala de embarque
departure lounge
sala de exposición
showroom
sala de exposiciones
exhibition hall
sala de juntas
boardroom
sala de subastas
auction rooms
sala de tránsito
transit lounge
salario (m) salary
or wage
salario inicial
starting salary
salario interesante
attractive salary
salario mínimo
minimum wage
**salario mínimo inter-
profesional** guaran-
teed minimum wage
salario neto net
income *or* net salary
saldar balance (v)
saldar una cuenta
settle an account
saldo (m) balance
(brought down *or*
brought forward)

saldo (m) [rebajas]
sale (n)
saldo a cuenta
nueva balance
carried down *or*
carrried forward
saldo acreedor *o*
saldo a favor credit
balance
saldo a (nuestro)
favor balance
due to us
saldo de caja cash
balance
saldo deudor debit
balance
saldo final closing
balance *or* bottom line
saldo inicial
opening balance
saldo insuficiente
insufficient
funds (US)
salida (f) departure
salidas (fpl)
departures
saliente retiring *or*
outgoing
salir go (out)
salón (m) de exposi-
ciones exhibition hall

salón VIP (salón de
personalidades)
VIP lounge
saltarse la cola
jump the queue
saltarse un plazo
miss an instalment
salud (f) health
saluda (m)
compliments slip
salvamento (m)
salvage (n)
salvar salvage (v)
salvedad (f)
proviso
salvo except
salvo error u
omisión errors and
omissions excepted
(e. & o.e.)
sancionar
penalize (v)
satisfacción (f)
satisfaction
satisfacción del
cliente customer
satisfaction
satisfacción laboral
job satisfaction
satisfacer satisfy
(v) *or* meet (v)

satisfacer una demanda meet a demand *or* satisfy a demand
satisfacer la demanda keep up with the demand
saturación (f) saturation
saturar saturate
saturar el mercado saturate the market
se admiten ofertas open to offers
sección (f) section *or* division
sección (de tienda) department
sección de 'marketing' marketing division
sección de compras purchasing department
sección de ventas sales department
secretario (-ria) secretary
secretario (-ria) de una empresa company secretary

secretario (-ria) eventual temp (n)
secreto (m) secret (n)
secreto (-ta) secret (adj)
sector (m) sector
sector primario primary industry
sector privado private sector
sector público public sector
sector terciario *o* **sector de los servicios** tertiary sector
secuestrar sequester *or* sequestrate *or* seize
secundario (-ria) subsidiary (adj) *or* secondary
sede (f) headquarters (HQ)
seguir follow *or* proceed
según depending on *or* according to *or* under
según contrato contractually

según factura as per invoice

según muestra as per sample

según nota de expedición as per advice

segundo (-da) second (adj)

segunda solicitud (f) reapplication

segundo trimestre (m) second quarter

seguridad (f) safety *or* security

seguridad de empleo security of employment

seguridad en el empleo job security

seguridad social social security

seguro (m) insurance

seguro (m) [de vida] life assurance

seguro (-ra) safe (adj)

seguro a todo riesgo comprehensive insurance

seguro contra incendios fire insurance

seguro contra terceros third-party insurance

seguro corriente de vida whole-life insurance

seguro de automóviles motor insurance

seguro de enfermedad health insurance

seguro de la vivienda house insurance

seguro de vida life assurance

seguro general general insurance

seguro marítimo marine insurance

seguro temporal term insurance

selección (f) selection *or* choice (n)

selección de artículos para preparar un pedido order picking

seleccionar candidatos (-tas) select *or* screen candidates

selecto (-ta) choice (adj)

sellar stamp (v)

sellar [precintar] seal (v)

sello (m) stamp (n)

semana (f) week

semana: a media- dos de semana mid-week

semanalmente weekly

semestre (m) half-year

señal (f) sign (n) *or* mark (n)

señal (f) [entrada] deposit (n)

señal de comunicar engaged tone

señal de línea dialling tone

señalar mark (v)

señas (fpl) address (n)

señas: poner las señas address (v)

sencillo (-lla) single

sentada (f) sit- down protest

sentencia (f) [fallo] award (n)

sentencia (f) [juicio] judgement *or* judgment

separado (-da) separate (adj)

separado: por separado under separate cover

separar separate (v)

ser despedido get the sack

ser distinto differ (v)

ser igual a equal (v)

ser responsable ante alguien be responsible to someone

ser válido [regir] run (v) *or* be in force

serie (f) [remesa] batch (n)

servicio (m) service (n)

servicio de contestación answering service

servicio de fotocopias
photocopying bureau
**servicio de habita-
ciones de un hotel**
room service
**servicio de man-
tenimiento** service
department
**servicio de paquetes
postales** parcel post
**servicio de post-
venta** *o* **servicio
posventa** after-
sales service
**servicio de recortes
de prensa** clipping
service
servicio deficiente
poor service
servicio rápido
prompt service
**servicios (mpl) de
informática**
computer services
servir serve
servir un pedido
deal with an order
signatario (-ria)
signatory
signatario colectivo
joint signatory

significado (m)
content
**signo (m) de cali-
dad** quality label
símbolo (m)
symbol *or* token
**símbolo de presti-
gio** status symbol
sindicalista (mf)
trade unionist
sindicato (m)
(trade) union
síndico (m) liquidator
or (official) receiver
síndrome del fénix
phoenix syndrome
sinergia (f) synergy
siniestro (m) total
dead loss
sistema (m) system
**sistema (m) [orga-
nización]** setup
**sistema de orde-
nador a tiempo real**
real-time system
**sistema de
recuperación**
retrieval system
sistema económico
economy *or*
economic system

sistema informático
computer system
Sistema Monetario Europeo (SME)
European Monetary System (EMS)
sistema operativo
operating system
sistema tributario
tax system
sistemas (mpl) de control control systems
sitio (m) [lugar]
site *or* place (n)
sitio web website (n)
situación (f)
situation *or* position
situación financiera
financial position
situado (-da)
situated
S.L. (= sociedad limitada) Ltd
(= limited company)
SME (Sistema Monetario Europeo) EMS
(= European Monetary System)

sobornar bribe (v)
soborno (m) bribe
(n) *or* backhander
sobre (m) abierto
unsealed envelope
sobre cerrado
sealed envelope
sobrecapacidad (f)
overcapacity
sobrecontratación (m) overbooking
sobregiro (m)
overdraft
sobrepasar exceed
sobreprima (f)
additional premium
sobreproducción (f) overproduction
sobrepujar [pujar]
outbid
sobresaliente
outstanding (adj)
sobrestimar [sobrevalorar]
overestimate (v) *or* overvalue (v)
sobretasa (f)
surcharge
sobretasa de importación import surcharge

sobrevalorar
overvalue *or*
overestimate (v)
social social
sociedad (f)
society
sociedad (f)
[asociación]
partnership
sociedad (f) [com-
pañía] company
sociedad anónima
(S.A.) Public Limited
Company (Plc)
sociedad comercial
trading company
sociedad coopera-
tiva cooperative
society
sociedad cotizada
en bolsa quoted
company
sociedad de
cartera holding
company *or* propri-
etary company (US)
sociedad de
responsabilidad
limitada (S.R.L.)
limited (liability)
company (Ltd)

sociedad en
comandita limited
partnership
sociedad ficticia
(para la compra de
acciones) shell
company
sociedad financiera
finance company
sociedad hipote-
caria *o* de crédito
hipotecario
building society
sociedad limitada
(S.L.) private
limited company
sociedad matriz
parent company
sociedad mercantil
corporation
sociedades (fpl)
industriales indus-
trialized societies
socio (-cia)
[asociado] partner
or associate
socio (-cia) [miem-
bro] member
socio comanditario *o*
socio en comandita
sleeping partner

**socio (-cia) princi-
pal** senior partner
**socio subalterno o de
menor antigüedad**
junior partner
socios: los socios
membership
solar (m) site (n)
**solicitación (f) de
votos** canvassing
solicitar apply for or
ask for or request (v)
solicitar pedidos
solicit orders
solicitar votos
canvass (votes)
solicitar por escrito
apply in writing
solicitar un trabajo
apply for a job
**solicitar una
patente** file a
patent application
solicitud (f) appli-
cation or request (n)
**solicitud de empleo
o de trabajo** job
application or
application for a job
solución (f)
solution

**solucionar un prob-
lema** solve a problem
solvencia (f)
solvency
solvente solvent or
credit-worthy
someter a prueba
test (v)
**sondeo (m) de
opinión** opinion poll
soporte (m) holder
soslayar get round
(a problem)
sostener keep up
or maintain
**S.R.L. (= sociedad
de responsabilidad
limitada)** Ltd
(= limited company)
stand (m) stand (n)
status (m) status
statutario (-ria)
statutory
sub judice sub
judice
subalterno (-na)
junior (adj)
**subarrendador
(-ra)** sublessor
subarrendar sub-
lease (v) or sublet (v)

**subarrendatario
(-ria)** sublessee
subarriendo (m)
sublease (n)
subasta (f) auction
(n) *or* bidding (n)
subastar auction (v)
subcontratar
subcontract (v)
subcontratista (mf)
subcontractor
subcontrato (m)
subcontract (n)
subdirector (-ra)
assistant manager
or deputy manager
subida (f) rise (n)
or increase *or*
appreciation
subir climb *or*
increase (v) *or* raise
(v) *or* mount up
subir [avanzar]
rise (v)
subir [en valor]
appreciate
subir de precio
increase (v) in
price
subproducto (m)
by-product

subsidiario (-ria)
subsidiary (adj)
subsidio (m) sub-
sidy *or* benefit (n)
**subsidio de
carestía de vida**
cost-of-living
allowance
**subsidio de paro o
desempleo** unem-
ployment pay
subvención (f)
subvention *or* subsidy
**subvención (f)
[beca]** grant (n)
**subvencionado: no
subvencionado**
unsubsidized
subvencionar
subsidize
suceder succeed
sucursal (f) branch
(office) *or* division
sucursal [tienda]
chain store
sueldo (m) wage
or salary
sueldo bruto gross
salary
sueldo neto net
income *or* net salary

sueldo por hora
hourly wage
suelo (m) floor
suelto (-ta)
loose (adj)
suelto (-ta) [des-parejado] odd
suficiente sufficient
sufragar defray
sufrir daños suffer
damage
sugerencia (f)
suggestion (n)
sujetapapeles (m)
paperclip
sujetar attach (v)
sujeto (-ta) a liable
to *or* subject to
sujeto (-ta) a
impuesto taxable
suma (f) sum *or*
addition
suma global
lump sum
suma total grand
total
sumar add up *or*
total (v)
sumar una columna
de cifras add up a
column of figures

suministrador (-ra)
supplier
suministrar
supply (v)
suministro (m)
supply (n)
superar exceed (v)
or top (v)
superávit (m)
surplus (n)
superficie (f) area
or surface
superficie útil
floor space
superior superior
(adj) *or* senior (adj)
or top (adj)
supermercado (m)
supermarket
supervisar
supervise
supervisión (f)
supervision
supervisión: de
supervisión
supervisory
supervisor (-ra)
supervisor
suplemeneto (m)
de póliza
endorsement

**suplemen-
tario (-ria)**
supplementary
suplemento (m)
supplement
**suplemento por el
servicio** service
charge
suplente (mf)
deputy (n)
suprimir delete *or*
remove *or* lift (v)
suprimir [extirpar]
excise (v) *or* cut out
suprimir controles
decontrol (v)
surtido (m) choice
(n) *or* range (n) *or*
selection
**suscribir una
opción** take up an
option
suspender suspend
or cancel
**suspender
[interrumpir]**
discontinue
**suspender un
acuerdo** call off
a deal

suspender pagos
stop payments
**suspender una
cuenta** stop an
account
suspendido (-da)
off *or* cancelled
suspensión (f)
suspension *or*
stoppage (n)
**suspensión de
entregas**
suspension of
deliveries
**suspensión de
pagos** suspension
of payments *or*
stoppage of
payments
sustituir replace
(v) *or* take over
sustituir a alguien
deputize for
someone
sustituto (-ta)
replacement *or*
substitute (n)

Tt

tablas (fpl) actuariales o tablas de mortalidad actuarial tables

tablero (m) panel

tablero de hojas sueltas flip chart

tabulación (f) tabulation

tabulador (-ra) tabulator

tabular tabulate

tachar cross out *or* cross off

tacógrafo (m) tachograph

talla (f) corriente stock size

talla muy grande outsize (OS)

taller (m) workshop

talonario (m) de cheques cheque book

talonario de recibos receipt book

tamaño (m) size

tamaño corriente stock size

tamaño normal regular size

tangible tangible

tanteo (m) trial and error

tanto (m) alzado flat rate

tanto por ciento percentage

taquilla (f) booking office

taquillero (-ra) booking clerk

tara (f) tare (n)

tara (f) [defecto] defect (n) *or* fault (n) *or* imperfection (n)

tarado (-da) damaged

tarde late (adv)

tarea (f) assignment *or* task *or* job

tarifa (f) tariff *or* rate

tarifa de horas extras overtime pay

tarifa de mercado market rate

tarifa horaria hourly rate *or* time rate

tarifa nocturna
night rate
tarifa por horas
time rate
tarifa postal
postage
**tarifa preferente o
tarifa preferencial**
preferential duty *or*
preferential tariff
tarifa reducida
cheap rate *or*
reduced rate
**tarifas (fpl) de
carga aérea** air
freight charges *or*
rates
tarifas de flete
freight rates
tarifas de seguros
insurance rates
tarifas diferenciadas
differential tariffs
tarifas postales
postal charges *or*
postal rates
tarifas publicitarias
advertising rates
**tarifas publicitarias
regresivas** graded
advertising rates

tarjeta (f) card *or*
business card
**tarjeta de cajero
automático o tarjeta
de dinero** cash card
tarjeta de crédito
credit card *or*
charge card
**tarjeta de desem-
barque** landing card
tarjeta de embarque
embarkation card *or*
boarding card *or*
boarding pass
tarjeta de saludo
compliments slip
tarjeta inteligente
smart card
tarjeta oro gold card
tarjeta postal card
or postcard
tasa (f) rate (n)
tasa de amortización
depreciation rate
tasa de cambio
exchange rate
tasa de conversión
conversion price *or*
conversion rate
tasa de crecimiento
growth rate

tasa de descuento
discount rate
tasa de errores
error rate
tasa de impuestos
normal standard
rate (of tax)
tasa de inflación
rate of inflation
tasa de interés
interest rate
tasa de rendimiento
rate of return
tasación (f)
valuation (n)
tasación de
acciones stock
market valuation
tasador (-ra) valuer
tasar value (v)
tasas (fpl) de
aeropuerto
airport tax
techo (m) ceiling
techo crediticio
credit ceiling
tecla (f) key
tecla de control
control key
tecla de mayúscu-
las shift key

teclado (m)
keyboard (n)
teclado numérico
numeric keypad
tecleado (m)
keyboarding
teclear keyboard (v)
tecleo (m)
keyboarding
técnica (f) skill *or*
technique
técnicas (fpl) de
'marketing' mar-
keting techniques
técnicas de dirección
de empresas man-
agement techniques
técnicas de sondeo
canvassing techniques
técnico asesor *o*
técnica asesora
consulting engineer
Telaraña (f)
mundial World
Wide Web
telefax (m) fax (n)
telefonear
telephone (v) *or*
phone (v)
telefonista (mf)
telephonist

teléfono (m)
telephone (n) *or*
phone (n)
teléfono celular
cellular telephone
**teléfono de confer-
encias** conference
phone
teléfono de tarjeta
card phone
teléfono interno
internal telephone
teléfono móvil
mobile phone
teléfono público
pay phone
teletarjeta (f)
phone card
teletrabajo (m)
teleworking (n)
télex (m) telex (n)
tema (f) subject (n)
temporada (f) season
temporada baja
off-season
temporero (-ra)
casual worker
temprano early
tendencia (f) trend
tendencia alcista
upward trend

**tendencias (fpl)
del mercado**
market trends
**tendencias
económicas**
economic trends
tendero (-ra)
shopkeeper
tenedor (-ra)
holder
tenencia (f) tenure
**tenencia de
acciones**
shareholding
tener hold (v) *or*
have *or* own
**tener: sin tener en
cuenta** regardless of
**tener como obje-
tivo** target (v)
tener en existencia
carry *or* have in
stock
tener existencias
stock (v)
tener éxito
succeed (v)
tener lugar take
place
tener tiempo
afford (the time)

tener una discusión hold a discussion
tercer trimestre (m) third quarter
tercero (m) third (n) *or* third party
terminación (f) termination *or* expiration
terminado (-da) finished
terminal terminal (adj)
terminal (f) de aeropuerto air terminal
terminal de contenedores container terminal
terminal del aeropuerto airport terminal
terminal (m) de ordenador computer terminal
terminar end (v) *or* terminate (v) *or* wind up
terminar de trabajar knock off *or* stop work

término (m) time limit *or* term
término: por término medio on average
términos (mpl) terms
terna (f) shortlist (n)
territorio (m) territory
Tesoro (m) treasury
testigo (mf) witness (n)
texto (m) text *or* wording
tiempo (m) time
tiempo: a tiempo on time
tiempo: a tiempo completo full-time
tiempo: a tiempo parcial part-time
tiempo: de hace tiempo long-standing
tiempo de preparación (de una máquina) make-ready time
tiempo invertido por el ordenador computer time

tiempo libre spare time

tiempo muerto down time

tienda (f) shop

tienda de barrio corner shop

tienda de fábrica factory outlet

tienda de rebajas cut-price store *or* discount store

tienda de regalos gift shop

tienda de una cadena chain store

tienda libre de impuestos duty-free shop

tiendas (fpl) al detall retail outlets

tierra (f) land (n)

timador (-ra) racketeer

timo (m) fiddle (n) *or* racket (n)

tipo (m) base de interés bancario bank base rate

tipo de cambio rate of exchange *or* exchange rate

tipo de cambio actual current rate of exchange

tipo de cambio cruzado cross rate

tipo de cambio desfavorable unfavourable exchange rate

tipo de cambio estable stable exchange rate

tipo de cambio para operaciones a plazo forward rate

tipo de descuento discount rate

tipo de gravamen tax rate

tipo de interés interest rate *or* rate of interest

tipo impositivo tax rate

tipo preferencial de interés bancario prime rate

tipos (mpl) de cambio flotantes floating exchange rates

tipos de interés money rates

tirada (f) circulation

tirar: de usar y tirar disposable

titulado (-da) certificated

título (m) deed

título (m) [acción] unit *or* share certificate

título (m) [bono] government bond

título al portador bearer bond

títulos (mpl) equities *or* securities

títulos del Estado government stock *or* gilt-edged securities

títulos profesionales professional qualifications

todo incluido all-in

todos los gastos pagados all expenses paid

toma (f) de decisiones decision making

tomar take (v)

tomar la iniciativa take the initiative

tomar medidas act (v) *or* take steps *or* make provision for

tomar nota take note *or* minute (v)

tomar posesión take over

tomar prestado borrow

tomar una decisión reach a decision

tomarse tiempo libre (durante el trabajo) take time off work

tonelada (f) ton

tonelada métrica tonne

toneladas (fpl) de peso muerto deadweight tonnage

tonelaje (m) tonnage

tonelaje bruto gross tonnage

total total (adj)

total (m) total (n) *or* sum (n)

total acumulado running total

total parcial
subtotal
totalidad (f)
total (n)
totalizar total (v)
trabajador (-ra)
working (adj)
trabajador (-ra)
worker *or* employee
trabajador (-ra) a
domicilio home-
worker
trabajador (-ra) a
tiempo parcial
part-timer
trabajador (-ra) eve-
ntual casual worker
trabajador (-ra) por
libre freelance (n)
or freelance worker
trabajadores (mpl)
pagados por horas
hourly-paid workers
trabajar work (v)
trabajo (m) labour
or work (n) *or* job
trabajo: sin trabajo
unemployed *or* out
of work
trabajo a contrata
contract work

trabajo a destajo
piecework
trabajo a tiempo
completo full-time
employment
trabajo bien
remunerado well-
paid job
trabajo de campo
field work
trabajo de oficina
clerical work
trabajo en curso
work in progress
trabajo eventual
casual work
trabajo manual
manual work
trabajo por horas
part-time work
or part-time
employment
trabajo por turnos
shift work
trabajo rutinario
routine work
trabajo urgente
rush job
traducción (f)
translation
traducir translate

traductor (-ra) translator

traer bring

tramitación (f) procedure

tramitación del pago de un cheque clearance of a cheque

tramitar process (v)

tramitar el pago de un cheque clear a cheque

trámite (m) formality *or* procedure

trampa (f) fiddle (n)

transacción (f) deal (n) *or* (business) transaction

transacción en efectivo cash deal

transacción global package deal

transbordador (m) ferry

transbordo (m) transfer (n)

transferencia (f) transfer (n)

transferencia bancaria bank transfer

transferencia de fondos transfer of funds

transferible transferable

transferir transfer (v)

transigir compromise (v)

tránsito (m) transit

transmisión (f) de títulos de propiedad conveyancing

transportar transport (v) *or* carry

transportar en contenedores containerize

transporte (m) transport (n) *or* freight *or* carriage

transporte en contenedores containerization

transporte por carretera (road) transport *or* road haulage

transporte por carretera o por vía marítima surface transport

transporte por ferrocarril rail transport

transporte público
public transport
Transporte
Internacional por
Carretera TIR
(= Transports Inter-
nationaux Routiers)
transportista (mf)
road haulier *or*
carrier *or* shipper
trasladar transfer
(v) *or* move to new
place
trasladar temporal-
mente second (v)
(member of staff)
trasladar(se) move
(house, office)
traslado (m)
transfer (n)
traslado (m)
[mudanza] removal
or move
traspaso (m)
premium *or* transfer
fee *or* key money
traspaso de bienes
assignment *or* cession
tratamiento (m)
de textos
word-processing

tratante (mf)
dealer
tratar handle (v)
tratar con alguien
deal with someone
trato (m) bargain
(n) *or* deal
trato difícil hard
bargaining
tren (m) train (n)
tren de mercancías
freight train *or*
goods train
tren de mercancías
de contenedores
freightliner
tribunal (m) court
tribunal de arbi-
traje arbitration
board *or* arbitration
tribunal
tribunal de
arbitraje laboral
industrial arbitration
tribunal
tribunal de justicia
adjudication tribunal
tribunal de rentas
rent tribunal
tribunales (mpl) de
justicia law courts

tributación (f) progresiva progressive taxation
trimestral quarterly (adj)
trimestralmente quarterly (adv)
trimestre (m) quarter *or* three months *or* term
triple triple (adj)
triplicado: por triplicado in triplicate
triplicar triple (v) *or* treble (v)
trocar barter (v)
trozo: en trozos pequeños fine (adv) *or* very small
trueque (m) barter (n) *or* bartering (n)
turno (m) shift (n)
turno de día day shift
turno de noche night shift

Uu

UE (= Unión Europea) EU (= European Union)
último (-ma) last *or* latest
último (-ma) [final] final
último requerimiento (m) de pago final demand
último trimestre last quarter
últimos en entrar, primeros en salir last in first out (LIFO)
umbral (m) threshold
único (-ca) [exclusivo] sole
único (-ca) [fuera de serie] one-off
único (-ca) [sencillo] single
unidad (f) unit
unidad de almacenaje storage unit

**unidad de produc-
ción** production unit
unidad monetaria
monetary unit
uniforme flat (adj)
or uniform
unilateral unilateral
unión (f) aduanera
customs union
Unión Europea (UE)
European Union (EU)
unir join *or* unite
urgente urgent
urgente [correo]
express (adj)
**usado (-da) [de
segunda mano]**
secondhand
usar use (v)
**usar: de usar y
tirar** disposable
uso (m) use (n) *or*
utilization
uso: de fácil uso
user-friendly
uso: en uso used *or*
employed
usual usual
usuario (-ria) user
usuario final
end user

**usufructo (m) vita-
licio** life interest
útil useful *or* handy
utilización (f)
utilization
utilizado (-da)
employed *or* used
utilizar use (v) *or*
run (v)
**utilizar capacidad
ociosa** use up spare
capacity

Vv

**vacaciones (fpl)
reglamentarias**
statutory holiday
vacante (f)
vacancy
vacante (adj) free
(adj) *or* vacant
vaciar empty (v)
vacío (m) gap
vacío (-cía)
empty (adj)

vagón (m) (de fer-rocarril) railway wagon *or* truck
vale (m) voucher
vale de caja cash voucher
vale para un regalo gift voucher
valedero (-ra) valid
valer cost (v)
validez (f) validity
válido (-da) valid
valla (f) publici-taria hoarding
valor (m) value (n) *or* worth (n)
valor: sin valor worthless
valor a la par par value
valor actual present value
valor contable book value
valor de activo asset value
valor de escasez o
valor de exclusivi-dad scarcity value
valor de mercado market value

valor de reposición replacement value
valor de rescate surrender value
valor declarado declared value
valor neto net worth
valor nominal face value *or* nominal value
valor total de factura total invoice value
valoración (f) valuation *or* assessment *or* estimation
valoración (f) [apreciación] appreciation
valoración de daños assessment of damages
valoración de existencias stock valuation
valoración de resultados performance rating
valorar value (v) *or* assess *or* estimate (v)
valorar [apreciar] appreciate

valores (mpl)
securities
**valores convert-
ibles en acciones**
convertible loan
stock
variación (f)
variation *or* variance
**variaciones esta-
cionales** seasonal
variations
vehículo (m) vehicle
**vehículo de
transporte** carrier
vencer mature (v)
or fall due *or*
expire (v)
vencido (-da)
overdue *or* due
vencimiento (m)
expiration (n) *or*
expiry (n)
vendedor (-ra)
salesman *or* seller
or vendor
**vendedor (-ra) a
domicilio** door-to-
door salesman
**vendedor (-ra) de
seguros** insurance
salesman

vender sell (v) *or*
market (v)
vender: sin vender
unsold
vender a futuros
sell forward
**vender a precio más
bajo que un rival**
undercut a rival
**vender con entrega
aplazada** sell forward
**vender las existen-
cias sobrantes** dis-
pose of excess stock
vender más barato
undersell
vender un bono
redeem a bond
vender un negocio
sell out *or* sell one's
business
**vender(se) al por
menor** retail (v)
vendible saleable
or marketable
**vendido: más
vendido** top-selling
**vendido: no
vendido** unsold
venirse abajo fall
through

venta (f) sale (n) *or* selling (n)

venta: a la venta on sale

venta: en venta for sale

venta a domicilio house-to-house selling *or* door-to-door selling

venta a prueba *o* en depósito sale or return *or* see-safe

venta agresiva hard selling

venta al contado cash sale

venta al por menor *o* al detalle retail (n)

venta con tarjeta de crédito credit card sale

venta directa direct selling

venta en la bolsa bargain (n) (on Stock Exchange)

venta en subasta sale by auction

venta forzosa forced sale *or* distress sale

venta por correo direct mail

venta sin presionar al cliente soft sell

ventana (f) window

ventanilla (f) counter

ventas (fpl) sales

ventas a plazo forward sales

ventas bajas low sales

ventas estimadas estimated sales

ventas nacionales domestic sales *or* home sales

ventas netas net sales

ventas por teléfono telesales

ventas previstas projected sales

ventas registradas book sales

verbal verbal

verdadero (-ra) real *or* true

verificación (f) verification

verificado: no verificado unaudited

verificar verify
vetar una decisión
veto a decision
vía via
viabilidad (f)
feasibility
viable viable
viajar travel (v)
viajar diariamente al trabajo commute (v)
viaje (m) voyage (n) *or* journey (n) *or* trip (n)
viaje de negocios business trip
viaje de regreso homeward journey
viajero diario o viajera diaria commuter
videoconferencia (f) videoconference (n)
viejo (-ja) old
vigente ruling (adj)
vigilante (m) security guard
vigor (m) energy *or* strength
vigoroso (-sa) strong

vinculante binding
vínculo (m) connection *or* link
violación (f) de contrato breach of contract
violación de garantía breach of warranty
violación de patente infringement of patent
violar violate *or* infringe
violar una patente infringe a patent
visado (m) visa
visado de entrada entry visa
visado de entradas múltiples multiple entry visa
visado de tránsito transit visa
visita (f) visit (n) *or* call (n)
visita comercial sin cita previa cold call
visita de negocios business call

visitar visit (v) *or* call on
vista (f) sight
vitrina (f) display case *or* showcase
vitrina de exposición display unit *or* display stand
volumen (m) volume *or* bulk
volumen comercial volume of trade
volumen de ventas volume of sales *or* sales volume *or* turnover
volumen de negocios volume of business
voluminoso (-sa) bulky
volver a comprar buy back
volver a nombrar reappoint
volver a presentarse reapply

volver a telefonear
ovolver a llamar phone back
voto (m) de calidad casting vote
voto de gracias vote of thanks
voto por poderes proxy vote
vuelo (m) flight (n)
vuelo chárter charter flight
vuelo de correspondencia connecting flight
vuelo de larga distancia long-haul flight *or* long-distance flight
vuelo regular scheduled flight
vuelta (f) [cambio] change (n)
vuelta (f) [regreso] return (n)

Ww Zz

Web (f) Web (n)
website (f)
website (n)
zona (f) zone *or*
area [of town]
**zona comercial
peatonal** shopping
precinct

**zona de libre
cambio** free
trade area
zona del dólar
dollar area
zona euro
eurozone (n)
zona franca
free (trade)
zone
zona industrial
industrial estate

Business correspondence

La corrispondenza commerciale

Sample Curriculum Vitae

CURRICULUM VITAE - Jacinta Terradas Bello
C/ Veza 3, 5° A, 28028 Barcelona
Teléfono: (020) 8868 9854   Móvil: (07914) 248553
E-mail: jterradasbello@hotmail.com

Objetivo:

Ser gerente de recursos humanos desempeñando el papel de responsable de equipo en una empresa puntera. En el futuro, gestionar las relaciones laborales a nivel nacional en España o a nivel internacional.

Experiencia laboral:

2000 — actualidad   ONDEA Sociedad Mercantil, Barcelona
Asesora del departamento de recursos humanos: *Asesoramiento profesional en todos los temas del departamento de recursos humanos, entre ellos las relaciones laborales y la formación de los empleados.Creación de un programa para España y puesta en práctica de cambios en el programa de la empresa.*

1996 — 1999   ONDEA Sociedad Mercantil, Barcelona
Asesora de recursos humanos: navegación, transporte marítimo y aviación commercial
Asesoramiento en la selección de personal en tres departamentos del grupo TEASA: productos de navegación, transporte marítimo y aviación comercial. Coordinación de varios procesos de selección

de personal internos y externos en todas las fases, desde el anuncio publicitario hasta la selección del candidato.

1993 — 1995   **ONDEA Producción, Barcelona**

Asesora de recursos humanos: ingeniería de explotación petrolera

Asesoramiento en una serie de temas, entre otros la gestión de una reubicación empresarial a gran escala.

Educación/Títulos:

1999 — 2001   **Máster en Relaciones Laborales,** *Universidad Autónoma de Madrid*

1996 — 1998   **Graduada por la Facultad de Personal y Desarrollo**

1990 — 1993   **Licenciada en Psicología Experimental,** *Universidad de Salamanca*

1982 — 1990   **Bachillerato y COU (ciencias y letras),** *Instituto de Bachillerato La Esperanza, Salamanca*

Curriculum Vitae

CURRICULUM VITAE for Ms. Josephine Catterall
5A, Hanton Street, London, SE13 1DF
Tel: (020) 8868 9854   Mobile: (07914) 248553
E-mail: jfcatterall@hotmail.com

Objective:

To become a professional HR manager with a team-leader role within a blue-chip company. Future positions to involve managing employee relations on a UK or global basis.

Work History:

Dec 1999 — present   GP International Trading and Shipping Company Ltd., London
Human Resources Policy Adviser
Provided professional advice on all HR policy matters including employee relations and training. Developed UK policy and implemented policy changes within the business.

May 1996 — Nov 1999 GP International Trading and Shipping Company Ltd., London
Human Resources Adviser: Marine, Shipping, and Aviation
Provided recruitment advice to 3 departments of the Global Businesses group:Marine Products, Shipping, and Aviation. Coordinated several internal and external recruitment processes through all stages from advertising to candidate selection.

**Sept 1993 — April 1996 GP UK Exploration and
Production, Southampton**
Human Resources Consultant: Oil-well Engineering
*Provided advice on a range of issues, including helping
to manage a large-scale company relocation.*

Education/Qualifications:

1999 — 2001	MSc in Employee Relations, *University of Westminster, London*
1996 — 1998	Graduate of the Chartered Institute of Personnel and Development
1990 — 1993	BA (Hons) Experimental Psychology (Class Iii), *University of Bristol*
1982 — 1990	'A' Levels: Biology (A), French (A), German (B), *St Stephen's School, Ely, Cambs*

Sample covering letter for job application

Adriana García Seoane
C/ Ramón Cabanillas, N° 20
28020 Barcelona

Sra./Srta. Sonia Ibero Fernández
Jefa de personal
ALFATEC
Columela 15
28002 MADRID

25 de marzo de 2003

Estimada Sra./Srta. Ibero Fernández:

Estoy muy interesada en el puesto de Jefa de ventas de ALFATEC que se ha anunciado el día 20 de marzo en el periódico *El País*.

Durante el año pasado en mi actual puesto de Delegada de ventas de InfoSoria he contribuido a aumentar en un 15% nuestra cuota de mercado. He podido apreciar en su página web y en su informe anual que ALFATEC también ha aumentado su cuota de mercado y pretende conseguir el mismo objetivo el próximo año fiscal.Creo que mis títulos y experiencia encajarían bien en este plan de desarrollo.

Tal como se indica en el anuncio, le envío adjunto una copia de mi Currículum Vitae en el que se incluyen todos los datos sobre mis títulos y experiencia laboral.Me sería muy grato poder ser considerada para este puesto.

Sin otro particular, quedo a la espera de sus noticias.

Le saluda atentamente,

Adriana García Seoane

Anexo

Carta de presentación

> Adrienne Griffiths
> 20 Shakespeare Road
> London
> SE18 2PB
>
> Jane Stevenson
> Senior Personnel Officer
> DataTech Ltd
> Botley Road
> Oxford
> OX2 1ZZ
>
> 25 March 2003
>
> Dear Ms Stevenson
>
> I am very interested in the position of sales manager at DataTech Ltd as described in your advertisement of 20 March in the Guardian newspaper.
>
> In my current position of deputy sales manager for Parker Smith Plc I have helped to increase our market share by 15% in the past year. I see from your website and annual report that DataTech have also increased their market share this year and are aiming to do the same in the next financial year, and I feel my track record and qualifications would fit in well with these plans for growth.
>
> As requested in the advertisement, I enclose a copy of my CV which gives full details of my qualifications

and work history. I would be very pleased to be considered for this position and I look forward to hearing from you.

Yours sincerely

Adrianne Griffiths

Encl.

Sample letter making a job offer

ALFATEC
Columela 15
28002 MADRID

Sra./Srta. Adriana García
Seoane
C/ Ramón Cabanillas, N° 20
28002 Madrid

10 de abril de 2003

Estimada Sra./Srta. García Seoane:

Asunto: Puesto de Jefa de ventas

Con relación a la entrevista mantenida la semana pasada, me complace poder ofrecerle el puesto de Jefa de ventas, dependiendo directamente de Francisco Aramburu Laguna, Director de ventas de la empresa.

Su salario inicial será de 31.600 euros, con una revisión del mismo al año de haberse incorporado a la empresa. Las demás condiciones serán según se han acordado en la entrevista.

Si desea aceptar esta oferta, le estaría muy agradecida que comunicara su confirmación por escrito.

A continuación se podrán ultimar los detalles de su contrato, la fecha de comienzo y estudiar los gastos que pueda ocasionar el cambio a su nuevo puesto.

Sin otro particular, reciba un cordial saludo,

Sonia Ibero Fernández
Jefa de personal
ALFATEC

Oferta de empleo

DataTech Ltd
Botley Road
Oxford
OX2 1ZZ

Ms Adrianne Griffiths
20 Shakespeare Road
London SE18 2PB

10 April 2003

Dear Ms Griffiths

Re: Post of Sales Manager

Further to your interview last week I am pleased to be able to offer you the post of Sales Manager, reporting directly to David Wardlock, our Company Sales Director.

Your starting salary will be £29,635, with an annual salary review on the date of your joining the company. Other terms and conditions will be as outlined in the interview.

If this offer is acceptable to you I would be grateful if you could send me confirmation in writing. We can then finalize details of your contract and starting date and discuss any relocation expenses you may have to claim.

Best wishes

Yours sincerely

Jane Stevenson
Senior Personnel Officer
DataTech Ltd

Sample letter of complaint

C/ Labastida 3, 47
20010 San Sebastián

> Sra./Srta. Marina Blanco Requejo
> INFOTÉCNICA
> Avda. Sancho el Sabio, 30 Bajo
> 20010 San Sebastián
>
> 20 de marzo de 2003

Estimada Sra./Srta. Blanco Requejo:

Impresora de chorro de tinta defectuosa (número de modelo A1234)

El jueves 13 de marzo hice la compra de una impresora de chorro de tinta (número de modelo A1234) en su establecimiento (adjunto copia del recibo).Desafortunadamente, la impresora no funciona y dos de los técnicos de su establecimiento no han podido establecer la causa del problema. Por consiguiente, le agradecería que se procediese lo antes posible a realizar el reintegro completo del importe de la impresora defectuosa.

No dude en ponerse en contacto conmigo en la dirección arriba indicada para poder acordar una fecha para el reintegro del importe y la recogida de la impresora.

Sin otro particular, quedo a la espera de sus noticias.

Le saluda atentamente,

Isabel Sandoval Ochoa

Carta de reclamación

47 Highfield Road
York
YO2 3BP

Ms H Naughton
The Computer Shop Ltd
123 High Street
York
YO1 7HL

20 March 2003

Dear Ms Naughton

Faulty inkjet printer (model number A1234)

I purchased an inkjet printer (model number A1234) from your shop on Thursday 13 March (copy of receipt enclosed). Unfortunately, the printer appears to be faulty, and two engineers from your shop have not been able to isolate the cause of the problem. I would, therefore, appreciate a full refund on the faulty printer at your earliest convenience.

Please contact me at the above address so that we may arrange a time when the printer can be picked up and returned.

I look forward to hearing from you.

Yours sincerely

Elizabeth Kendall